PRAISE FOR
AMERICAN GENERAL

"The blood and thunder of the Civil War comes alive in John S. D. Eisenhower's *American General*, a brilliantly written and researched biography of William Tecumseh Sherman. Eisenhower's delineation on Sherman's Scorched Earth strategy is a must read. Highly recommended!"

> —Douglas Brinkley, professor of history at Rice University, CBS News historian, and *New York Times* bestselling author of *The Wilderness Warrior*

"John S. D. Eisenhower, who knows something about generals and soldiering, has written a marvelous biography of a much misunderstood man. Yes, Sherman did say 'War is Hell' and made it so waging 'total war' against the South. But he was at the same time a shrewd, colorful, brave man, and Eisenhower brings him vividly to life."

> —Evan Thomas, *New York Times* bestselling author of *Ike's Bluff* and *Sea of Thunder*

"Veteran soldier, former general, acclaimed historian, renowned military biographer, and son of America's preeminent twentieth-century general, John S. D. Eisenhower brings William Tecumseh Sherman to life as only he can. The eminently readable *American General* takes you beyond the standard-issue portrayals of Sherman—avenging angel for the North, devastating demon to the South—and reintroduces you to the man himself. On the hundred fiftieth anniversary of Sherman's fiery March to the Sea, this book will help you understand the man behind the legend."

> —Daniel P. Bolger, author of *Why We Lost: A General's Inside Account of the Iraq and Afghanistan Wars*

"Only U. S. Grant could have written a truer portrait of William Tecumseh Sherman. John S. D. Eisenhower had Grant's gifts for lucidity, exactness, and concision, as well as keen military insight."

> —Sidney Blumenthal, *New York Times* bestselling author of *A Self-Made Man: The Political Life of Abraham Lincoln*

"Highly recommended . . . should be read by anyone interested in the Civil War."

> —*Library Journal*

"The late historian Eisenhower, son of the president and a general and West Point graduate in his own right, does a service in presenting this solid, useful biography of William Tecumseh Sherman . . . a readable, evenhanded work."

> —*Kirkus Reviews*

AMERICAN GENERAL

THE LIFE AND TIMES OF
WILLIAM TECUMSEH SHERMAN

JOHN S. D. EISENHOWER

NAL
CALIBER

NAL CALIBER

NAL CALIBER
Published by New American Library,
an imprint of Penguin Random House LLC
375 Hudson Street, New York, New York 10014

This book is a publication of New American Library. Previously published in an NAL Caliber
hardcover edition.

First NAL Caliber Trade Paperback Printing, October 2015

NAL CALIBER TRADE PAPERBACK ISBN: 978-0-451-47136-9

THE LIBRARY OF CONGRESS HAS CATALOGED THE HARDCOVER EDITION OF THIS TITLE AS FOLLOWS:
Eisenhower, John S. D., 1922–2013.
American general: the life and times of William Tecumseh Sherman/John S. D. Eisenhower.
p.   cm.
Includes bibliographical references and index.
ISBN 978-0-451-47135-2
1. Sherman, William T. (William Tecumseh), 1820–1891.   2. United States—History—Civil War,
1861–1865—Biography.   3. Generals—United States—Biography.   4. United States. Army—
Biography.   I. Title.
E467.1.S55E37   2014
355.0092—dc23   2014013270
[B]

Printed in the United States of America
10 9 8 7 6 5 4 3 2 1

Set in Minion   •   Designed by Elke Sigal

PUBLISHER'S NOTE
While the author has made every effort to provide accurate telephone numbers and Internet
addresses at the time of publication, neither the publisher nor the author assumes any responsibility
for errors, or for changes that occur after publication. Further, publisher does not have any control
over and does not assume any responsibility for author or third-party Web sites or their content.

Penguin
Random
House

CONTENTS

BOOK I

THE RISE OF WILLIAM T. SHERMAN

CONTENTS

BOOK II

SHERMAN ASSUMES COMMAND

To Percy W. Thompson

★

FOREWORD

by
Susan Eisenhower

It is hard to articulate the sum of a life. But my father, John S. D. Eisenhower, who died before the publication of this book, produced a loving family and accomplished his professional goals. The only surviving son of Mamie and General and President Dwight D. Eisenhower, John Eisenhower wore his father's fame with dignity and resolve. By midcareer, he had gotten into "the writing game" to fulfill his desire to be an author. He also knew it would help him create an identity of his own. In the succeeding decades he made an independent reputation for himself, becoming what the *Washington Post* called "a soldier, diplomat and acclaimed historian."

John Eisenhower's life was utterly shaped by the military. As a young man, he moved with his parents from army assignment to assignment, in places like Panama and the Philippines. After high school he sought an appointment to West Point. After three years he graduated from the Academy coincidentally on June 6, 1944, just hours after the invasion of Normandy had begun. He served in intelligence posts in Europe before the war ended, and later in combat operations in Korea. He left the Army in 1963 to pursue his love of writing.

Becoming a military historian was, for John Eisenhower, more than a vocation. "Putting pen to paper" is not just what he did; being a writer is who he was. He knew this even before he graduated from West Point. After VE Day he got a master's degree at Columbia University and was assigned to the English Department at West Point. Between 1948 and 1951, he was, in his own words, "able to learn much of what he and the Class of 1944 had missed because of West Point's [foreshortened graduation schedule] during the war." His master's thesis was on the role of the military in William Shakespeare's work. In addition to military histories, he loved humorists like Mark Twain and P. G. Wodehouse and appreciated the lean, evocative style of Ernest Hemingway.

In the late 1960s, after serving as an editor on Ike's two-volume White House memoirs, my father wrote his first book, *The Bitter Woods*, on the Battle of the Bulge. He undertook extensive research on the subject, which included doing interviews at all echelons in the chain of command, including those who fought on the German side. I remember vividly dining with the 5th Panzer Army General Hasso von Manteuffel after his interview with my father at our house in Pennsylvania. The German general had played a significant role in the Battle of the Bulge.

After *The Bitter Woods* appeared on bestseller lists, my father was appointed as U.S. Ambassador to Belgium, and he served in that capacity from 1969 to 1971. During his tenure my parents rented a small cottage in the Ardennes forest, and on my visits "home" he would take me out on battlefield excursions, much like he did with my other siblings.

As my father's career developed, he and I made trips to a number of Civil War battlefields, family landmarks and other points of historic interest. There he would try to learn more, all the while he told me stories and explained the significance or the strategic importance of the place.

My father was a cerebral man—a quiet observer of the many things to which he'd been exposed. He had done a lot of living. During the war in Europe, he'd been to Buchenwald and seen the Holocaust firsthand. He was a combat officer in the Korean War, and that conflict also left a deep imprint on him. Perhaps, notably, he may have been the last person alive who had dined with both Churchill and Stalin—and he went with his father to Normandy just after the invasion. He wrote several books on World War II, but on subjects he later tackled—from General Winfield Scott and the War of 1812 to the United States' intervention in Mexico and World War I—he used his love of writing as a gateway to a lifetime of intellectual discovery. He had an instinct for detail and an eye for spotting uncommon capabilities, historic ironies, and the elements of a good story.

What impressed me the most was his extraordinary ability to connect the intellectual dots across centuries of history and articulate them as simple principles, often associating them with the events of the day. He had a striking ability to identify the exceptional qualities in people that made them leaders, as well as the ones that made others fall short.

With respect to our society, it was the changing mores and attitudes that fascinated him. In this, he saw the hand of time as a mysterious "fourth dimension," which altered things as no physical change ever could.

My father also liked colorful characters—he knew a few in his day. Perhaps this is what drew him to General Sherman in the first place. It was Sherman who famously said: "War is hell." Indeed, fact and lore reveal a quick-witted Sherman who didn't hesitate to speak his mind. One such example relates to Sherman's disdain for journalists, whom the General deemed as nothing better than battlefield spies and gossipmongers. On hearing that three correspondents had been killed near Vicksburg, Sherman is said to have quipped, "Good! Now we shall have news from Hell before breakfast."

In the course of his lifetime, John Eisenhower edited three books and wrote thirteen others. *American General* was his fourteenth. It was under way in the last two years of his life. Just as my father was preparing this book for the editor, he died on December 21, 2013, at age ninety-one. In fact, the manuscript was the subject of my last conversation with him, shortly before he passed away. He asked that I serve as his "stand-in" for getting the book ready for publication.

While no one could ever hope to substitute for John Eisenhower, I have been privileged to play a small role in helping to bring this project to fruition, an important piece of his body of work.

My father's legacy will become clearer with the fullness of time. But it was gratifying to read the many articles written about his life and to receive countless letters from people who'd read his books. The field of military and leadership history, many observers wrote, is richer today because John Eisenhower devoted himself to the writing craft.

Sage insights on world leaders, observations about strategy and its impact, and sensitivity to the fighting man's condition are part of what my father leaves behind. His determination to be his own man, to pursue his talents and to forge his own identity, is also how he will be remembered—and another reason for why he will be missed.

AMERICAN GENERAL

INTRODUCTION

The Tactical Department at the United States Military Academy, West Point, in evaluating the Class of 1840, dubbed the sixth-highest-ranking cadet in the class, William Tecumseh Sherman, as "no soldier." A century later, General George S. Patton would use the same term in describing Terry Allen and Teddy Roosevelt Jr., two of the most pugnacious infantrymen of World War II. Both the West Point tacs and "Old Blood and Guts" made the same error; they equated spit and polish with "soldiering." Sherman's appearance was rough-hewn, with scraggly red hair. His uniforms were always rumpled. Using that criterion, of course, they were both right.

Sherman was not concerned with that evaluation. Indeed, in later years he reveled in it. Even at the time, it seemed to cause him no grief. Actually, if required to summarize this otherwise complex man, I for one would be inclined to call him a "soldier's soldier."

Sherman's basic attitudes were typically military. He was physically fearless—or appeared so. He distrusted politicians and the press, considering the latter to be licensed spies. He was loyal to a fault, both to the office of his superiors and certainly to Ulysses S. Grant personally. But

Sherman could never be put in a mold. He was one of the most colorful figures of the American Civil War, or any other American war. To many people he is best remembered for his answer to the suggestion that he run for the presidency: "If nominated, I will not run. If elected, I will not serve. If given the choice between four years in the presidency or four years in prison, I will choose prison, thank you." He put a new word in our language: "Shermanesque."

These idiosyncrasies, however, are not the reason we remember Sherman. The military historian B. H. Liddell Hart called him "the first of the modern generals." If that evaluation seems to be a bit of an exaggeration, it must be admitted that Sherman was a truly independent thinker. Conventionality was not part of his makeup. And part of his original thinking was the concept that to conquer a nation determined to resist, the attacking force cannot limit its efforts to that people's armed forces; the war must be waged against the will of the civilian populace as well. Hence the term "total war." Only one other Civil War general, the venerable Winfield Scott, also realized what has become a truism. But not until Sherman made his vaunted march from Atlanta to Savannah in late 1864 did it come to be universally acknowledged. The victims of this concept, the American Confederacy, have never forgiven him for it.

Actually, it is too much to give Sherman credit for discovering the feasibility of an army's living off the land of the enemy, free of its own supply lines. He seems to have learned that lesson from U. S. Grant at Vicksburg, when Grant, having secured a foothold on the lands south of the city, attacked Jackson, Mississippi, without a supply line. In fact, the discovery was not even Grant's. Henry W. Halleck, in 1862, lived off the land in his large-scale movement from Shiloh to Corinth. But Sherman was the first to adopt the policy for purposes beyond feeding his troops: that of depriving the enemy of all matériel necessary to war as well as making use of it himself.

In writing this short book I found his personality even more interesting than his deeds. The contrast between Sherman's true affection for the people of the South and his actions toward them is to me mind-boggling. (Of course, unreconstructed Southerners hardly return that affection.) When the military phase of the Civil War was finished, he made a sentimental trip to Charleston, South Carolina, to check on the welfare of the friends of twenty years earlier. (He found almost none.)

It is the combination of military genius and complexity of character that has made this book a joy to write. Sherman's major role in bringing about the ultimate Union triumph in the Civil War, along with being the most unlikely general, is unique in American military history.

PROLOGUE

In early 1861, a forty-one-year-old ex-soldier named William Tecumseh Sherman, then president of the Louisiana State Seminary of Learning & Military Academy (later Louisiana State University), was dining with Professor David F. Boyd, a dear friend from Virginia, a state contemplating secession from the Union. As recalled by Boyd, Sherman minced no words:

> You people of the South don't know what you are doing. This country will be drenched in blood, and God only knows how it will end. It is all folly, madness, a crime against civilization! You people speak so lightly of war; you don't know what you're talking about. War is a terrible thing! You mistake, too, the people of the North. They are a peaceable people but an earnest people, and they will fight, too. They are not going to let this country be destroyed without a mighty effort to save it. . . . Besides, where are your men and appliances of war to contend against them? The North can make a steam engine, locomotive, or railway car; hardly a yard of cloth or pair of shoes can you make. You are rushing into war with one of the most powerful, ingeniously me-

chanical, and determined people on Earth—right at your doors. You are bound to fail. Only in your spirit and determination are you prepared for war. In all else you are totally unprepared, with a bad cause to start with. At first you will make headway, but as your limited resources begin to fail, shut out from the markets of Europe as you will be, your cause will begin to wane. If your people will but stop and think, they must see in the end that you will surely fail.[1]

Sherman knew whereof he spoke. With remarkable prescience, he described as concisely as can be imagined the tragedy that was about to befall the United States, the American Civil War. He had no inkling of the major role he would play in this drama, something that seemed to come about almost by chance. There was little in his background that would presage it.

BOOK I

THE RISE OF WILLIAM T. SHERMAN

CHAPTER ONE

EARLY LIFE

On a cold and windy day in mid-February 1891, an elaborate funeral was held in New York City for general of the army William Tecumseh Sherman. All the important people were there: Among them were President Benjamin Harrison, former presidents Rutherford B. Hayes and Grover Cleveland, and thirty thousand troops, including the entire corps of cadets from West Point. One of the honorary pallbearers, present at Sherman's previous request, was an unlikely member: Joseph Eggleston Johnston, a onetime general of the Confederate States of America and Sherman's fierce antagonist. The two men—with a fourteen-year difference in their ages—had fought hard against each other during the Civil War, but in later years they had developed a warm friendship, working together to repair the Union that had been rent asunder between the years 1861 and 1865.

Johnston's friends were worried about him, for despite the icy winds, his eighty-four years of age, and frail health, he insisted on remaining bareheaded throughout the ceremony. Johnston would have none of his friends' protests. "If I were in [Sherman's] place, and he were standing in mine, he would not put on his hat." A month later Johnston died of pneumonia, presumably the result of exposure at Sherman's funeral.

Johnston's affection for Sherman, expressed at risk to himself, was contrary to the feelings of his fellow Southerners; Sherman's name, in fact, still stands as a symbol of the destruction he visited on their lands while marching from Atlanta to Savannah in late 1864. The contrast between those who knew him as a warm and somewhat sensitive man and those who knew him only by the measures he took in war characterizes the contrasts of Sherman's life. He was a man who hated war and all it stood for, but whose duty, as he saw it, called for measures designed to finish off a failing enemy.

Sherman came from a prominent family, but little in his ancestry indicated that one day he would be recognized as one of the nation's most brilliant generals. If anything, his background should have led him to the legal profession. He was born in 1820 in Lancaster, Ohio, to Charles Sherman, Esq., and his wife, Mary Sherman. Charles Sherman was a distinguished lawyer, a member of the Ohio Supreme Court. The Sherman family had come from Essex County, England, in two groups; William Sherman's family came to Connecticut in 1636. A cousin, Roger Sherman, had been a signer of the Declaration of Independence. The boy's grandfather, Taylor Sherman, had moved out to the west and settled in Ohio. Charles R. Sherman, William's father, had moved his family to Lancaster, Ohio, just in time to get involved in the War of 1812, fought between the United States and Great Britain. For some reason he had become an ardent admirer of the statesmanlike qualities of the Shawnee chief Tecumseh, even though Tecumseh had fought on the British side. As a result Charles Sherman named the son born in 1820 William Tecumseh, which the family quickly abbreviated to the nickname of "Cump."

Cump's boyhood, as with so many others in days when many people died young, was uprooted in 1829. When he was nine years old, his father suddenly passed away, leaving his widow, Mary, practically penniless, and saddled with a family of eleven children. Of these, two had grown up and had left home, but Mary, with nine still to care for, was faced with starvation. Deciding to keep the youngest three at home, she gave up six. Fortunately, those six were kindly taken in to be raised by friends and relatives.

Cump's situation, sad though it was, could have been worse. His foster parents were nearby neighbors and distant relatives. Thomas Ewing, like Judge Sherman, was a highly successful lawyer, and in 1830, the year after Cump joined his household, was elected to the United States Senate from Ohio. Fortunately, Ewing was a kind man, and he recognized the deep debt he owed to Cump's father for having assisted in launching his own law career years earlier.* Ewing and his wife had four children of their own and were also acting as foster parents for three others besides Cump.

The Ewings were a congenial family, and their residence was sufficiently close to that of Mary Sherman that the Sherman children had been playmates with those of the Ewings even before tragedy struck. While living with the Ewings, young Cump occasionally went to his own family's house for dinner. Though Sherman was only nine years old at the time of his father's death, Judge Charles had had an influence on him. Sherman always remained proud of his family's accomplishments, and he appears to have inherited an unusually strong sense of duty and a passionate belief in the Union, a conviction that would give him the strength to perform unpleasant duties in his years of service to his country.

According to one biographer, however, Cump never got over the feeling of being abandoned, the child who'd been sent away. Dangerous as such theorizing may be, Sherman throughout his life exhibited characteristics that could well stem from that circumstance. He was intelligent and imaginative but extremely touchy and sometimes nervous, though cool in battle. His loyalties to such men as Grant and later (though not at first) to

---

* In 1841, Ewing was appointed secretary of the treasury by President William Henry Harrison, but resigned when Harrison's successor, John Tyler, took measures that Ewing disapproved of. He was later the secretary of the interior for the eighteen months of Zachary Taylor's tenure in office.

Lincoln were so strong as to work sometimes to his peril. On the other hand, his hatred of the press and politicians was also exaggerated, sometimes with dire results.

A strong figure in the Ewing household was the wife and mother, Maria. She was a staunch, devout Roman Catholic, and she raised her children strictly. Her husband, Tom, and Cump did not share her views on religion, but they respected her. The family situation has given rise to the story that Cump's father had not named him William; rather he had named him Tecumseh. It was Maria, so the story went, who was responsible for William's Christian name. She is said to have been unable to tolerate the boy lacking a Christian name, and even though the Ewings never formally adopted their four foster children, she insisted that Tecumseh be baptized. Apparently any Christian name would do, and the officiating priest, noting that the date of the baptism was St. William's Feast, is given credit for naming the boy William. From then on, his name would be William Tecumseh Sherman. It makes a good story, but Sherman, in his memoir, does not mention it. He simply states that his father named him William Tecumseh.[1]

During the seven years that Sherman resided with the Ewings, he developed an affectionate relationship with one of the Ewing daughters, Eleanor ("Ellen") Boyle Ewing. Their mutual affinity had to be platonic for a long time because William was five years older than Ellen. (She later admitted being interested in him when she was four years old and he had just arrived at the Ewing home.) Their personal contact was interrupted in 1836, however, when Senator Ewing secured William an appointment to West Point. By then William and Ellen were sufficiently close that the two of them maintained an extensive correspondence while he was a cadet and beyond. West Point regulations forbade a cadet's leaving the post for a full two years from the date of entry. Fortunately for the two of them, an upperclass cadet from Lancaster was willing to act as a sort of go-between. The letters Cump wrote to Ellen were both lengthy and literate, as well as upbeat and detailed. On one occasion, Ellen sent William a present that included some welcome candy.

Sherman was apparently a happy cadet, and in his letters he described various features around West Point, which provided scenery close to breathtaking. He mentioned such landmarks as Fort Putnam, which had been so important in the American Revolution. He admired the Kosciuszko Monument, dedicated to the Polish engineer who had laid out the West Point defenses that had stopped the British in 1778. In 1839, the nineteen-year-old Cadet Sherman urged the fifteen-year-old Ellen to visit West Point to see all these wonders for herself.[2] These letters, many of which have survived and even been published, cast considerable light not only on Sherman himself but also on the American society as it then existed. History is richer for the preservation of their correspondence.

Sherman's record as a cadet at West Point was creditable but unremarkable. He was highly intelligent, and of the ninety-four "new cadets" who had entered the academy in 1836, his final class standing was sixth out of the forty-seven who had survived that stringent curriculum. He seems to have been driven by no ambition to emulate such model predecessors as Robert E. Lee, who had graduated the same year that Judge Charles Sherman had died in Lancaster. As Sherman described his cadet career,

> At the Academy I was not considered a good soldier, for at no time was I selected for any office, but remained a private throughout the whole four years. Then, as now, neatness in dress and form, with a strict conformity to the rules, were the qualifications required for office, and I suppose I was found not to excel in any of these. In studies I always held a respectable reputation with the professors, and generally ranked among the best, especially in drawing, chemistry, mathematics, and natural philosophy. My average demerits, per annum, were about one hundred and fifty, which reduced my final class standing from number four to six.[3]

One feature of Sherman's years as a cadet would prove invaluable in the future: the opportunity to become acquainted with many of the cadets he would later serve with and against. The most important of these was

Ulysses S. Grant, who entered the academy as a plebe in 1839, Sherman's first class year, his final at West Point before graduation. Nobody could predict the close relationship that would blossom later, but Sherman took an interest in Grant, especially because both youngsters were from Ohio. In one letter, Sherman described to Ellen his perplexity over the question of how Grant had picked up the nickname of "Sam." The cadets finally concluded that Grant's initials, [U]lysses [S]impson, stood for "Uncle Sam," and the nickname derived from it. Never mind that Grant's true given name had previously been "Hiram" before some minor official at West Point decided to designate it otherwise.[4]

In any event, the tall, redheaded boy of twenty graduated from West Point in the Class of 1840 and was assigned to the 3d Artillery, which was stationed along the east coast of Florida. His company, "A," was located at Fort Pierce, on the Indian River. He was a good officer, and he was content. The assignment, even though the Second Seminole War was still officially on, offered very little by way of orthodox combat experience. By then the Seminoles, who never reconciled themselves to being moved to Oklahoma, had been fairly well scattered, and aside from one attack on the camp gave little trouble. The most valuable aspect of that assignment was common to all new West Point graduates: indoctrination into the realities of the army as it truly existed, in contrast to the high standards, observed under ideal conditions, that all cadets had known on the Hudson River.

Sherman long remembered dramatic incidents. Fort Pierce was a lonely place, and men were allowed to bring their wives, if a woman could be induced to live under such primitive conditions. But the fact that some men had families present and others did not was a potential source of trouble. In one instance a relatively frail soldier found that a husky, burly comrade was hanging around his quarters and paying what he considered undue attention to his wife. After consulting with friends and apparently receiving some encouragement, the husband shot and killed the intruder. No action was taken against him.

Another tragedy, a result of the elements, involved Sherman. A lonely soldier went from Fort Pierce to St. Augustine to meet his young wife and her younger sister, who were to join him at his duty station. The seas were rough, and for some reason the skipper of the small boat was able to get the two women ashore but not the husband. Eventually the boat floundered on a reef in rough waters infested with sharks. The two women, onshore, long held hope that a miracle would save the husband's life. It was not to be, and it was the duty of Second Lieutenant Sherman to so inform a weeping widow. Other excitement was confined to patrols that were occasionally sent out, and the duty was a good breaking-in.

In 1841, about the time of Sherman's promotion to first lieutenant, the 3d Artillery was transferred to Fort Moultrie, a fortress located just outside Charleston, South Carolina. In contrast to the wild, primitive existence in Florida, the men of the 3d Artillery enjoyed congenial relations with the citizens of Charleston, who were known for their hospitality. Sherman circulated among the elite. In a country in which affairs were conducted by a small group of oligarchs, it was known that Sherman had close connections with a former senator and cabinet officer, and he was treated especially warmly. The four-year tour gave Sherman his first exposure to Southerners, and he could not have failed to sense some of the steel and determination that lay hidden beneath the hospitality and charm. Sherman and General Winfield Scott, who was a Southerner himself, would, in a far-off day, be among the few who understood the mettle of the enemy they were facing in the Civil War.

During all this time Sherman kept up his correspondence with Ellen Ewing. In 1843 he was granted leave to visit his home at Lancaster, and while he was there he became officially engaged to his lifelong confidante. This they arranged over the objections of her father, who, though fond of Sherman, hated to allow his rather sickly daughter to marry into the army and share the rigorous life of a frontier officer. For that reason, as well as Ellen's poor health, the engagement dragged on for seven years.

Three years later, in April 1846, the United States went to war with Mexico. A year earlier, President James K. Polk had ordered Brigadier

General Zachary Taylor to concentrate a small army of about 3,500 men on the Texas border, anticipating annexation of that independent country to the United States. Mexico broke off relations, and Taylor's army was sent to Corpus Christi, on the Sabine River, and in early 1846 was sent across disputed territory to the spot on the Rio Grande where Brownsville, Texas, now stands. Then, in late April 1846, a Mexican force crossed to the American side and killed or captured the members of an American patrol. President Polk claimed that "American blood" had been shed on "American soil," and the two countries were at war. It was a heady period, though few Americans expected full-scale war at the time.

Sherman's days of peacetime military duty were now at an end.

CHAPTER TWO

CALIFORNIA

B efore the dramatic news from the Mexican border reached Washington—or even Charleston—Sherman received orders to report to the army's Eastern Command at Governors Island, New York. On arrival he was assigned to recruiting duty, an important activity, and was to be stationed at Pittsburgh. Accordingly, he and a small contingent took a stagecoach and set up headquarters within a couple of weeks. He was pleased to learn that his area of responsibility included a substation at Zanesville, Ohio, not very far from Lancaster. Any inspection trip to Zanesville could easily afford him a chance to visit home.

In late May events began to move rapidly. On a trip back to Pittsburgh from Zanesville, Sherman learned that war had been formally declared between the United States and Mexico. After the skirmish on the Rio Grande that precipitated the conflict, the Mexican commander at Matamoros, General Pedro de Ampudia, had brought his army across the Rio Grande, where Zachary Taylor's men, though vastly outnumbered, had fought him to a standstill at Palo Alto. On May 9, the next day, the Mexican army at Resaca de la Palma had been shattered, inflicting heavy loss and forcing Ampudia to flee back across the river. The details were probably not in the dispatches that Sherman received, but the fact that actual fighting had broken out put him in a state of excitement. He decided on the spot that he could no longer tolerate recruiting duty; he had to get into the action.

On arrival back at Pittsburgh, Sherman found a letter waiting for him from Governors Island. His West Point roommate Edward O. C. Ord, like Sherman a member of the 3d Artillery, had received orders to proceed to California, and he was inviting Sherman to join him. Sherman grasped at the opportunity. He was not part of Taylor's army, but he saw California as the coming theater. He wrote the adjutant general,[1] who placed him on orders to join a group traveling by ship to California. Among the others, besides Ord, was a friend from West Point days, Lieutenant Henry Wager Halleck.

On July 14, 1846, Sherman's packet departed New York City aboard the USS *Lexington*, an aged warship that had been converted into a "store ship" (freighter) carrying artillery pieces and a great amount of gunpowder. She was bound for California by way of Rio de Janeiro, the Strait of Magellan, and Valparaiso. As Sherman calculated it, the voyage would be twenty-two thousand miles in length and would require several months to complete. (He noted that the trip overland would be something like two thousand miles.)

The *Lexington*'s long route had her sailing eastward across the Atlantic to a point near Africa in order to make use of the prevailing winds from the west. After crossing the equator she would travel from east to west. Sherman at first hoped that this route would allow a stopover at Madeira, but the captain's orders specified that the only refueling stations to be visited would be Rio de Janeiro and Valparaiso. So he missed a bit of sightseeing.

The *Lexington* was a congenial ship. As the men expected action at the end of the voyage, they were buoyed by a spirit of adventure. The captain was an experienced old sailor who had crossed through the critical and dangerous Strait of Magellan several times. Though his position gave him the power to administer severe discipline, Sherman noted that such action was seldom necessary. There was, in fact, room for a bit of levity on occasion. A great deal, for example, was made of the fact of crossing the equator. In a letter home, Sherman described to Ellen how it was observed:

The ship was pronounced on the equator at eight this forenoon when I was summoned to the Captain's cabin where a holystone [piece of hard stone used for cleaning decks] was presented for me to rest my hand upon when the following oath was administered by the Captain in person: "You do swear that you will not chew pig-tail when you can get good Cavendish, that you will not eat hard tack when you can get soft bread, unless you like the hard best, that you will not kiss the maid instead of the mistress, unless you like the maid best, and in all other things comport yourself like a true son of Neptune. So help you salt water"—a dash of which was sprinkled in my face. I was then duly initiated, and in my turn administered the same oath to all of our officers on the quarter deck, taking care to baptize them well in salt water.[2]

The *Lexington* was carrying ten officers, six from the army and four from the navy. Sherman, as a senior first lieutenant, was the highest-ranking army officer, and according to custom was the channel through whom the captain issued all his orders to the soldiers.

Life for the officers centered around a wardroom, which was sur-rounded by several officers' cabins. Sherman shared a stateroom with Ord, and the other four army officers, including Halleck, roomed together. The space in the staterooms was limited, however, and they were used only for sleeping.

The main problem, which each man solved in his own way, was boredom. Fortunately, the running of the ship itself required the full-time efforts of about half the sailors, assisted by a quarter of the soldiers. Since an army officer had to be present to command the soldiers, Sherman found himself on deck duty about one day in four. Otherwise, he passed the time reading and writing letters. As he had great volumes of writing paper on hand—and an amazing eye for detail—his letters to his fiancée were voluminous and informative.[3]

Arranging for his letters to be delivered was a major problem. In the two ports of call where the *Lexington* stopped, he found ships heading for the United States to take his letters with them. Selection of couriers was a matter requiring great care. Since the route being followed by the *Lexington* was well traveled, it was possible at times to join up with a ship at sea bound for home. Not every ship encountered on the ocean would stop, however, and when one did heave to, Sherman would not always find her heading for home. A ship going to New York by way of Le Havre, France, would suffice. As the *Lexington* went farther along on her voyage, Sherman became less choosy in selecting his couriers.

The *Lexington* covered the first leg of the trip, to Rio de Janeiro, in two months almost to the day. She stayed in port for nine days, during which Sherman divided his time between sightseeing, which was ample and rewarding, and writing to Ellen. On September 21 the *Lexington* raised anchor and left Rio, setting out on the most dangerous part of the voyage, the passage around Cape Horn.

At first the *Lexington* enjoyed generally smooth sailing, with only a couple of storms along the coast of Patagonia, in South America. Even though the time of year corresponded to springtime in the northern hemisphere, the conditions were grim. The land areas were covered with snow, the winds from the west were fearsome, and the ocean currents flowed from the Pacific to the Atlantic.

As had become common practice for all vessels crossing from the Atlantic to the Pacific, the captain of the *Lexington* avoided using the Strait of Magellan itself, which is a narrow, extremely dangerous channel. Ferdinand Magellan had discovered it in 1520, after thirty-eight days waiting at the east entrance while scouting parties determined whether the strait actually led to open ocean on the west. The next significant traversing was that of Sir Francis Drake, 150 years later. Drake actually used Magellan's strait, but he made a note that he believed a wider, safer passage existed south of Tierra del Fuego, the island south of Magellan's passage. Thus, when this much wider passage was confirmed in the 1600s, it was named after Drake. That route was the one selected by the captain of the *Lexington*.

Though the Drake Passage is preferable to the Strait of Magellan, both have been generally considered the most dangerous waterways on the globe. Temperatures are extremely low and the winds strong, creating monster waves, some of them reaching crests of a hundred feet. The captain of the *Lexington* was forced to wait at the eastern entrance for thirty days before beginning passage. The passage itself took only twelve days.

Such a long wait was nothing unusual; nor was it uncommon for a ship to be tossed around. Sherman noted, with a touch of amusement, that tradition of the sea forbade complaint. An individual might be hurled from his seat at the dinner table, or his plate dumped into his lap, but anyone undergoing such an experience—it happened to everyone at least once— was required to laugh; any other reaction was verboten among his fellows.

On October 28, Sherman wrote Ellen, "The Horn is passed, and all now look upon our arrival at Valparaiso as a matter of course."[4] That optimism, however, was premature. An unexpected gale of wind blew the ship from the Pacific Ocean back into the Drake Passage. Once more out of the passage, however, sailing was smooth. The *Lexington* arrived at Valparaiso on November 24, 1846.

Unlike the enthusiasm Sherman had held for everything in Rio, he did not care much for Valparaiso. For some reason, when his cohorts Ord and Halleck made the sixty-mile trip inland to Santiago, Sherman did not accompany them. He was, he claimed, too busy with business and pleasure in the town. The business probably involved sending and receiving mail, but Sherman also witnessed a steeplechase, attended church, and took in an opera. He visited the British minister and conferred with the officers of some of His Majesty's ships in the harbor. He noted an interesting matter of social structure. Whereas in Rio de Janeiro all manual labor and toting of bales was done by black slaves from Africa, in Chile no such slaves existed. Physical labor was performed by free men. Sherman was slightly amused to observe the efforts that menial laborers exerted to assure visitors that they were, despite the nature of their work, *caballeros*—gentlemen.

During the *Lexington*'s stay in Valparaiso, a couple of ships from California arrived, bound for Cape Horn. They brought jarring news. The Americans, they reported, had already taken possession of California, overcoming the weak resistance of the *Californios*. Having done so, the conquerors had begun squabbling among themselves as to who among them was actually in charge. The important thing to Sherman, however, was that the *Lexington*, with all its guns and ammunition, was arriving in a region where the fighting had ceased. He was therefore going not to a combat zone, but to an occupied territory where his duties would be administrative. It was quite a blow to an officer with career ambitions.

Sherman pondered issues wider than his own career. The United States had now become a power that owned foreign territory. In his conversations with a newly arrived British admiral at Valparaiso, he gathered that the British were not happy with America's entrance onto the international stage. Yet he finally concluded that President Polk had been justified in annexing the area. He conjectured that in the absence of such action, another country, possibly Britain, would have taken California instead.

On December 5, 1846, the *Lexington* set sail from Santiago, bound for California. Sherman had little to report on that leg of the voyage other than a couple of severe storms, which were to be expected. The final destination of the *Lexington* was uncertain. The captain divulged only that they were bound for some somewhere in northern California—probably either Monterey or San Francisco. Sherman hoped that they were headed for San Francisco, eighty miles beyond Monterey,[5] because that region was relatively pristine. The Monterey area had been occupied by the Mexican *Californios* since 1821. He had been told that the barracks in Monterey were "flea-bitten." Rumor had given him much by way of previous knowledge.

The mere fact that this leg of the journey was relatively uneventful did not mean it was short. On January 26, some fifty days after leaving Valparaiso, the *Lexington* pulled into the Bay of Monterey. Whether Sherman's artillery would remain there or go on to San Francisco was not certain.

Sherman, it turned out, was to be assigned to headquarters at Monterey. Once there, he learned the details of the American takeover of California, of the aggressive and probably illegal actions of Commodore Robert F. Stockton in Los Angeles, of the role of the exploration party of John C. Frémont, and of Commodore John D. Sloat's taking Monterey. He was also aware that Brigadier General Stephen Watts Kearny had arrived at San Diego, after a grueling trip overland, on December 12, 1846, and that Frémont had defied him by declaring himself governor, despite the fact that Kearny carried orders from President Polk to take over as governor.

The matter had been finally settled with the arrival of Commodore William Shubrick in early February, with a regiment of troops. As a regular soldier, Sherman personally favored Sloat and Kearny in that unfortunate internecine quarrel. Frémont and Stockton, it is widely held, had done more harm than good. One *Californio* advised Sherman that had it not been for their antics, the native population would have submitted to American rule without firing a shot.[6]

Kearny was a hero to Sherman. It was a big day, therefore, when the general came from the *Cyane* and visited the *Independence* while he was there:

I was dining with the ward room officers of the *Independence* . . . General Kearny came on board and received a hearty welcome to the Bay of Monterey. I had met him before. He looked haggard, worn, and rough, for he had endured a hard march from Santa Fe, had got into a tight place, lost two of his captains, one lieutenant, and twenty men out of forty-five. He too had received two lance wounds in the fight, but nevertheless, his face wore that smile so characteristic of him. He has always been a favorite model of mine and I was peculiarly glad to see him.[7]

Apparently Sherman's admiration for Kearny was reciprocated, because the general took him as an aide on various explorations around California.

———

The situation in California may have been stabilized, but Sherman, like most other professional soldiers, was hoping that the war would not completely end before he had a chance to participate. Since news required six months to travel from Washington to California, he had very little idea how much action had taken place. He knew that Zachary Taylor had taken the Mexican city of Monterrey, but he did not know that on February 22 and 23, a month before his letter about the Kearny affair, Taylor had won a battle—"survived" is a better word—at Buena Vista, just south of Saltillo.[8] In March, Winfield Scott had landed ten thousand men at Veracruz and was preparing to move inland toward Mexico City. Sherman's chances for active fighting in this war were gone.

———

In California, however, Sherman had experiences that would have been considered quite memorable had they not been compared to the dramatic events taking place in Mexico. He was assigned as an aide to Colonel Richard Barnes Mason, who had succeeded Kearny as governor of California in early May of 1847. His duties were not crushing, but they included maintaining order and discipline. One day his duties required him to take a small detachment and track down a sailor who had deserted. The man knew that his punishment would be death, and Sherman knew it as well. But Sherman's duty was plain. He delivered the victim into the hands of the proper authorities, never checking up to learn of the man's fate.

Sherman was curious about John C. Frémont, the colonel who had once called himself governor of California. He went to visit this renegade, who received him cordially. They visited about an hour, including sharing a cup of tea. Like so many others, Sherman was puzzled how such a plain, ordinary-looking man could exert such a dynamic influence over his band of explorers. Some fire must have lit up in Frémont when in action that escaped the observer when he was in repose. This visit occurred before Frémont, still under arrest, left for the east with Kearny.

Sherman had a similar experience with the famed explorer Kit Carson, who had sided with Frémont in the previous controversy. Carson was carrying the rank of a mere lieutenant despite his national acclaim, and his modest status seemed to give him no problems. Carson seemed unimpressed by all the public attention he had received; his sole thought was to head east and join his wife in Taos, New Mexico. With all his bravery on land, Carson regarded travel by water with sheer terror. He had once ridden on horseback for five hundred miles between Monterey and Los Angeles to avoid making the trip by steamship. Since Sherman had been shipboard for 198 days on the way around the Horn, he found this puzzling. Carson also refused the offer of a detachment of troops to accompany him as he headed eastward. He took a couple of men and rode off from San Diego alone.

One day in early May 1848, two men walked into Colonel Mason's headquarters in Monterey with a request: to file a claim for a piece of land near a place called Sutter's Mill, California, about forty miles northeast of Sacramento. With them they carried a small packet of dust in which were small nuggets they claimed were gold. If such turned out to be the case, they wanted exclusive legal rights to that piece of land, a development they believed would make them rich.

Mason was doubtful about a proposition of such potential importance. First he had to determine whether the nuggets were actually gold. Here Sherman was able to help. Mineralogy had been an important academic subject at West Point, and, more important, Sherman had, as a young officer in Georgia, become familiar with the characteristics of the substance that was to cause the Cherokees to be evicted from their lands.

He bit the substance and then took a hammer and pounded it. Its malleability convinced him—and therefore Mason—that the shiny particles were what the two men claimed they were.

Another, more serious problem remained, however. At the time of the incident, both Mason and Sherman regarded California as Mexican territory, with themselves only military occupiers. That being the case, Mexican law, not American, would apply. In view of these doubts, Mason wrote an innocuous letter that did not grant the rights. The two visitors, probably disappointed, went on their way.

Mason and Sherman were disturbed by the encounter, and they still held hopes that the discovery of gold would escape general notice. They knew that small quantities of gold had been discovered weeks before, and nothing had come of it. Mining interests up to that time had been centered on mercury, not gold. A man who shared their concern was John Sutter, a Swiss immigrant who had adopted Mexican citizenship and had built the trading post called Sutter's Fort on the road leading from the Sierra Madre westward to San Francisco. His business of supplying exhausted and depleted travelers coming from the East had been lucrative, and he could foresee that a gold rush on his property would ruin him. So when one of his workers, James W. Marshall, had discovered gold the previous January, Sutter had demanded silence. He had thus far been able to maintain secrecy about the discovery.

Such a thing as gold in the streams, promising instant wealth, could not be kept a secret long. When word got out and was spread in banner headlines in the newspapers, the famed gold rush began.

Finally, Colonel Mason decided it was time for him to take a personal look. So in late June 1848, he took a small detachment, including Sherman, on an expedition to Sutter's Fort. It was not an easy trip. Bodies of water had to be crossed, and it took the party three days to make the journey. To make things even more difficult, their horses got away just as they reached the fort. Fortunately, Sutter was able to send out a group of Indian employees and recaptured them.[9] Time was not urgent, so the party spent several days of relaxation and celebration. It was only then that Mason and Sherman received the details of Marshall's discovery of gold months before. Then, on July 4, the party left Sutter's Fort, accompanied by Sutter, for Coloma, forty miles away.

The party spent several days on the American River, where Coloma was located. They encountered Marshall himself, who was originally a lumberer but was now digging for gold. A couple of systems for gold removal were in use, the principal one being a mere sifting of the sands of a creek in a pan of water. But whatever system, in a letter to his brother John, Sherman estimated that as many as four thousand men were mining in the area, taking out of the ground about $30,000 to $50,000 a day.[10] It was an awesome sight.

Back at Monterey, Sherman saw the gold rush only in negative terms. He had a right to do so. His first concern was for the economy of the region. Prices for goods, being paid for in gold, became astronomical. The most ordinary of commodities carried prices so high that people of fixed income, such as officers like himself, could not make ends meet. Of equal concern to a conscientious officer was the effect of the panic on members of the army and navy; desertion was rampant. (Even Sherman's own clerk deserted.) The terms of service of the volunteers who had fought in the war with Mexico had expired, and many of them simply headed for the Sierra Madre and the American River. Ironically, though Sherman's duties called for him to quell desertions and maintain order, he was unable to share in the bonanza himself.

Sherman, however, was a practical man, a survivor. To cope with his own personal financial problems, he secured two months' leave and, with a couple of other officers, set up a store in the gold mining area. Sherman hired himself out as a surveyor—land claims were highly important—and invested in some landholdings. By dint of these actions he was able to get by. He did not forget his brother John. Sherman advised a way in which his brother could profit:

. . . if you can, even when you receive this, despatch a cargo of assorted articles ready for immediate consumption or use, you can realize more than a hundred per cent. Indian goods of all kinds command any price that is asked.[11]

Sherman's advice was a big order, and it is doubtful that John was adventuresome enough to take it.

Though Sherman coped satisfactorily with the effects of the gold rush, he could never shed his concern that by his own mistake he had missed participating in the exploits of the men under Zachary Taylor and Winfield Scott. At one point he contemplated resigning from the army while he was still in California. General Persifor Smith, who had succeeded Colonel Mason as governor of California, successfully dissuaded him by promoting him to the position of adjutant, a jump above that of aide.

In December 1849, General Smith ordered Sherman to deliver some dispatches to General Winfield Scott in New York City. Sherman therefore left Monterey on January 2, 1850, on the steamer *Oregon*. By this time it was no longer necessary to go around Cape Horn. One ship took him to Panama, and another from there to New York. He arrived at New York about the close of January.[12]

CHAPTER THREE

THE BLEAK YEARS—1850–1861

As Sherman contemplated his future in early 1850, the prospects were mixed. He was glad to leave California, which he considered a backwater, and he was anxious to return to civilization and to Ellen. On the other hand, his prospects in the army appeared bleak. And though he had every intention of marrying Ellen, he knew that she and her father would pressure him to resign from the army. Though Ellen had made it clear that she wanted to marry him, she did not look forward to being an army wife. Further, she could not understand why Cump, having been baptized in the Catholic faith, did not bother to attend Mass. That last concern was minor at the moment, but it was destined to cause tension between them during their later married life.

The first stop on Sherman's journey, once he had reached the East Coast, was New York, where the general in chief, Winfield Scott, kept the headquarters of the army.* Scott, a giant of a man, both physically and in

---

* President Zachary Taylor had been Scott's subordinate for many years, including, technically, during the relatively recent Mexican War. As political rivals in the 1848 election, they had experienced a falling-out. Since the headquarters of the army had no need to be in Washington, Scott had obtained Taylor's permission, readily granted, for him to keep his headquarters in New York. Scott had not attended Taylor's inauguration as president.

prestige, greeted him cordially, and Sherman was honored to be invited to dinner. He should not have been surprised, however, when he discovered that the venerable old soldier was interested in him primarily as the foster son of Thomas Ewing. Scott, at age sixty-four, was planning to run for the presidency in 1852, two years hence, and he needed Ewing's help as a senior Whig. What made Sherman more unhappy, however, was Scott's descriptions of the dazzling successes of his campaign from Veracruz to Mexico City three years earlier. As Scott recounted the events of that time, Sherman was reminded of how much he had missed out professionally for having been in California.[1]

From New York, Sherman went on to Washington, where he delivered dispatches from California. He then obtained a leave of absence from the army of seven months. Conveniently, the Ewing family was in Washington, where Thomas Ewing was serving as Zachary Taylor's secretary of the interior, a newly created post. Sherman lost no time in confirming his engagement to Ellen, and the two were married on the first of May. It was a lavish affair, as befitted the dignity of a father of the bride of Ewing's stature. Such luminaries as President Zachary Taylor and his cabinet attended, as well as senators Henry Clay and Daniel Webster, and all the justices of the Supreme Court. Taylor, like Scott, was another top official who courted the goodwill of Sherman's foster father. The gifts, not surprisingly, were generous.[2]

One dark cloud, however, hovered on the horizon. The entire Ewing family—the father, Thomas; the mother, Maria; and Ellen herself—were convinced that Cump was wasting his time in the army. After ten years of service, he was only a lieutenant, and he had done nothing to amass any kind of money. Even his brother John, who at thirty-seven years of age was a successful lawyer entering politics, joined the rest. But Cump refused to resign. The military was the only profession he was truly familiar with, and he liked the army. If he resigned, the only position in sight would be to manage the saltworks that Thomas Ewing owned near Lancaster. The relations between Ewing and Sherman were cordial enough, but Sherman's pride was such that he refused to be an employee of the older man. The

Ewings already had enough hold on Ellen, and working for her father, as Sherman saw it, would be the ultimate in captivity.

The issue was never solved; it was only deferred. Cump received orders to report to Jefferson Barracks, Missouri, in September, but he had to go alone. Ellen, pregnant, chose to stay with her parents until the baby, which they would name Minnie, arrived in late January 1851. She then joined her husband.

The Shermans did not stay long at Jefferson Barracks. Shortly after Ellen arrived, Cump was transferred to New Orleans. At first things went well. Their house was roomy, and the surroundings were congenial. A second daughter was born there. After a while, however, Sherman began to feel a financial pinch. The pay of a captain could never keep up with the prices of everything in the stores. And Ellen, raised in wealthy circumstances, was anything but thrifty. Sherman concluded that he could not afford their lifestyle if he remained in service.

For once Sherman, the most independent of men who asked few favors, turned to a friend, Major Henry S. Turner, whom he had met at St. Louis while he was stationed at Jefferson Barracks. Turner was a partner in an expanding bank by the name of Lucas, Turner & Co., which was opening a branch in San Francisco. Knowing of Sherman's experiences in California, Turner urged him to obtain a six-month leave from the army to revisit his old haunts and weigh the prospects. Sherman did so, and he liked what he saw. Accordingly, on September 6, 1853, he turned in his resignation, thus ending his first army career. He agreed with Turner to remain in San Francisco for seven years, to January 1, 1860.[3]

As usual, Sherman again encountered resistance from the Ewings. Thomas Ewing made another offer for his employment, and again Cump refused on the same basis as before. He held his ground, and on September 20, Sherman, Ellen, and the new baby left for San Francisco. To secure the permission of the elder Ewings for Ellen's departure, they agreed to leave Minnie back in Lancaster.

Once again, the relations between Sherman and Ellen ran into difficulties; Ellen was miserable in San Francisco. She hated the Western topography, with its sand and hills. She hated the rented house they occupied. She missed Minnie. Beneath it all was the fact that she could not stand to be away from home. She was blunt about her feelings. "If you prefer this outlandish place because of business advantages," she reportedly said to Sherman, "that is no reason why I should be willing to give up home, parents, and friends for life."[4] Sherman, by now accustomed to such tirades, held his ground. In the meantime their problems were heightened by the arrival of a third child, this one a boy, whom they named Willie.

During the summer of 1856 Sherman underwent an experience that stayed with him for the rest of his life. For a short period, at the request of Governor William N. Johnson, he served as the commander of the state militia of California. The position carried with it the rank of major general, a considerable jump from his previous rank of captain, but it was hollow; the state militia had little by way of resources. Fortunately, the position was only a part-time job and did not interfere with Sherman's conducting business at his bank.

Commanding the state militia was no sinecure. Within a couple of days after Sherman had taken office, an incident occurred that proved the impossibility of his position. The recent gubernatorial election had been hotly contested, with many accusations of ballot-box stuffings and the like. Corruption was rife and fairly open.[*] In that atmosphere a newspaper editor named James Casey began writing scurrilous stories attacking prominent men, causing another editor, James King, to look into Casey's past. His investigation revealed that Casey had once been imprisoned in Sing Sing for some felony unknown in San Francisco. An enraged Casey shot King, inflicting a mortal wound.

There was no question about Casey's guilt; his fate was sealed. But a controversy arose around who would try and execute him. Governor

---

* Sherman estimated that the sheriff had paid the Democratic machine a whopping $118,000 for the nomination to a position that paid only $12,000. Sherman, *Memoirs*, p. 118.

Johnson wanted Casey tried by the state supreme court, but the sheriff, a law unto himself, wanted it done under his own jurisdiction. The sheriff had Casey in his custody and he allowed another group of unofficial law enforcers, who called themselves the Vigilantes, to get ahold of Casey and hang him. All this was done outside the governor's jurisdiction, in fact in defiance of him.

Sherman was helpless to interfere. He had the organization to disperse the Vigilantes, but his men were totally lacking in arms. To rectify that vital shortcoming, he and the governor visited Major General John E. Wool, commanding general, Pacific.

General Wool, a hero of both the War of 1812 and the recent Mexican War, received the visitors cordially, and in the presence of witnesses promised Sherman that he would provide from army stocks all the weapons that Sherman requested. Sherman knew the armaments were there; his keen eye identified the unopened boxes of ammunition that had been aboard the *Lexington* as far back as 1846.[5] He left assured.

Something, however, happened. Wool changed his mind and sent letters to both Governor Johnson and Sherman saying rather vaguely that he disapproved the request for arms. Sherman immediately wrote out his resignation as major general in the California militia.[6] He returned to his bank without regret and never went near California politics again. The episode had a profound effect on Sherman's respect for the usefulness of volunteer troops.

What brought Sherman's time in California to an end was, purely and simply, the conclusion of the gold rush. The Sacramento area had been overbuilt to accommodate thousands of miners, but the supply of gold was not inexhaustible. Bank after bank failed. Sherman was a good businessman, and he managed to keep his own branch of the Lucas bank afloat. However, the financial situation in San Francisco was continuing to degenerate, and Turner saw no chance for a reversal. With no prejudice against Sherman, he and the other owners decided to close that branch down. In early 1857, therefore, the Shermans headed for home, as usual by way of Panama.

The experience had been hard on Cump; he was haggard, and the asthma that plagued him at times in his life returned. Reassigned to the New York branch of Lucas and Symonds, he went through the humiliation of another failure. The panic of 1857 had reached Wall Street, and the central Lucas bank in St. Louis closed in August. Sherman seems to have kept the New York branch open for a short while, but in October the owners decided to close down that branch also. Sherman was on the verge of what he dreaded most: becoming dependent once more upon the Ewings.

For the next couple of years, Sherman appeared to live the life of a drifter. Though his talents were recognized, he did not stay in any job for very long. Immediately after closing down the Lucas and Symonds bank in New York, he returned to St. Louis to help pick up the pieces. He then went to San Francisco to salvage what he could from that location. That chore finished, Sherman headed back to the East.

A memorable incident occurred when Sherman returned to St. Louis to participate in planning for the final closing of the Lucas bank. On the street he encountered Ulysses S. Grant, whom he had known at West Point but had not seen since. The conversation was casual, but Grant had fared worse in civilian life than had Sherman. When asked about the encounter in later years, all Sherman could recall was that "West Point and the Regular Army were not good schools for farmers and bankers."[7] Nothing more came of their meeting.

Sherman was once more out of work, and once more Ellen and her father attempted to induce him to manage the salt mines near the Ewing home in Lancaster. Sherman once more refused. He did, however, accept an offer to join a law firm that Ewing had set up in Leavenworth, Kansas. On January 1, 1859, the firm of Sherman, Ewing, and McCook was established. Sherman soon learned, however that the term "law office" was misleading. While he practiced some law, he soon discovered that he and his partners performed only odd jobs, one of which was to manage his father-in-law's extensive landholdings in the area. He stayed only a short time and was again looking for work.

Finally, in desperation, Sherman applied for readmission into the regular army. There he again ran into a roadblock. The incredibly small establishment was unable to commission all the young men who were graduating from West Point, much less take on those who had resigned. Four years, four jobs.

———————

Sherman was definitely down on his luck, but it would be an exaggeration to call him a failure, as so many are wont to do. Turner, for example, appreciated his worth, and when other banks had failed in San Francisco, Sherman's did not. Turner, in fact, had shown a great deal of confidence in Sherman when he transferred him to their New York branch. It was only when the central branch in St. Louis closed down that the whole Turner network closed.

A major cause for Sherman's continued run of hard luck was his pride. He was, however, wise in his refusal to accept employment with Thomas Ewing. Ewing, with all his kindly disposition, was a man who exercised authority. And though the two men worked together well as equals in later years, Sherman could never tolerate Ewing as a superior.

In applying for readmission to the army, Sherman was doing what he probably had wanted to do all along. The act led to a position that turned out to be among the most rewarding in his career.

CHAPTER FOUR

THE UNION ABOVE ALL

In June 1859, while visiting the Ewings, Sherman received a message from his old friend Don Carlos Buell, currently the adjutant general of the army. The message was disappointing, in a way, because no vacancy existed for Sherman in the army. But Buell had an intriguing suggestion: The state of Louisiana, he disclosed, was about to open up a new military school near present-day Baton Rouge, carrying the impressive name of the Louisiana State Seminary of Learning & Military Academy.[1] Sherman might apply for the position of superintendent.

At first glance, Sherman's prospects for gaining the position might have seemed to be unlikely, since he was from Ohio, not Louisiana, but actually they were not. Despite his hard luck in business and law, Sherman was known as a capable man with a creditable military record. He was known to have spent a great deal of time in the South and to be fond of the residents of that region. And there was always the prominence of his father-in-law. His application was accepted on November 12, 1859.

A cloud, however, loomed on the horizon. At the time of Sherman's appointment the newspapers were full of an event that had occurred at Harpers Ferry, Virginia, on October 16. An abolitionist by the name of

John Brown, leading a small band of fanatic abolitionists, had seized the federal arsenal in the town and held it for a while, unrealistically expecting a surge of slaves from all over the South to escape their plantations and join him. Brown and his group had been quickly captured and subsequently put on trial. Brown himself was hanged for treason. The long-term consequences of this seemingly small incident were incalculable, but they were probably not much on Sherman's mind at that moment.

Though Buell was the man who had suggested Sherman's application for his new position, the official who had made the appointment was General Thomas O. Moore, the head of the education department of Louisiana, soon to become governor of the state. He and Sherman made something of an odd couple. Their views on the troubles between North and South, centered on slavery, were far apart, and yet the two men developed a personal friendship that survived the war.* It was at a dinner given by Governor Moore that Sherman had the opportunity to explain his political position to the guests, many of whom suspected that he was an abolitionist, possibly a spy. Those who had doubts about the new superintendent were uncomfortable that Sherman was the foster son of Thomas Ewing, an antislavery man, and worse, the brother of John Sherman, a man known to be of the same persuasion.

Sherman, in the address he made, assured the dinner guests that neither of his relatives was an abolitionist, which he defined as a man ambitious to enforce his antislavery views on the South. He also clarified his own position. Personally, he admitted, he disapproved of slavery as a human institution, but he strongly rejected the use of force to settle the problem. The audience largely accepted his words.

Sherman was happy with his new situation. His salary of $5,000 a year

---

* At the end of the Civil War, Moore, who had served as a general in the Confederate Army, fled to Mexico to escape being tried for treason. Sherman interceded with President Andrew Johnson to secure a pardon for Moore and even aided him in restoring his properties near Alexandria, where Moore lived out the rest of his life in peace.

was generous for the time, and it was totally independent of any connection with Thomas Ewing. Still, Ellen, who never wanted to be far from her family, persisted in coming up with other ideas. From Lancaster she wrote a letter suggesting a banking position in London. Once again Cump refused. He made it quite clear that as soon as possible he would bring her and the children to live in Alexandria, a town near the seminary. He intended to spend the rest of his active life at the school. In one letter, he added a bit of ironic humor:

> I suppose I was the Jonah that blew up San Francisco, and it took only two months' residence in Wall Street to bust up New York, and I think my arrival in London will be the signal of the downfall of that mighty empire.[2]

Sherman gave his new job his all. He was devoted to the seminary, and he was careful to care for both the faculty and the fifty-three cadets who were his charges. He made a point of speaking to each cadet every day, and he did everything possible to make them all feel happy with his tutelage, while still insisting on very high standards. He brooked no foolishness, though his discipline was far from autocratic. He was not dealing with people who were necessarily docile; in one letter to Ellen, for example, he described a fight between two cadets in which one boy threatened the other with a knife. Sherman actually enjoyed the company of the cadets socially. He was known to enjoy telling them stories of the army in the West, all of which they ate up. But he was still utterly in charge.

Sherman's most intimate friend at the seminary was the professor of modern languages, Dr. David French Boyd, whose observations of Sherman have been invaluable to anyone attempting to understand the man. Impressed with Sherman's ability to play the role of the father to the cadets and to mingle with them without lowering standards, Boyd observed that the superintendent was "no scholar" and lacked any "literary and scientific acquirements." Nor was he much of a reader. But, he continued,

He was rather a tough, unpolished diamond made great by nature of deep discernment, needing little the ideas of other men. But brilliant and original as he was in thought, he had not the usual accompaniment of genius—want of practicality. Sherman was eminently practical.

"It was this combination of brilliance, originality, and practicality," a Sherman biographer has written, "that set Sherman apart from many other people of his day."[3]

But clouds continued to gather above this congenial scene. Relations between North and South degenerated daily, and though the gathering storm did not affect Sherman's situation for the moment, they caused him anguish. At Christmas dinner in 1860, he received a telegraph message from the East that the legislature of South Carolina had seceded from the Union in protest against the election of Abraham Lincoln as president. According to his host, Boyd, the news brought tears to Sherman's eyes. Boyd recorded how Sherman stomped up and down the floor for a period of about an hour. In the course of his orating, he came up with ideas that, in hindsight, predicted the dire future of the South with remarkable accuracy. As quoted by Boyd, he declared that the people of the South "didn't know what they were doing." He predicted that the country "would be drenched in blood." He depicted the overpowering strength of the North compared to that of the South. Sherman may have been located far from the seats of power, but he knew whereof he spoke. He had been in contact with Tom Ewing, John Sherman, and others.

Even though South Carolina had seceded, Sherman still held hopes that the secession movement might stop with that single state. After all, South Carolina had threatened a similar action back in 1832, withdrawing the threat only when faced down by a forceful Andrew Jackson. Perhaps, since he was so convinced that war between the sections would be utterly destructive to the South, Sherman hoped that those south of the Mason-Dixon Line might see the light.

Sherman's future was here put to the test. On the one hand, his loyalty to the Union and to the rule of law was fierce, due partly to the influence of Thomas Ewing, and partly to his experiences in California, where he saw anarchy at its worst. On the other hand, he dearly hoped to stay at the seminary.

In the end, of course, Sherman would inevitably stick with the Union, which meant the North. A breakup of the Union, even though the Constitution contained no objection to such an eventuality, was to Sherman's mind a form of anarchy, and he would have none of it.

Still Sherman watched with dismay as the Union disintegrated. He was angry at the halfhearted measures being taken by President James Buchanan to halt it. When General Winfield Scott attempted to resupply Fort Sumter at Charleston by use of the SS *Star of the West*, Sherman was disgusted. He wrote to Ellen that this was the ship on which they had made a trip to California—they should have sent a warship that could defend herself against the Charleston shore batteries. Sherman's fears came to pass. The *Star of the West* was turned back.

Faced with this stark reality, Sherman soberly and methodically laid his plans. As long as Louisiana remained in the Union, he would be able to stay in his present position. But if Louisiana should secede, Sherman's duty was to resign it. Even if the seceded states agreed not to use his military talents directly against the United States, his activities at the seminary would be contributing indirectly to the Southern cause.

On January 26, 1861, the worst happened: Louisiana seceded from the Union. Despite his grief—and the urgings of Governor Moore—Sherman submitted his resignation as superintendent of the Louisiana State Seminary, effective that date. He did not leave immediately, however; he was determined to be meticulous in his accountings for property and other odds and ends. Then, in Boyd's words,

> When the day for his departure arrived, the cadets were formed up in his honor on the parade ground. He passed down the line bidding each officer and cadet goodbye. At the end of the last column Sherman attempted to deliver the speech he had prepared, but emotion choked his efforts. Finally, after a long silence, he simply placed his hand over his heart and said, "You are here." Turning on his heel, he quickly disappeared.[4]

From Alexandria, Louisiana, Sherman made his way home to Lancaster, where Ellen and their five children were still living with the Ewings. As he traveled north, his frame of mind began to shift from grief at leaving the South to a deep concern for the welfare of the North. The people of Louisiana were talking war and making preparations for it, accumulating arms and mobilizing volunteers. In contrast, Sherman saw no sense of urgency as he surveyed the countryside of the North. It was all business as usual.

Sherman was keenly conscious of what was happening between Washington and the authorities in the South. Kept up-to-date primarily by his brother John, he was well aware that a focus of conflict was now the future of the Union forces located at Charleston, South Carolina. He knew that the presence of Union troops would be intolerable to the people of that city if secession became an established reality. He also had a personal concern as to the fate of Fort Sumter's commander, Major Robert Anderson, who, at fifteen years his senior, had been a sort of mentor to him. Sherman had felt great pride some weeks earlier when Anderson had boldly transferred the Union garrison from the vulnerable Fort Moultrie to Fort Sumter out in Charleston Harbor. Now he wrote to Ellen with vehemence, "Let them hurt a hair of [Anderson's] head in the execution of his duty, and I say

Charleston must [be] blotted from existence." The Union garrison at Charleston must be reinforced, he added, "if it cost ten thousand lives."[5]

Yet Sherman had no desire to participate in what he foresaw as an inevitable conflict. He was too emotionally torn between his veneration for the Union and his affection for the people of the South to want to take sides. Therefore, while staying temporarily with his family at the Ewing home, he decided that he would once again cast his lot with the ever-faithful Major Turner in St. Louis, who had already secured a position for him as president of the Fifth Street Railroad. It was not a spectacular job, but it was adequate, and it promised to pay enough to support his growing family. He determined to go there soon.

In the meantime, however, Sherman received a letter from his brother John, who had just been elected a United States senator from Ohio. John was urging him to visit Washington, a thinly disguised effort to bring his older brother into governmental service. Open to anything at the moment, Sherman rationalized that loyalty to John required him to accept the invitation.

On Sherman's arrival in Washington, John immediately took him to the White House to meet the new president, Abraham Lincoln. According to Sherman's account, he and John entered the president's office to find the room filled with crowds of men milling around. Lincoln was sitting at the end of a long table, talking casually with three or four men, who quickly disappeared on John's arrival. John Sherman and Lincoln shook hands. John produced some papers, perhaps from the Ohio legislature, and Lincoln looked them over briefly and promised to take care of them. John then introduced his brother and announced grandly, as if expecting Lincoln to be impressed, that he had just returned from Louisiana. "Mr. President, this is my brother Colonel Sherman, who is just up from Louisiana; he may give you some information you want."

"Ah," said the president, "how are they coming along down there?"

Sherman spoke eagerly. "They think they are coming along swimmingly," he said. "They are preparing for war."

"Oh, well," said Lincoln. "I guess we'll manage to keep house."

Sherman was shocked by this noncommittal, disinterested response and said no more. Once outside the building, however, he turned on John. As he quoted himself in his memoir, he damned all politicians, saying, "You have got things in a hell of a fix, and you may get them out as best you can."[6] Despite John's efforts to keep him around a bit longer, Sherman would have none of it.

After his disappointing visit with President Lincoln—and his outburst at his brother John—Sherman lost no time in returning to Lancaster and picking up his family for the journey to St. Louis. This time Ellen, though pregnant with their sixth child, accompanied him with the rest of the family. They settled down in a comfortable house, where they could live satisfactorily, though Sherman's yearly salary was only half that which he had enjoyed at the seminary.

Sherman's letters from that period indicate that he still hoped, perhaps unconsciously, to return to the army. He was not, however, willing to do so on any terms except his own. He would not, for example, be involved with the militia, so when Frank Blair Jr.,* a prominent local citizen, proposed to secure an appointment for him as a brigadier general in the Missouri militia, he flatly refused. Missouri, an important slave state, was going through the throes of deciding whether or not to secede from the Union, and the outcome of the matter would be of much consequence. But Sherman showed little interest in the local situation; his mind was focused on much broader issues.

Despite his temporary disillusionment with the government in Washington, Sherman remained in close contact with John, who agreed that he should be choosy as to the nature of his participation in the war that all

---

* Blair's father, Frank Blair Sr., was a prominent Washington journalist, friend of presidents, and onetime owner of the Blair House, now an adjunct of the White House. His son, Frank Blair Jr., had moved to St. Louis.

now knew was inevitable. Perhaps because of John's promotion of his cause, Cump received an offer in early April 1861 to be chief clerk of the War Department, with the promise of appointment as assistant secretary when Congress came back into session. Sherman did not specify the reason for his flat refusal, but John knew his brother well enough to surmise that he desired active duty in the field, not in the bureaucracy. John agreed with his brother's action.

Three days after Sherman's letter of refusal, on April 12, 1861, Confederate forces at Charleston demanded that Major Anderson surrender Fort Sumter to Confederate forces under the command of Sherman's old friend Pierre Beauregard. Eventually Anderson had to comply. That incident triggered the secession of the upper South* and, depending on President Lincoln's actions, a major war. Under these circumstances Sherman's participation as a soldier was now inevitable. And yet he was still particular in his selection of a position.

A letter came from John on April 14, the day that Anderson surrendered Fort Sumter. Men in Washington, he wrote, were well aware of Sherman's capabilities, and if he wanted a position in the War Department, it was his for the asking. But John had another suggestion: Sherman could return to Ohio—safe Union territory—and raise a regiment of volunteers; he could do so without difficulty.[7] Sherman again refused; he did not trust volunteers.

In the meantime, the correspondence between the brothers covered many other aspects of the war besides Sherman's personal career. Sherman's letters were not confined to military matters; he trespassed into broad aspects of the war. It would be fought, he advised, on two premises, the "national integrity" (union) and slavery. He was adamant that the Union must be the issue. If the issue were slavery, the South would fight to the last man, creating a war of attrition. If negotiations could be conducted

---

* States in the upper South—Virginia, Tennessee, North Carolina, and Arkansas—seceded by the spring of 1861. Kentucky, Missouri, Maryland, and Delaware became "border states"—slaveholding states of the upper South that remained loyal to the Union.

on the basis of the Union and set the slavery issue aside, a major war might be averted. Sherman had only a secondary sympathy with the slaves themselves, and he held Lincoln responsible for much of the crisis by failing adequately to court the border states while there was still time.

Finally Sherman swallowed his pride. On May 8, 1861, he wrote Secretary of War Simon Cameron virtually asking for a command:

> Dear Sir: I hold myself now as always, prepared to serve my country in the capacity for which I was trained. I cannot and will not volunteer for three months because I cannot throw my family on the cold support of charity, but for the three years' call made by the President an officer could prepare his command and do good service. I will not volunteer because, rightfully or wrongfully, I feel myself unwilling to take a mere private's place, and having for many years lived in California and Louisiana, the men are not well enough acquainted with me to elect me to my appropriate place. Should my services be needed, the Record or the War Department will enable you to designate the station in which I can render best service.[8]

Cameron's answer was not long in coming. The authorities in Washington were willing to give Sherman the choice between appointment as a colonel of the regular army or as a major general of volunteers. He chose the former and was given command of the 13th Infantry, a regular regiment that would be recruited in St. Louis. Before assuming command, however, he was ordered to report to Washington. He left St. Louis for that destination in the middle of May 1861.

CHAPTER FIVE

BULL RUN

On his arrival in Washington, Sherman reported at once to Lieutenant General Winfield Scott, who was still the general in chief of the army. There he found the old warhorse, now seventy-five years old, working around the clock in an effort to create an army out of the collection of volunteer regiments coming in from the states. On the insistence of Simon Cameron, the army would be made up almost entirely of volunteer regiments known by their state designations, such as the 71st Pennsylvania Volunteer Regiment. This decision had been made much to the displeasure of the generals, most of whom were regulars.

The meeting with Scott brought on one small disappointment: Sherman had been expecting to leave Washington at once to begin recruiting his regiment at St. Louis, but Scott had other ideas. Sherman was to remain in his own office for a time to serve as the army's inspector general. The general insisted that Sherman's lieutenant colonel, in Missouri, could tend to the business of recruiting the regiment.

Sherman soon discovered, however, that his job as inspector general had one pleasing aspect: It allowed him a chance to travel around and get a feel for the overall situation in the eastern theater. Events were happening rapidly. Scott, Sherman soon learned, was organizing the troops around Washington into two separate armies. One was located directly across the Potomac from Washington, under the command of a newly appointed brigadier general, Irvin McDowell. The other, located farther west at Hagerstown, Maryland, was under the command of Major General Robert E. Patterson, who had been a prominent general in the Mexican War thirteen years earlier.

Neither was a good choice. McDowell, who owed his position partly to his friendship with Treasury Secretary Salmon P. Chase, had neither sought nor desired the command. His career in the army had always involved administration, and he had never commanded a troop unit of any size. His counterpart, Patterson, who had always been mediocre, was advancing in age. While not doddering, he was lacking in the energy necessary for arduous duty. But as of that moment, as Sherman observed, the authorities in Washington, with the exception of Scott, were convinced that this would be a short war, with the South giving up without much of a fight. The tragedy that awaited both sections of the country was not yet foreseen. Sherman visited his brother John, who had temporarily left his seat in the Senate to serve as a volunteer aide to General Patterson. All was optimism.

That hubris would cost the nation dearly. Scott, one of our greatest generals, was now too old and overweight to take the field in person. He was, however, a military student, and he bore no illusions that the people of the South would succumb easily. In this realization, Scott and Sherman were remarkably close. The Mississippi River, they contended, would be critical in the coming conflict. The Union would have to occupy it for its full length, isolating the cotton states from Texas and Arkansas, cutting off resupply from the West.

The trouble with Scott's plan, scornfully termed the "Anaconda Plan" by its critics, was that it would take months, even years, to put into effect. The temper of the times called for immediate action: "On to Richmond," cried the New York Tribune. Abraham Lincoln, much as he respected the views of his general in chief, could not resist the pressure of public opinion. He ordered McDowell and Patterson to move forward against Beauregard's army at Manassas on July 16, 1861.

Sherman was destined to be part of this offensive. At the last minute, just before McDowell marched off, he was placed in command of a brigade. It was not what he would have preferred.* All of the units, with the exception of the 3d Artillery, were volunteers. Sherman took a jaundiced but philosophical view of his command. He later wrote, "We had good organization and good men but no cohesion, no real discipline, no respect for authority, and no real knowledge of war."[1] He took solace in reminding himself, however, that the Confederates were in no better condition than the Union troops.

Sherman's brigade was assigned to a division commanded by Brigadier General Daniel Tyler, basically a good man but unqualified to be a high commander. A West Point graduate from the class of 1819, he had resigned his commission in 1834 to pursue a successful career in business. Now, at the age of sixty-two, he was going into the field after an absence from the army of twenty-seven years. He had reentered service commanding a volunteer Connecticut regiment, but so desperate were Lincoln and Scott for men with military backgrounds that he had been given a division soon after.[2] The division consisted of four brigades—Sherman's, Erasmus Keyes's, Robert Schenck's, and Israel Richardson's.

As of the morning of July 21, both sides were deployed behind Bull Run, a stream that ran about halfway between Centreville and Manassas. Both sides planned to attack. McDowell and Confederate general Beauregard were each concentrating his force on his right wing, planning to

---

* The units were the 13th New York Volunteers (Quinby), the 69th New York (Corcoran), the 79th New York (Cameron), the 2d Wisconsin (Peck), and Company E, 3d Artillery (Ayres).

envelop the other one's left. Beauregard, with Brigadier General Joseph Johnston having joined him after eluding Patterson in the Shenandoah, was based on Manassas Junction. McDowell, on the Warrenton Pike, intended to send Tyler across Bull Run by way of the Stone Bridge, largely as a demonstration. He planned to move the bulk of his forces, two divisions under brigadier generals Samuel P. Heintzelman and David Hunter, northward to cross Bull Run at Sudley Springs and attack southward, rolling up Beauregard's left. Both McDowell's and Beauregard's plans were good, but McDowell struck first. Beauregard, realizing his plight, moved northward across Henry House Hill to meet him.

Of Tyler's three brigades, he sent Schenck's directly to the Stone Bridge. Keyes was to march northward behind Hunter's division, and Sherman was to follow Schenck and take position at a point behind Bull Run about a mile north of Stone Bridge.

Sherman left Centreville at two thirty a.m. on the morning of July 21, arriving at his destination around six a.m. He deployed his four regiments along the riverbank and waited. During the morning Hunter's division, bound for Sudley Springs on the north, began its northern movement, followed by Heintzelman's. The road leading to Sudley Springs was no highway; it was a rough trail. Sherman knew that it would take a long time for the two divisions to get into position.

Sometime during the morning a small but significant incident occurred. A Confederate officer on horseback crossed Bull Run to the Union side, rode toward Sherman's position, and then, staying out of musket range, shouted curses and insults at the Yankees. Then, apparently satisfied, he returned back across the stream. Sherman's sharp eye followed him; he carefully noted the place where the hotheaded rebel horseman had forded the stream.

It was midmorning before Sherman detected the sound of battle off to the right, where he correctly surmised that Hunter's division had made contact with the Confederates. He had no way of knowing that Hunter was being faced by only a single Confederate brigade commanded by an iras-

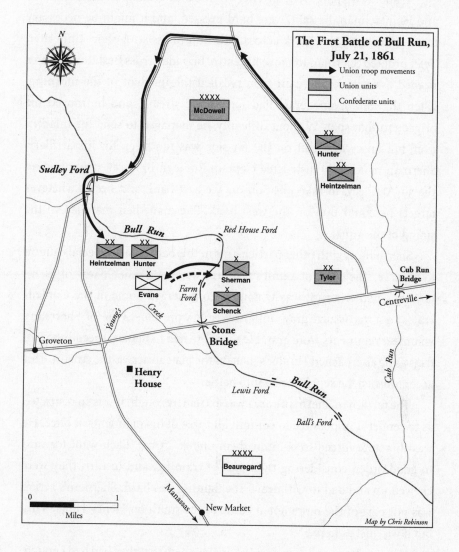

The First Battle of Bull Run,
July 21, 1861

→ Union troop movements
▨ Union units
☐ Confederate units

N

XXXX
McDowell

XX
Hunter

XX
Heintzelman

Sudley Ford

Bull Run

Red House Ford

XX
Heintzelman

XX
Hunter

X
Sherman

XX
Tyler

Cub Run
Bridge

X
Evans

Farm
Ford

XX
Schenck

Centreville →

Young's

Creek

Stone
Bridge

Cub Run

Groveton

■ Henry
House

Bull Run

Lewis Ford

Ball's Ford

XXXX
Beauregard

Manassas

0   1

Miles

New Market

Map by Chris Robinson

cible, hard-drinking member of the West Point class of 1848, Nathaniel "Shanks" Evans.[*]

At about two p.m. General Tyler arrived at Sherman's position. Hunter and Heintzelman, he said, were hard-pressed, and it might be necessary to send the 69th New York across Bull Run to assist. A short time later, Tyler ordered Sherman to move his entire brigade across Bull Run; Hunter needed assistance. Sherman then recalled the incident of the morning, when the lone Confederate had forded the stream, and he moved his brigade to that spot. Without difficulty, he managed to send his infantry over, but an escarpment on the far side was too steep for his artillery. Sherman reluctantly instructed Captain Romeyn B. Ayres, commanding the 3d Artillery, to take position on the east bank and fire at whatever targets he could find on the west bank. Sherman then marched to the sound of the guns.

Sherman, as with other participants in this battle, had a special caution to observe. The color of a unit's uniform was not a reliable way of ascertaining whether a unit was Union or Confederate. Some of the Confederates, not yet issued gray uniforms, still wore blue. One of Sherman's volunteer regiments wore gray. He therefore had to make a special show of flags as he approached Hunter's men on the plateau across the stream. This accomplished, he sent his men into battle.

The terrain in Sherman's area was extremely rough. It was so restricted as to render it impossible to commit all three of his regiments at once. He was therefore forced to commit them one at a time. Each went forward in good order, considering their lack of training, and in turn they were chewed up and had to withdraw. The fighting was hard. Sherman's action was not part of the more noted battle to the south on Henry House Hill, but it was just as fierce.

Finally, Sherman's men decided on their own that they had had enough.

---

[*] Evans had a spotty career because of his disposition and alcoholism. He was, however, a brave and skillful soldier. He was later given the thanks of the Confederate Congress for his victory in October 1861, at Ball's Bluff, near Leesburg, Virginia.

Despite their commander's urgings to stay in the fight, each regiment began making its way slowly and deliberately to the rear. There was as yet no panic, but the move was inexorable. Sherman, a realist, soon concluded that these men had had all the fighting they were going to do that day. He therefore guided them back to the ford they had originally crossed. Late in the day they were safely on the east side of the stream.

The fighting done by Sherman's brigade was obviously only a small part of the story of Bull Run. Furthermore, the actual fighting was not the most memorable aspect of the day's events. The worst was the panic that soon developed once the Union soldiers had escaped back across Bull Run. Sherman kept his men in better order than did most brigade commanders; in fact, his performance was noticed.* At Centreville, Sherman encountered McDowell, who was still hoping to make a stand at that position. But it was too late; the men could not be stopped. The rout continued through the night, led by the carriages of civilian spectators who had come out from Washington. Sherman himself did not reach his former headquarters, Camp Corcoran, until noon the next day, July 22.

Sherman's brigade had lost heavily. In his official report, submitted on July 25, he listed his total casualties (out of a brigade of 3,500) as 609, of which 111 had been killed. More than twice that number were missing. The casualties had been particularly heavy among the officers. He mentioned Lieutenant Colonel Haggerty (killed), Colonel Cameron (mortally wounded), and Colonel Corcoran (missing).[3]

Even though Sherman had performed well, he was in a black depression. Never mind that he had predicted a poor performance from his volunteer

---

* At one point, for example, when his men were hit by a detachment of Confederate cavalry, Sherman formed his men up in a hollow square, British style, and repulsed the assault handily.

troops. Never mind also that his good performance had been noticed by his superiors. Such matters were trivial compared to defeat. On July 24 he wrote Ellen, principally to assure her that he had survived the battle. Then, on the twenty-eighth, he wrote her a long account, which is more lucid than the official report he had submitted to General Tyler. In particular he was angry about the pursuit:

> Here [Centreville] I suppose we should assemble in some order the confused masses and try to stem the tide. Indeed I saw but little evidence of being pursued, though once or twice their cavalry interposed themselves between us and our rear. I had read of retreats before, having seen the noise and confusion of crowds of men at fires and shipwrecks, but nothing like this. It was as disgraceful as words can portray, but I doubt that volunteers from any quarter could do better. Each private thinks for himself. If he wants to go for water, he asks leave of no one. . . . No curse could be greater than invasion by a volunteer army. No Goths or Vandals had less respect for the lives and property of friends and foes, and henceforth we ought never to hope for any friends in Virginia.[4]

Despite this anguish, Sherman had other, immediate problems to deal with. Fort Corcoran was located on the Virginia side of the Potomac, but many of his troops did not consider the position strong enough and they continued to flee into Washington. Sherman recovered almost all of them.

As always Sherman was methodical in restoring order in his sector of the defense. He first consolidated his four regiments, bringing them as close together as possible. The 69th New York, their colonel still missing, returned to Fort Corcoran, and the 79th New York and the 2d Wisconsin were moved in closer to it. By the twenty-fifth of July, only a couple of days after reoccupying that position, Sherman was reasonably confident that he could defend against the Confederate attack that everyone presumed was inevitable. His success was duly noted.

It was not, however, an easy job. To restore a sense of discipline, Sherman drilled his men hard. To stem desertion he held three musters a day to ascertain how many men, if any, were missing. The men were not docile; so many wanted to leave camp that at one point Sherman unlimbered an artillery battery with a threat to blast some would-be deserters if they really tried to leave.

July 26, 1861, was a memorable day for the commander of the 3d Brigade. In the morning, just following reveille, Sherman noticed a few men from the 69th New York heading for a nearby drawbridge across the Potomac. As far as they were concerned, their three-month enlistment was up; they had, in fact, applied for discharge just before the move on Bull Run a week earlier. Among the departing group was a doughty captain who lightly asked the colonel whether there was anything he could do as a favor when he and his men reached New York.

Sherman bristled. In a positive manner he pointed out that he had signed no orders granting any leaves of absence. The captain reiterated the oft-repeated argument that since his unit's time was up, his men were no longer soldiers; they needed no leave.

Sherman sensed a crisis. If he allowed these men to depart, he could soon be a colonel without a command. He therefore played his trump card. "Captain," he later recalled saying, "this question of your term of service has been submitted to the rightful authority, and the decision has been published in orders. You are a soldier, and must submit to orders till you are properly discharged. If you attempt to leave without orders, it will be mutiny, and I will shoot you like a dog! Go back into the fort now, instantly, and don't dare to leave without my consent."[5] In recalling the incident, Sherman was not certain whether or not his right hand was near a firearm, but in any event, the captain looked at him a long time and then obeyed his orders. The men scattered; none left.

The story did not quite end there. Later in the day, when Sherman was inspecting some installations down near the river, he was surprised to see a carriage being ferried across the river from Georgetown. The occupants of the carriage were unmistakable; they were President Abraham Lincoln and his secretary of state, William Seward. Sherman went down to meet them and asked whether their destination was his position. It was. Upon Sherman's offer to provide him a guide, the president invited him to join the party and guide them himself.

As the carriage labored up the hill, Sherman was impressed by the depth of Lincoln's feelings. Asked whether he wished to address the troops, Lincoln said he would very much like to. Sherman sent word ahead to assemble the troops of one regiment, but he had an earnest and unusual request: that Lincoln discourage the men from cheering. "I asked him," Sherman later wrote, "to please discourage all cheering, noise, or any sort of confusion; that we had had enough of it before Bull Run to ruin any set of men, and that what we needed were cool, thoughtful, hard-fighting soldiers—no more hurrahing, no more humbug." Perhaps Sherman was surprised by the good-humored way the president took this admonition from a colonel.[6]

By the time Lincoln's carriage reached the first camp, he found the men drawn up in proper fashion. Lincoln stood up straight in his carriage to address them. Sherman was struck by the quality of his speech, later calling it "one of the neatest, best, and most feeling addresses I ever listened to." At one point the men began to cheer, but Lincoln stopped them: "Don't cheer, boys. I confess I rather like it myself, but Colonel Sherman here says it is not military; and I guess we had better defer to his opinion." The president finished by promising that his soldiers would have everything they needed. Sherman considered the effect of the speech excellent.[7]

Lincoln was able to speak to only one regiment at a time, and the second one was the New York 69th. His talk was similar to the earlier one, but while it was in progress Sherman spied the captain he had threatened that morning working his way through the crowd, pale faced and tense. When the captain reached Lincoln's side, he shouted, "Mr. President, I have a cause of grievance. This morning I went to speak to Colonel Sherman, and he threatened to shoot me."

Lincoln paused before speaking; he looked at the captain and then looked at Sherman. Finally, he leaned way over and said in a loud stage whisper for all to hear, "Well, if I were you, and he threatened to shoot, I would not trust him, for I believe he would do it."

The crowd laughed, and the captain disappeared in the crowd. When Sherman later explained the circumstances of the incident, the president was relieved. Lincoln's support made Sherman's task easier in the future, and he was happy when Seward remarked that the visit had been "the first bright moment they had experienced since the battle."[8]

Lincoln's visit did not, however, mean an end to the discontent in the army. Some discipline was enforced by sending regiments or parts of regiments to Fort Jefferson, in Florida. But the real solution to the problem came when the three-month men were sent home and were replaced by three-year volunteers. Sherman was reinforced and was able to move his line of defense out ahead of the ramparts at Fort Corcoran.

———

Sherman's chagrin over the defeat at Bull Run was such that in spite of his pleasant encounter with President Lincoln, he expected to be cashiered. So did Heintzelman, Porter, and others. One evening, however, as the officers were gathered at Arlington House—a Virginia mansion converted into the headquarters of the Army of the Potomac—a message came in carrying a list naming several officers who were to be promoted to the grade of brigadier general.* Sherman was one. The officers scoffed at the idea, but it later turned out to be true.

———

* Arlington House, built between 1802 and 1818, had been the home of George Washington Parke Custis, stepgrandson of George Washington. In 1831, Custis's daughter, Mary, married a young West Point cadet named Robert E. Lee. Lee lived at Arlington House in the decades prior to the Civil War, and upon the outbreak of hostilities made his fateful decision to resign his U.S. Army commission in a second-floor bedroom at Arlington. Positioned on Arlington Heights along the Potomac River, the house sat directly across from the nation's capital and was quickly commandeered by federal troops at the start of the war. In a less than subtle act of retaliation, federal commanders soon transformed Lee's former estate into a massive cemetery for Union dead—today known as Arlington National Cemetery.

General Irvin McDowell remained in command of the Army of the Potomac for a short while. From his headquarters at Arlington House, he organized his army and awaited the arrival of his replacement, Major General George B. McClellan. In due time, McClellan arrived and assumed command. Sherman felt his first doubts about the showy little engineer from Ohio. Instead of taking station with the army across the river at Arlington House, McClellan took a house in Washington and visited the army only occasionally. Sherman developed his first inkling that McClellan had political as well as military ambitions. Still, "Little Mac," as McClellan was soon dubbed by his troops, was a good organizer, and soon the Army of the Potomac began to take shape.

Sherman did not have long to stay at Fort Corcoran, located along the Potomac River, just southwest of the nation's capital. In the middle of August he received a note from Robert Anderson, former commander at Fort Sumter, now catapulted from the grade of major to that of brigadier general. Sherman was elated to read that Anderson was asking him to ride into the city to confer with him at the Willard Hotel. He readily agreed, and they joined a small group that included Senator Andrew Johnson of Tennessee.

Anderson had just been appointed to a newly organized command, the Department of the Cumberland, which consisted of Union forces in Kentucky and Tennessee. It was an important mission and an urgent one. The legislature of Kentucky was in session, and Anderson's first challenge would be to convince that body to remain with the Union. The chances were good, and Union troops were being provided to protect the area from invasion by Confederate forces. To help him, Anderson had been authorized to select four assistants. Sherman's name headed the list, which also included George H. Thomas,* Ambrose Burnside, and Don Carlos Buell, all four men destined for prominent roles in the war. Sherman readily agreed.

---

* Lincoln had some doubts about Thomas because that officer came from Virginia. He and Winfield Scott were the only two Virginians to remain loyal to the Union.

A couple of days later, Anderson and his newly appointed aides met personally with President Lincoln to discuss the mission. At that time, Sherman made a strange demand: He exacted a promise from the president that he would serve only in a subordinate capacity, not in a high command. Sherman had apparently not yet recovered from what he considered his own failure at Bull Run, and a realistic assessment of his own strengths and weaknesses was one of his most remarkable aptitudes. But he was also influenced by his contempt for volunteer soldiers. As he saw it, the first members of the Union high command would be sacrificial lambs. He did not want to be one of them. He would wait until the Union finally developed a trained army.

With some surprise, Lincoln agreed. "He promised," Sherman later wrote, "making the jocular remark that his chief trouble was to find places for the too many generals who wanted to be at the head of affairs . . ."[9] Orders were issued by General Scott on August 24, 1861. Sherman's future service in the Civil War would be in the West, as he preferred.

CHAPTER SIX

SHERMAN FINDS HIS NICHE— WITH GRANT

Sherman's departure from Washington was delayed a short time, because General George B. McClellan, fearful of an attack on Washington—and recognizing Sherman's worth—refused to release him until the threat from Beauregard had passed. When Sherman finally got loose, he reported to General Anderson, arriving at the latter's Ohio home on September 1. Of the three key staff officers assigned to assist him, only Sherman and George H. Thomas were present.

Anderson, they found, was in a depressed state of mind. At the age of fifty-six he was finding himself unable to cope with the confusion that was raging in the border state of Kentucky. Anderson was somewhat exaggerating.

The confusion was being caused by the fact that most of the citizenry, though it included many slave owners, tended to hold the Union as more important than slavery. In a referendum held the previous June the legislature had voted by a ratio of four to one to refuse the offer of the cotton states to secede from the Union and join them. Governor Beriah Magoffin, on the other hand, was an avid secessionist and declared his intention to veto any action the legislature might take to declare its loyalty to the Union.

As befitted the tradition of Henry Clay, the "Great Compromiser," the people of Kentucky had found an interim answer: The governor and the legislature had agreed to declare Kentucky neutral in what was expected to be the coming conflict. In that status, virtually as an independent country, Kentucky had selected as their military chief a capable man, Simon Bolivar Buckner, a West Pointer from the class of 1844, a year behind Grant. In 1860 Buckner had joined with other officers from the South in resigning from the United States Army. But he had worked, as long as it was feasible, to make Kentucky's neutrality succeed.

As of the time Sherman reported to Anderson, there were neither Union nor Confederate troops on Kentucky's soil; neutrality was holding up. That fact did not, however, prevent the Union from building up forces in Ohio and the Confederates from doing likewise in Tennessee. Though neither side admitted it, neither expected neutrality to last long, and both were preparing to cross into Kentucky once its borders were violated. Anderson had established camps at Dick Robinson, across the Ohio River, and Albert Sidney Johnston had camps at Nashville.

Anderson knew that the Confederate forces were well organized and prepared. Their overall commander, Albert Sidney Johnston, was a man considered by President Jefferson Davis as the number one Confederate officer. Johnston's gray-clad rebels were numerically smaller than the Union forces, but he used them so cleverly, through raids and demonstrations, that their weakness was not apparent.

―――――――――

Almost immediately after Sherman's arrival, events began moving rapidly. On September 4, Kentucky's neutrality was shattered by a blunder on the part of Confederate lieutenant general Leonidas Polk, who crossed the Mississippi River into southern Kentucky and seized the city of Columbus. In retaliation, Brigadier General Ulysses S. Grant, commanding the Union troops in southeast Missouri, moved south from his position at Cairo, Illinois, and occupied Paducah, Kentucky. Both sides now invaded Kentucky, but the Kentucky state legislature, holding Polk responsible for taking the first step, ordered the Confederate forces to leave Kentucky and decreed that the United States flag should be raised above the statehouse in Frankfort. Politically, Kentucky had been saved for the Union, but it was now a potential battleground between the opposing armies.

Anderson, with his headquarters now established in Frankfort, was still in a difficult spot, because he was not being provided with troops to maintain his position. Volunteer regiments were being recruited and trained throughout the West, especially by the governors of Ohio, Illinois, and Indiana, but Anderson, with no cadre to organize volunteers, sorely needed help. Unfortunately for Anderson, Lincoln and McClellan were focused on Washington, D.C., and St. Louis, Missouri, and were therefore giving those theaters priority in resources. Some sixty thousand men had been sent to Major General John C. Frémont, commanding in St. Louis. Each of these commands, Washington and St. Louis, held fronts of only a

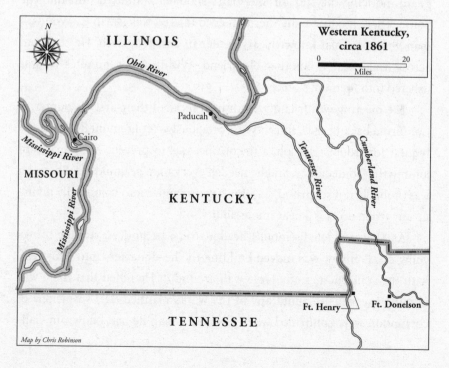

Map by Chris Robinson

hundred miles each; Anderson, with only about eighteen thousand men, was charged with defending a front of three hundred miles.

Sherman's first assignment, therefore, was to visit the governors of Ohio, Illinois, and Indiana to ask them for help, to send at least a portion of their newly recruited volunteers to Anderson. Cordially received at all three capitals, he was unsuccessful in securing any resources.

At this point Anderson decided to resort to unusual measures. He sent Sherman to St. Louis to try to wheedle some troops from Frémont. Sherman headed for St. Louis and arrived late in the day. In view of the hour, he decided to wait until the next morning.[1] While at his boardinghouse that evening he was subjected to dire warnings from his companions: He would never, they warned, be granted the privilege of even securing an audience with Frémont, who was preoccupied with converting the sumptuous house he was living in into a fortress. Sherman scoffed.

The next morning Sherman arose early and reached the gate of Frémont's headquarters before the normal workday. The corporal of the guard, noticing the star on Sherman's shoulder, admitted him into the house. There the first man Sherman encountered was Isaiah C. Woods, a man whom he had known years earlier in San Francisco. He then ran across Major Eaton, another old friend. Within a few minutes he was ushered into Frémont's office.

The meeting was friendly. Both men recalled their first encounter in California back in 1847, fifteen years previously. Yet Frémont declined the request for troops. His job, a major one, was to prevent Missouri from joining the Confederacy, and he needed every man he could get. Sherman was probably not surprised. Talking a commander into voluntarily giving up any troop units is a near impossibility.

As Sherman left Frémont's headquarters, he noticed strange things going on. Frémont was indeed building the headquarters into a fortress, with the construction of a large wall around it. He noted that there was nothing inexpensive about any of the works planned. His suspicions of corruption were confirmed when he spied a man he had known in California, a shady but prosperous entrepreneur, "Baron" John B. Steinberger, noted for his ability to plunder the United States treasury. Though Sherman avoided the baron, he admitted he saw him doing nothing wrong. Yet he recalled thinking, "Where the vultures are, there is a carcass close by."[2] His conjecture soon appeared to be at least partially correct.

Frémont was replaced after his visit by Sherman's old friend Major General Henry Wager Halleck. Frémont's wrongdoings had involved more than the simple matter of corruption. On August 30, 1861, General John C. Frémont declared martial law in the border state of Missouri, a measure that included the immediate emancipation of Missouri slaves. Frémont issued the order without consulting President Lincoln. When Lincoln learned of his actions, he publicly rescinded Frémont's order and removed him from command. Lincoln feared the emancipation edict might push the state of Missouri (and perhaps even neighboring Kentucky), with its heavy Southern sympathies, into the arms of the Confederacy.

———

Soon after Sherman's return to Louisville, the development he had feared most came to pass. General Anderson, under strain from his days at Sumter and basically a Confederate sympathizer, concluded that the political confusion and the threat of Confederate attack from Tennessee were too much for him to contend with. His request for relief as commander of the Department of the Cumberland was readily accepted, and his departure automatically made Sherman the commanding general. Rather than being elated over this elevation in status, Sherman was furious. He did not yet consider himself ready, and he blamed President Lincoln for breaking a promise. Assurance from McClellan that General Buell would soon arrive to replace him did little to assuage his anger.

Part of Sherman's deep concern was his conviction that the Civil War was to be won in the West, not the East. He considered the Ohio–Indiana–Illinois region the true heart of the United States, and contended that whoever controlled the Mississippi River would win the war. And to his mind, Washington, with Scott gone,* placed all emphasis on the Washington–Richmond front at the expense of the West.

———————

Sherman was a tense and nervous man by nature, and his concern was exacerbated by the skill of his principal opponent, Albert Sidney Johnston, who continued to maneuver his troops so swiftly that Sherman's intelligence reports, not too competent, vastly multiplied the real strength of Johnston's force. Accordingly, Sherman began sending messages from Louisville back to Washington, sometimes to Lincoln, and in his agitated state of mind sometimes overstepping the bounds of propriety for a general writing to a president. At one time he demanded an answer.

On October 16, Sherman saw his chance to express his views directly to someone in authority. Secretary of War Simon Cameron was on his way back from St. Louis to Washington and came by Louisville, planning to stay over for only a few hours. When he sensed Sherman's state of mind, however, he changed plans and booked a later train. In the meantime he conferred with Sherman in the company of the secretary's entire entourage, including the newspaper reporters who were traveling with him. It was a disastrous scenario. Sherman detested the press, and he was forced to deal directly with its members because Cameron, in bad health, lay on a bed while the others conferred. Cameron did, however, take in everything.

The conference might have been quickly forgotten except for one aspect: Cameron asked from his bed how many troops Sherman would need to hold Kentucky or commence operations into Tennessee, adding that the latter was something that Lincoln very much desired. Sherman answered without hesitation: He would need sixty thousand men to defend Kentucky, he said, but it would take two hundred thousand to drive southward to the sea. "Great God!" Cameron burst out. "Where are they to come from?"[3]

———————

* Scott retired on November 1, 1861, worn-out. Yet he had already lost Lincoln's confidence. The army now had virtually a single commander, McClellan.

Sherman's statement and Cameron's reaction were reported with zest by the newsmen, who began a not-so-muted whispering campaign against Sherman, magnifying a casual remark made by Cameron that Sherman's requirements were "insane." The press interpreted Cameron's words as meaning that Sherman himself was insane. A reporter for *The New York Times* told another correspondent that Cameron saw Sherman as "unbalanced," questioning whether it was wise to leave Sherman in command. The *Chicago Tribune* went so far as to accuse Sherman of disloyalty.[4] These comments cut Sherman to the quick. His rage grew stronger, and he was once quoted as saying, "I know they will ruin me, but they will ruin the country too. Napoleon himself would have been defeated with a free press."[5]

By now it was generally accepted that Sherman was at least temporarily unbalanced. The situation continued for a month, pending Buell's arrival at Louisville to take command on November 12. Sherman then headed for St. Louis to consult with his old friend Henry Halleck, who was in command there.

Fortunately for Sherman and for the Union, those close to him stuck by him. Ellen, Thomas Ewing, and his brother John were familiar with his nervous nature and eccentricities, but they also appreciated his intelligence, basic stability, and rigid set of personal principles. More important at the moment, the only man who could render real help to Sherman was Halleck. While aware of Sherman's unacceptable behavior, Halleck acted as if nothing untoward had occurred. He gave Sherman an assignment as an inspector general to examine the conditions at Sedalia, Missouri.

The change in assignment, surprisingly, did not alleviate Sherman's condition; instead it seemed to grow worse. As described by one biographer,

By now Sherman was almost a completely other-directed person. Extremely concerned about his image in the eyes of others, he grew even more nervous and hyperactive. Instead of relaxing and approaching his new duties calmly, he set a frantic pace. Inspecting, planning, and training filled most of his working hours. Burning the candle at both ends, he attempted to compensate for the negative things people were reading and saying about him. Instead of improving his situation, he worsened it. To [his brother] John, he wrote, "Some terrible disaster is inevitable. . . . Could I now hide myself in some obscure corner, I would do so, for my conviction is that our Government is destroyed . . ."[6]

And Sherman himself later admitted his condition:

. . . I saw and felt, and was of course deeply moved to observe, the manifest belief that there was more or less in the rumor that the cares, perplexities, and anxiety of the situation had unbalanced my judgment and mind. . . . Of course I could not deny the fact, and had to submit to all its painful consequences for months, and, moreover, I could not hide from myself that many of the officers and soldiers subsequently placed under my command looked askance and with suspicion. Indeed, it was not until the following April that the battle of Shiloh gave me personally the chance to redeem my good name.[7]

Sherman's condition finally reached a point where Halleck decided to take further action. On November 29, 1861, Sherman received a message from Halleck's aide saying that the general was now satisfied that the Confederates intended no attack on Sedalia and therefore Sherman should return to St. Louis to report his observations. Sherman returned immediately and, on finding Ellen in a distraught mood, on December 18 applied for a twenty-day leave of absence, which was granted. In so doing, Halleck wrote graciously,

The newspaper attacks are certainly shameless and scandalous, but I cannot agree with you, that they have in their power "to destroy us as they please." I certainly get my share of abuse, but it will not disturb me. . . . I hope to see you well enough for duty soon. Our organization goes on slowly, but we will effect it in time.[8]

Sherman and Ellen returned to Lancaster, where the two were afforded a chance to relax. With the assistance and sympathy of Ellen, Thomas Ewing, and John, Cump made a miraculous recovery in the short period of three weeks. He then considered himself fit for at least a limited form of duty.

When Sherman returned to St. Louis, Halleck could see the change, but was not certain whether his friend was yet fit for assignment to a field command. He therefore played it safe by assigning him to a training unit at Benton Barracks. There he could be well watched.

Sherman never allowed personal grief to interfere with his performance of duty, and he trained the twelve thousand men at Benton Barracks well. Nevertheless, his depression continued to haunt him. He wrote home to Ellen in pathetic terms: ". . . having so signally failed in Kentucky, I am in about the same health as at Lancaster but the idea of having brought so much disgrace on all who are associated with me is so horrible to contemplate that I really cannot endure it."[9] Eventually, by February 13, 1862, Halleck gave him an active assignment in command of a support unit. The officer he was to support was Brigadier General Ulysses S. Grant, whose headquarters were still located at Cairo, Illinois.

Fate had been kinder to Grant than to Sherman since the two had met by chance at St. Louis five years earlier, and a word about that period is in order. Grant, like Sherman, had waited until he was absolutely certain that war was inevitable before negotiating a commission. When Beauregard pulled the lanyard on the first shot at Fort Sumter, Grant joined throngs of other citizens attempting to sign up for duty. But he was still cautious. Fortunately his fifteen-year record as an army officer was well-known in Galena, and he was able to assist the Illinois governor, Richard Yates, in organizing the volunteers that were streaming in—such of those as could be accepted. Eventually the governor himself asked him to stay on longer. Grant was glad to do so.

In organizing the six regiments that Lincoln had levied on Illinois, Grant had no intention of joining them himself. Instead, he wrote a modest letter to the secretary of war offering his service. He was realistic in evaluating his capabilities:

> Having served for fifteen years in the regular army, including four years at West Point and feeling it the duty of everyone who has been educated at the Government expense to offer their services for the support of that Government, I have the honor, very respectfully, to tender my services, until the close of the war, in such capacity as may be offered. I would say, in view of my present age and length of service, I feel myself competent to command a regiment, if the President, in his judgment, should see fit to intrust one to me.[10]

Eventually, on June 14, 1861, Grant received notice that he was to command the 21st Illinois Volunteer Infantry Regiment, in charge of defending the southern tip of the state. He was soon replaced by another, more senior officer, however, and reported to Halleck at St. Louis. After a very brief command of another regiment, he was made a brigadier general and placed in command of the Department of Southwest Missouri. He established his headquarters at Cairo, Illinois, a short distance away, and his command now became known as the District of Cairo.

The assignment was an important one. Cairo was located in one of the most critical areas in the West, where all the main waterways of the eastern part of the country converged. Cairo and Paducah, Kentucky, were about a hundred miles apart along the roaring Ohio River. It was at Cairo that the Ohio joined the Mississippi, more than one hundred and thirty miles downriver from St. Louis, where another gigantic tributary, the Missouri, joined it.

Two other smaller but strategic rivers also joined the Ohio at Paducah, both from the southeast. They were the Cumberland River, which flowed westward from Nashville, in northern Tennessee, and the Tennessee, flowing northwestward from southern Tennessee. For the last few miles of their courses, the two rivers run only about a dozen miles apart. In an effort to dominate the state of Tennessee by controlling these rivers, General Albert Sidney Johnston had erected two forts, Henry and Donelson, south of the state border between Tennessee and Kentucky. At the time of their construction, Kentucky had not yet decided whether or not to remain neutral, and Johnston respected Kentucky's insistence that military force was not to come on her soil, even though slightly better positions were farther north across the border.

Grant, at Cairo, was not constitutionally disposed to defend southern Illinois passively. He eyed the two forts, Henry and Donelson, and applied to Halleck for permission to take offensive action against them. After one rebuff he finally received permission on February 1, 1862, to advance against Fort Henry.

Grant was fortunate to win his first, all-important battle. The garrison at Fort Henry was small compared to Grant's seventeen thousand men. Furthermore, the fort was poorly located, actually underwater at times. Another crucial help to Grant was the cooperation of Flag Officer Andrew Foote, whose seven ironclad gunboats had been attached to him for this operation. Therefore, when Foote's gunboats appeared at Fort Henry on February 6, Confederate general Lloyd Tilghman put up no fight; he simply evacuated the fort and managed to deliver most of the garrison to Fort Donelson, though becoming a prisoner himself.

With Fort Henry in Union hands, Grant left on February 7, not bothering to ask Halleck's permission, hoping to seize Fort Donelson by the eighth. But it was not to be so easy. Unlike Fort Henry, Donelson was a hard nut to crack. It had twelve thousand in the garrison. Its commander, Brigadier General John Floyd, had once been secretary of war in the administration of President James Buchanan. Also present were Gideon Pillow, a prominent troublemaker from the Mexican War, and Simon Bolivar Buckner, who had by now joined the Confederates. The future cavalry leader Nathan Bedford Forrest was also part of the garrison.

Fort Donelson itself was only the core of the position. A total of twenty-one thousand Confederates defended the area. Surrounding it were strong fortifications. Here Grant's familiarity with some of the Confederate generals came to good use. He considered Floyd no soldier, and knew Gideon Pillow from the Mexican War. Grant therefore dared to take the risk of besieging Donelson closely, assuming that Pillow would not venture far out from his fortifications. Grant's judgment was borne out, and by February 13, in bitter cold weather, he was investing Fort Donelson closely on three sides, the rear being on the Tennessee River.

The siege lasted only three days, involving a confused melee of small units outside the fort. At one point Floyd made an attempt to break out of the perimeter by hitting Grant's right flank along the river. Initially successful, Floyd apparently lost his nerve; in any event he pulled back into the fort. He did not seem to recover his courage, because he called a conference of war with himself, Pillow, and Buckner, to discuss surrender.

At that meeting the three generals decided that surrender was necessary. Furthermore they decided—or Floyd ordered—that he and Pillow should make their escapes before the capitulation and that Buckner should be left behind to execute the unpleasant duty of negotiating the surrender. Floyd, in particular, had every reason to avoid falling into Yankee hands. As the secretary of war he was known to have taken every possible measure to weaken the Union Army, such as scattering it into small garrisons instead of concentrating it. He could well be tried for treason. Pillow, once a major general of volunteers in Mexico, had less cause for fear, but he still elected to flee.

That decision made, Floyd and Pillow escaped by water in the early hours of February 16. Soon thereafter Buckner sent a message to Grant proposing a meeting to negotiate a surrender. He was jolted to receive Grant's reply:

Sir: Yours of this date, proposing armistice and appointment of Commissioners to settle terms of capitulation, is just received. No terms except an unconditional and immediate surrender can be accepted. I propose to move immediately upon your works.[11]

Simon Buckner, a friend and classmate of Grant's from West Point, was doubtless sincere in expressing his resentment at the tone of Grant's message. Nevertheless, he had no choice:

Sir—The distribution of forces under my command, incident to an unexpected change of commanders, and the overwhelming strength of the forces under your command, compel me, notwithstanding the success of the Confederate army yesterday, to accept the ungenerous and unchivalric terms which you propose.[12]

Grant had established a new concept in what had previously been a matter of military courtesy. He had put a new term in the English language, "unconditional surrender." And he had achieved the first significant Union victory in the Civil War.

————————————

Sherman watched Grant's exploits at Henry and Donelson from the sidelines, but he had an excellent vantage point, because Fort Belmont, where he was still commanding, was located near Halleck's headquarters in St. Louis. When it came to giving credit for the operation, Sherman was inclined to favor Halleck, as Grant had been serving under Halleck's orders. His judgment was also influenced in all likelihood by the fact that he and Halleck had been friends ever since the long voyage from New York to San Francisco in 1846. More important, Halleck had been instrumental in bringing Sherman back from the depths. At this point Sherman owed Halleck a great deal.

Of one thing Sherman was certain: Halleck had always intended to take forts Henry and Donelson as his first move south. One night in January, when Sherman was visiting with Halleck in St. Louis, Halleck laid out a large map on a table and asked, "Where is the rebel line?" His chief of staff, General George Cullum, took a pencil and drew a line that ran roughly east to west in southern Kentucky. On the east was Bowling Green, in the center were Forts Henry and Donelson, and on the west was Columbus, Kentucky, still under the command of General Leonidas Polk.

Halleck, possibly testing his subordinates, asked, "Now, where is the proper place to break it?" Either Sherman or Cullum—Sherman could not recall which—blurted out that the place was in the center. Halleck then drew another line running southward from Cairo and Paducah, through forts Henry and Donelson and up the Tennessee River. "That," he declared, "is the true line of operations." Sherman noted later that this incident took place a whole month before Grant moved out along that line in early February.[13]

Despite Sherman's close relations with Halleck, his career took a critical turn as a result of Grant's campaign. On February 13, 1862, after the capture of Fort Henry but before the fall of Fort Donelson, Halleck finally began to grasp what Grant had done—pushing on without orders. Highly concerned about Grant's supply situation, he ordered Sherman to turn over the command of Fort Benton and proceed immediately to Paducah, Grant's vital supply hub. Sherman left immediately.

Sherman's arrival in a supporting role was potentially the cause of some embarrassment, because he was senior to Grant by three years and by law should have assumed command. But Sherman had better sense than to do so. He made it easy. As Grant described their meeting,

During the siege General Sherman had been sent to Smithland at the mouth of the Cumberland River to forward reinforcements and supplies to me. At that time he was my senior in rank and there was no authority of law to assign a junior to command a senior of the same grade. But every boat that came up with supplies or reinforcements brought a note of encouragement from Sherman, asking me to call upon him for any assistance he could render and saying that if he could be of service at the front I might send for him and he would waive rank.[14]

The problem of rank was quickly solved, because in the national exhilaration of Grant's victory he was appointed to the grade of major general. But Sherman's offer began an association immortal in American military history. Joining Grant gave Sherman the chance to rise out of the depths he had been suffering in for months.

CHAPTER SEVEN

SHILOH RESTORES SHERMAN'S REPUTATION

In Grant, Sherman had found a man he could serve under with zest. They were personally compatible, and equally important, they shared extremely high standards. Sherman's regard for Grant was lavish; Grant returned the admiration, though probably not quite so intensely. The outside world, even in the army, was as yet unaware of the extent to which Sherman's efforts had contributed to Grant's successes, and recognition of his worth would require further evidence. That evidence would soon be provided by Sherman's role in the gigantic battle of Shiloh, or Pittsburg Landing.

Sherman saw Grant as a man who would fight, who would even ignore accepted rules. As an avid reader of military history, Sherman recalled a formula laid down by the iconic Napoleonic staff officer Baron Antoine-Henri Jomini. Jomini had pontificated that, in order to conduct a successful siege, the besieging force needed a strength five times that of the defender. Here, Sherman observed, Grant had invested Donelson with a force actually inferior to that of Floyd and Pillow.

Grant fully appreciated what Sherman had done in relieving him of the need to fret over his supplies and reinforcements during that action. But

Sherman's reward was more tangible than mere admiration: His command at Paducah was redesignated as a combat unit. He was now a brigadier general in command of a division, one of the six under Grant's command.

Others, higher ranking and better-known, were given even greater kudos. The greatest credit was given to Halleck, whose Department of the Missouri was expanded to include Buell's Army of the Ohio, with which Halleck had previously been on an equal status. Both Grant and Brigadier General Charles F. (C. F.) Smith, his second in command, were promoted to the grade of major general of volunteers. The Union was beginning to develop the team that would eventually bring victory. Oddly, at this point, they were all in the West.

Halleck's star was now at its zenith. Not only had he been placed over his rival Buell, but he had been given credit for the fact that, with the Cumberland and Tennessee rivers closed, the Confederate commander, Albert S. Johnston, had been forced to evacuate Bowling Green on the Tennessee River and Nashville on the Cumberland. Johnston retained scattered positions,[1] but the all-important fact was that Kentucky was now safe for the Union. Future battles east of the Mississippi River would be fought in West Tennessee and farther south.

Halleck now decided to concentrate his two armies, Buell's and Grant's, into one, over which he would assume personal command. With that powerful combined force, he hoped to drive south to the Gulf of Mexico. But arranging for that ambitious project would take some time, during which he intended to cut the Memphis and Charleston Railroad, which ran west–east from Columbus on the Mississippi River, through Corinth to Memphis and Richmond beyond. In a day when the road net was primitive, rivers and railroads were the critical means of delivering supplies that made operations possible. That railroad fit the bill exactly.

————

Grant's command at Paducah was ready for action, and it was given a mission to drive up the Tennessee River, which in western Tennessee flows south to north. But for Grant personally there was a catch:

To Major-General U. S. GRANT,

Fort Henry:

You will place Major-General C. F. Smith in command of expedition, and remain yourself at Fort Henry. Why do you not obey my orders to report strength and positions of your command?

H. W. HALLECK,

Major-General.[2]

It was an indication of Sherman's newly attained status that on March 10 Halleck gave him an independent mission: He was to take his division southward from Paducah and move up the Tennessee River, and to make a forced march all the way to Corinth to destroy the Memphis and Charleston Railroad.

Sherman set out as scheduled, and on the way he observed a spot on the Tennessee River called Pittsburg Landing, where C. F. Smith had already stationed one of his divisions, that of Major General Stephen A. Hurlbut. When Sherman neared his destination, however, he met floods and downpours so severe as to endanger the naval vessels he was dependent on. He therefore withdrew down the Tennessee River to Pittsburg Landing, where he disembarked. He landed his division on the west side of the river at a position on the Corinth road near a church named Shiloh. There he set up camp and prepared for training, something his men still badly needed. He sent messages to a reinstated Grant touting the value of the position.[3]

Grant honored Sherman's recommendation and moved his men by water to Pittsburg Landing, arriving on April 3. By the sixth, five of his six divisions, totaling fifty thousand men, were in place or nearby. Four of them, Sherman and three others, were encamped on the west side of the Tennessee River south of Pittsburg Landing. They did not consider it necessary to prepare defensive positions, because all seemed quiet. Grant knew that Buell's wing of the combined army was closing in after a month's march from Nashville. Together the two wings would make a powerful force.

Grant appeared to have no feeling of urgency. He did not even take station personally at Pittsburg Landing, preferring more comfortable quarters at Savannah, nine miles up the river. Grant later admitted that he had no knowledge of the whereabouts of Johnston's Confederate forces—an astonishing admission—and he was not concerned. On the evening of April 5, he sent a message to Halleck, advising, "I have scarcely the faintest idea of an attack (general one) being made upon us, but will be prepared should such a thing take place." He overstated his preparedness, considering that only four of his divisions were on the west bank of the river.[4] When the Sixth Division arrived during that same evening, Grant told the commander to camp on the east bank and cross over the next day.[5]

Sherman was nearly as complacent as Grant. His only nod to the matter of security was to send out a reconnaissance patrol on the evening of April 5, but when it ran into a considerable firefight, he brushed the matter off, assuming that the Confederate troops were a patrol sent out by Confederate refugees from the Battle of Pea Ridge, Arkansas.[6]

In the meantime, things were unsettled among the Confederates at Corinth. Anger and frustration reigned among soldiers and citizens alike, much of the blame laid at the feet of Johnston himself. Some discontents even contemplated removing their onetime hero in favor of someone else. Though they could not quite bring themselves to such a drastic move, they did the next-best thing: They saddled him with a prestigious subordinate, Pierre G. T. Beauregard. It was a bad move; Beauregard made matters worse, because his more cautious views were opposite those of Johnston. He protested against Johnston's plan to hit Grant at Pittsburg Landing. But Johnston was in command, and he doubtless felt keenly the criticisms that were being directed toward him. He gathered troops from Nashville, Bowling Green, and Corinth and set out to strike. His army of forty-four thousand men left Corinth on April 3, the day that Grant arrived at Pittsburg Landing.

Johnston organized his army into four corps, which he concentrated on the west of the Tennessee River, and made his way to the Corinth road, near which stood Shiloh Church.[7] He moved in a column of corps, Major

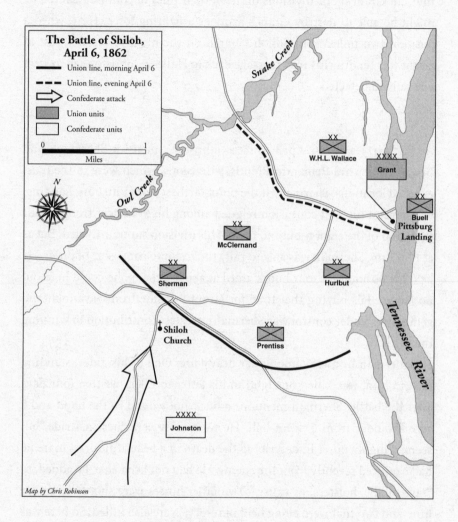

The Battle of Shiloh,
April 6, 1862

Union line, morning April 6
Union line, evening April 6
Confederate attack
Union units
Confederate units

0   1
Miles

N

Snake Creek

Owl Creek

Tennessee River

XX
W.H.L. Wallace

XXXX
Grant

XX
Buell
Pittsburg
Landing

XX
McClernand

XX
Sherman

XX
Hurlbut

† Shiloh
Church

XX
Prentiss

XXXX
Johnston

Map by Chris Robinson

General William J. Hardee leading. Johnston's plan was to penetrate Grant on the Union left, with his objective Pittsburg Landing itself. If he could thus cut Grant's four divisions off from their lines of communication, he might be able to destroy Grant's army as a fighting force. He reached a position two miles from Shiloh Church on the night of April 5, just as Grant was sending his rosy message back to Halleck. Johnston's men were virtually undetected.

At six thirty a.m. on April 6, 1862, Johnston's men hit Sherman's and Brigadier General Benjamin Prentiss's divisions, which were in the most exposed locations. Sherman, at the point farthest from Pittsburg Landing, was hardest hit, and confusion reigned among his volunteer troops. Four thousand of the eight thousand men of his division summarily fled. But as at Bull Run, Sherman was able to rally the rest into some sort of order. He held his position for four hours, until at about ten a.m. he could hold out no longer. His buying that time for Grant to come from Savannah and get matters under control was Sherman's greatest contribution to winning the battle.

Sherman himself came under heavy fire. One of his aides, standing next to him, was killed outright; in his letter to Ellen, written four days after the battle, Sherman mentions a buckshot wound in the hand and a sore shoulder from a spent ball. He took these scratches in stride, but seemed highly upset in describing the death of a beautiful sorrel mare he had captured recently from the enemy. He had not been able, he added, to "save saddle, holsters, or valise." Two other horses were shot from under him, and two that were being held in reserve were also killed. So here was a major general "completely unhorsed."[8]

Sherman's slow retreat took his troops to the northwest. The position he finally held at four p.m. was critical to Grant's defense, in the line of Johnston's main attack.

Unfortunately for the Confederates, their general Albert Sidney Johnston was killed in the early afternoon. His death was unnecessary. In mid-morning, he had been hit in the left leg, and the leg was apparently numbed. He considered the wound minor, and sent the nearby medical corpsmen off to tend some wounded soldiers. As a result he bled to death. The South had lost its most prominent general.

When Grant arrived at Pittsburg Landing around nine a.m. on April 6, he set about to restore order. General Lew Wallace's division, at Crump's Landing nine miles down the river on the western bank, was ordered forward into the battle. Somehow the orders became mixed up and Wallace wandered around, never participating in that day's battle. On the positive side, however, Buell's divisions, camped nearby, began crossing the Tennessee River along with the last of Grant's own reinforcements.

The critical fight of the battle occurred on Sherman's left, where Prentiss and W. H. L. Wallace held out in a sunken road called the Hornet's Nest. Though finally captured, they blocked the Confederate drive to Pittsburg Landing.

Beauregard, now in command of Confederate forces, decided at the end of the day not to press the attack, giving Grant's army a respite and time to build up and organize. Sherman, coming back to report, found Grant standing casually in the rain under a tree, smoking a cigar. "Well, Grant, we've had the devil's own day, haven't we?" Sherman asked.

"Yes," replied Grant. "Lick 'em tomorrow, though."[9]

Through the night of April 6 and 7, Grant's last division and three of Buell's were ferried across the Tennessee River, past the long lines of men huddled against the near banks seeking shelter from the battle. Buell's twenty thousand men fell in on the left at Pittsburg Landing, and drove directly south. Despite Grant's seniority and the fact that the bulk of the troops came from the Army of the Tennessee, Buell insisted that he was commanding his three divisions independently. Grant did not make an issue of Buell's outrageous claim, though the result was poor coordination and therefore less effectiveness.

This time it was Beauregard who was surprised by a dawn attack. The

Confederate troops were not completely reorganized from the fighting of the day before, but they fought in place. Despite the surprise and the fact that Grant now outnumbered him by about two to one, Beauregard managed to bring some order by noontime, and the fighting went on for five more hours. At about dusk, the Confederate commander realized that he had had enough, and he ordered his force to retreat back to Corinth, which they did in remarkably good order. Grant did not pursue, despite Buell's later claim that he could have continued the attack for another hour of daylight. Sherman's division, depleted from the fighting the previous day, had fought all day but did not play a major role. By dusk he was back near his position of the morning before. Writing home, he estimated that of his eight-thousand-man division, half had fled, three hundred and eighteen had been killed, and more than twelve hundred had been wounded. Assuming these figures were reasonably accurate, his division now numbered fewer than twenty-five hundred officers and men.[10]

It had been a grim experience, the bloodiest battle in the nation's history up to that time, and the first one to convince the public that they were in for a long war.

———————

Though Shiloh was by all definitions a Union victory, the "butcher's bill" of casualties shocked everyone in the North. By no means did the end of the battle and the burying of the dead end the unpleasantness. In fact, Sherman, who was fairly matter-of-fact when describing scenes of nearly unimaginable horror, now rose in wrath, not against the Confederates, but against Buell.* Buell retaliated in kind. He seems to have suffered from considerable ego and a lack of generosity when dealing with his fellow

———————

* He had good reason. Buell, a native of Kentucky, was an honest and brave soldier who had fought in the Second Seminole War, and with Zachary Taylor and Winfield Scott in Mexico. He appeared as a commander to be overly cautious and lackadaisical. For some reason, it had taken him a whole month to march his Army of the Ohio from Nashville to Pittsburg Landing, a distance of only ninety miles.

officers. Hardly was the battle over before Buell began making claims that he had come to the "rescue" of Grant. Further, he said, had Grant followed his advice, the victory would have been more decisive. Many of the press believed him, and, more important, Henry Halleck believed him. Therefore, while Sherman's reputation had been restored by his performance at Shiloh—he had justifiably been hailed as a foremost hero—that of Grant plummeted. The former hero was now considered a failure despite what was really a great victory, and the onetime crazy man was a shining light.

As is usually the case, the elation that followed right after a great victory was superseded by a terrible letdown. Fatigue previously suppressed by the excitement of battle set in, and the horrible sights of the dead and dying took their toll on victors and vanquished alike. Thus, though Sherman received a promotion to major general, he showed no elation when writing to Ellen:

> I have worked to keep down, but somehow I am forced into prominence and might as well submit. . . . The scenes on this field would have cured anybody of war. Mangled bodies, dead, dying, in every conceivable shape without heads, legs; and horses.[11]

The letdown, unfortunately, soon translated into public rage. When visiting reporters witnessed the scenes of the battle's aftermath, they pounced on the supposed incompetence of the generals in command. Surprise, not the fact of victory, was the theme.[12] This was particularly so, ironically, in Ohio, Grant's native state. On receiving news that Ohio regiments under Sherman had been among the four thousand men who had fled the field, Governor David Tod, who took pride in his nickname of "the soldier's friend," immediately concluded that the flaw had been faulty command, not the greenness of the troops. He castigated the "criminal negligence" of the commanders, and, needing a scapegoat, chose Grant. Sherman was largely spared, possibly because of the influence of Tom Ewing and Sherman's younger brother John. The "accepted wisdom" that Grant had blundered previously at Belmont and had been saved from disaster at Fort Donelson only by General C. F. Smith was again exhumed. Lieutenant Governor Benjamin Stanton came to Shiloh, visited with Sherman among others, and then returned to Ohio, publishing an article in a Bellefontaine newspaper confirming the worst about the incompetence of the high command.

This was too much for Sherman. Though Lieutenant Governor Stanton had not included him in his accusations, Sherman wrote in severe terms for a soldier addressing a politician. "As to the enemy being in their very camps before the officers were aware of their approach," he started out, "it is the most wicked falsehood that was ever attempted to be thrust upon a people sad and heartsore at the terrible but necessary casualties of war." Then, somewhat disingenuously, he called it "ridiculous" to talk about a surprise. In finishing up, Sherman pulled out all the stops:

> If you have no respect for the honor and reputation of the generals who lead the armies of your country, you should have some regard for the welfare and honor of the country itself. Our whole force, if imbued with your notions, would be driven across the Ohio in less than a month and even you would be disturbed in your quiet study where you now in perfect safety write libels.[13]

Fighting the trend of public opinion was of no use when the commander in the field was Henry Halleck. Already jealous of Grant's growing reputation, he once more relieved his aggressive subordinate. He went through with his original plan of assuming personal command, departing St. Louis and joining the army in the field for the drive to Corinth. His subordinate commanders were Buell, John Pope, Thomas, and Brigadier General John McClernand. After a slow advance described derisively by Simon Buckner as a "long siege," he reached Corinth. Beauregard had evacuated.

Grant meanwhile was temporarily without a command. But he retained the support of a man far more important in the scheme of things than Halleck: Abraham Lincoln. And Grant now recognized Sherman as a foremost general.

CHAPTER EIGHT

A HARD WINTER AT VICKSBURG

The period between Halleck's capture of Corinth on May 30, 1862, and the surrender of Vicksburg on July 4, 1863, was a time of hardship for Union forces. Corinth was occupied shortly after McClellan had essentially admitted failure in his Peninsular Campaign to take Richmond, and that was followed by Second Bull Run (August 1862), Antietam (September), Fredericksburg (December), Chancellorsville (May 1863), and Gettysburg (July 1863). If we consider Antietam as a drawn battle, the only Union success among them was Gettysburg; all the others were Confederate victories. Yet the campaigns in the West, which cost the nation only a small fraction of those in the East, arguably produced greater eventual results. Nearly all the efforts were eventually concentrated on that small town that had only one reason for importance: control of the Mississippi River.

The central figure in the capture of Vicksburg was Ulysses S. Grant, ably assisted by William T. Sherman and Flag Officer David Dixon Porter. So much did Grant dominate the scene that one is tempted to assume that he had been in comfortable control throughout the period. Such an idea is misleading. Grant was always in a struggle to retain whatever position he occupied, and the unswerving loyalty of others, especially Sherman, was what made his efforts a success.

―――――――

After Halleck had relieved Grant as commander of the Army of the Tennessee following Shiloh, he doubtless would have liked to remove him from the scene. However, Grant had too many supporters in high places to be relieved outright. Halleck therefore did the next best thing: He retained Grant as his "deputy commander" of the Army of the Tennessee and left the subordinate units more or less intact. Sherman, for example, remained in command of the Fifth Division for some time before being sent to Memphis, without prejudice, on special duty.

In contrast to the mutual hostility that existed between Halleck and Grant, Sherman retained his warm friendship for "Old Brains," so a few days before leaving for Memphis, Sherman rode to Halleck's headquarters for a farewell visit. There, in the course of an otherwise pleasant conversation, Halleck mentioned, almost casually, that Grant had applied for a thirty days' leave, which Sherman interpreted to mean that his friend was intending to leave the army.

Sherman, in an alarmed state, headed straight for the latter's headquarters. He soon found it a short distance off the road. What he saw alarmed him further; Grant's aides were outside the tent, and piled up on the ground was all the office equipment, organized as usual for a move. Sherman asked to see Grant and was immediately ushered in.

"After the usual compliments," in Sherman's words, he asked whether it was true that the general was going away. Grant affirmed that he was:

"Sherman," he said, "you know that I am in the way here. I have stood it as long as I can, and can endure it no longer." Asked where he was going during his leave, Grant confirmed that he was going to St. Louis. When asked whether he had any special business in that city, he admitted that he had none.

Sherman lost no time in begging Grant to stay. To support his arguments he gave a long description of his own case, how downcast he had been a few months earlier when all the newspapers had declared him crazy. He went on to describe how the recent battle had restored him to "high feather." If Grant went away, Sherman continued, things would go right along without him. On the other hand, if he stayed, some "happy accident" might restore him to his rightful place. Grant did not appear instantly convinced, but he promised to delay a bit and think the matter over. After Sherman left Corinth—he remembered the date, the sixth of June—he received a note from Grant advising that he had thought the matter over further and had decided to stay.

Sherman sat down and penned a quick note.

Chewalla, June 6, 1862

Major General Grant:
 My dear Sir. I have just received your note, and am rejoiced at your conclusion to remain; for you could not be quiet at home for a week when armies were marching, and rest could not relieve your mind of the growing sensation that injustice had been done you.[1]

Then, for a time at least, the paths of Grant and Sherman parted.

———

Grant's situation, fortunately, was improved somewhat when Halleck approved his request to move his personal headquarters to Memphis. There he would have a job to do. Memphis had only recently been taken by the Union and the usual confusion reigned. Add to that, most of the people held strong hostility toward their conquerors, and Grant's administrative chores kept him occupied.

On July 11, Sherman's prediction regarding Grant's situation became reality. The authorities in Washington, fed up with McClellan's failed Peninsular Campaign at Richmond—and overly impressed by Halleck's capture of Corinth—brought Halleck back to Washington, appointing him general in chief of the U.S. Army. Grant was selected to succeed him at Corinth. Halleck departed on July 17, without uttering a single friendly word.

Sherman was personally unaffected by the animosity between Halleck and Grant. When Halleck left, Sherman wrote him a letter wishing him well:

> I cannot express my heartfelt pain at hearing of your orders and intended departure. . . . That success will attend you wherever you go I feel no doubt. . . . I attach more importance to the West than to the East. . . . The man who at the end of the war holds the military control of the Valley of the Mississippi will be the man. You should not be removed. I fear the consequences. . . .
>
> Instead of that calm, steady progress which has dismayed our enemy, I now fear alarms, hesitation, and doubt. You cannot be replaced out here.[2]

That letter, implying a lack of faith in Grant, is puzzling, and can be explained only by Sherman's complex nature and his tendency to hyperbole. His opening sentence expressing grief at Halleck's departure is not surprising given the long friendship the two had shared. Nor is it surprising that Sherman feared that Halleck's transfer from the Western Theater to the less important Eastern was a bad sign.

Sherman's expression of fear for the future, however, is astonishing, especially since his friend Grant would be assuming Halleck's position. Possibly with all his admiration for Grant's aggressiveness and coolness, Sherman had not yet developed the degree of respect that would grow in the future. In any event, the letter accurately represents Sherman's views at the time, since he wrote letters to other friends praising Halleck. For the moment, perhaps, Sherman's passion for order was getting the best of him.

———

Halleck's departure as commander of the Department of the Mississippi was not done gracefully. On the personal side, he was, as always, less than considerate of Grant. But far more serious than personal discourtesy was Halleck's destruction of the powerful 120,000-man army he had assembled at Corinth. He had previously sent Buell from Corinth to Nashville with his Army of the Ohio, and now he ordered Grant to send Buell two more divisions. The result was that Grant would be unable to continue offensive action against Beauregard; the best he could do would be to defend what territory Halleck's once great army had taken.

Why did Halleck disperse his army so? It would be unfair to assume that his sole motive was to prevent Grant's earning more glories at his expense. It seems more likely that, as a cautious man, he believed that Union forces had captured all the Confederate territory possible, and that they now must simply defend what had been taken. In any event, Halleck had ensured that major offensive action in the Department of Mississippi was, for the time being, at a standstill.

Though they were separated, the next few months were not completely lost for the growing comradeship between Grant and Sherman. Grant at Corinth and Sherman at Memphis communicated often and constructively. Each man had much to offer: Sherman had the advantage of broader experiences through his connections with Thomas Ewing and John Sherman, and his experiences in California; Grant somewhat assumed the role of pupil, but he provided stability and common sense to the exchange of views. Only on one all-important matter did they fully agree: The South would never give in until treated in a most brutal manner.[3]

The period of quiet came to an end in early October 1862, at about the time that Grant was officially assuming command from Halleck. Major General John A. McClernand, one of Grant's corps commanders at Shiloh, visited President Lincoln in Washington and sold him on the idea of raising a new army—to be under McClernand's command, of course—to advance on the Confederate bastion of Vicksburg, on the Mississippi River. Lincoln heartily agreed to the operation, but to McClernand's disappointment he assigned the new formation to Grant's command. Grant and Halleck, for once seeing eye to eye, both considered McClernand, a political general, unfit for the job.[4] On Halleck's urging, therefore, Grant took over the expedition personally. Thus was born the historic campaign of Vicksburg.

Taking Vicksburg did not seem at the time to be a major undertaking. True, its critical importance on the Mississippi was widely recognized,* but the strength with which it was defended was underestimated. That development was tragic in that Halleck, once he had taken Memphis, had neglected to seize the city at a time when it could easily have been taken. Since then Vicksburg had received substantial reinforcements.

Vicksburg was not the only Confederate bastion remaining on the Mississippi. Far to the south, General Nathaniel Banks was attempting to reduce another strongpoint, Port Hudson. Banks's force was actually larger than Grant's, though the position he was attempting to take was less formidable. The relationship between himself and Banks would remain a factor in Grant's planning throughout most of this campaign.

Months earlier, Banks and Admiral David Farragut had attempted to take Vicksburg even before the city's garrison had been reinforced. The effort had failed because Farragut's guns had lacked the punch to subdue those of Vicksburg, and Banks lacked sufficient ground strength to make an assault. Banks had therefore attempted to dig a canal across a strategic point in the river to open north–south traffic, out of the sight of Confederate guns. He succeeded in creating a canal of about fourteen feet wide and fourteen feet deep, but that size was not nearly enough to be useful. Banks and Farragut returned to New Orleans.

But that was a thing of the past. At of the end of 1862, Grant eagerly seized the opportunity for action and began making his plans to take that all-important objective.

---

* Confederate President Jefferson Davis referred to it as the nail that held the Confederacy together, as Vicksburg and the land around it provided the avenue through which vital men and supplies, especially horses, were brought from Texas and Arkansas for the use of Lee's armies in Virginia. Lincoln, using another metaphor, called Vicksburg the key to the war. "We cannot win the war," Lincoln is quoted as having said, "until we have that key in our pocket." Lewis, pp. 224–48.

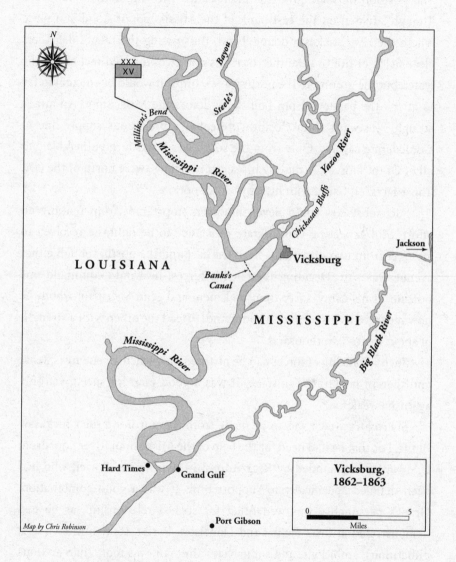

N

XXX
XV

Millikens' Bend

Bayou

Steele's

Mississippi   River

Yazoo River

Chickasaw Bluffs

LOUISIANA

Vicksburg

Jackson

Banks's
Canal

MISSISSIPPI

Mississippi River

Big Black River

Hard Times

Grand Gulf

Port Gibson

Vicksburg,
1862–1863

0   5
Miles

Map by Chris Robinson

The position of Vicksburg was often called the Gibraltar of the West. Though situated on the east bank of the Mississippi, it stood at a place where the river makes a double bend, thus giving the town's defenders clear fields of fire to rake the river. It stood two hundred feet above the water, but the ground to the north was swampy. It would be suicidal to try to attack the bastions from Louisiana, across the Mississippi. An attack straight westward from Corinth presented a precarious supply line to Confederate cavalry. Only from the south was Vicksburg vulnerable, but all of Grant's forces, including his seven ironclads, were north of the city. Those facts left Grant with little by way of options.

Such obstacles could never, however, stop Grant from making an effort. Still expecting Confederate resistance to be light, he resolved to attack it from two directions, from the east and the north, though either avenue was bad. Deciding to split his forces, he would command one portion of his army, forty thousand men, and send Sherman, whom he now regarded as his second in command, to lead the other, with a strength of about thirty-two thousand.

Such a splitting of forces can be justified only when an enemy is weak, and therein lay Grant's mistake. It was a good plan for speed, yet only against a weak foe.[5]

Sherman's attack was to be made from the north, up the Chickasaw Bluffs. For that he had need for the help of the Mississippi River Squadron, U.S. Navy, commanded by Rear Admiral David Dixon Porter, who had been detailed specifically to support him. It was a good combination. Grant's personality was well fitted for such a relationship, as he had demonstrated at forts Henry and Donelson. Porter, though known as a punctilious, ambitious, and somewhat vain man, was more than anxious to help in any way possible.

Grant and Porter met for the first time at a dinner aboard an army vessel at Corinth in early December. At first Porter was taken aback by Grant's rumpled informality of dress, but the admiral soon noticed that

Grant was an unusual man, with only one thing on his mind: Vicksburg. The general, Porter noticed, was so focused on the pending operation that he neglected to eat the luxurious roast duck that had been served to him. The two men spent only a half hour together, and Grant filled the time explaining his plans. At the end of the short meeting, Porter cheerfully promised the navy's full-fledged support.[6]

The meeting with Grant had been called for by protocol, but Porter's actual role in the operation was to cooperate with Sherman. He therefore went to Sherman's headquarters in Memphis to meet. When Porter arrived, he was at first impressed by the businesslike atmosphere of the staff, but was offended when he was kept waiting for a whole hour before Sherman appeared. Sherman apologized profusely, insisting that nobody had informed him of the admiral's arrival. Porter accepted the apology, but then, when Sherman interrupted the conversation to dictate a short message, he nearly left. He soon realized, however, that Sherman could keep several things going in his mind at once. Within a short time Porter and Sherman had "bonded as if they had known each other for years."[7]

———————

Both efforts to take Vicksburg quickly failed. Porter carried Sherman's four divisions down the Yazoo River, but on December 26, Sherman's men were unable to scale the heights at Chickasaw Bluffs. The strength of the Vicksburg garrison resulted from reinforcements available to the fortress because of the failure of Grant's efforts to take the city by land. After three days of futile repulses, Sherman gave up the effort and returned north to Cairo. Waiting for him there was General McClernand, with orders from Lincoln himself to take over Sherman's wing of Grant's army. It was only at that time that Sherman learned of Grant's failure, which had enabled the Confederates to reinforce Vicksburg.

———————

Grant's wing had never had a chance. Driving a pencil-like thrust through hostile territory made his men too vulnerable to Confederate cavalry leaders Nathan Bedford Forrest and Earl Van Dorn. Grant's major supply base at Holly Springs was raided and utterly destroyed, and he dropped back to Natchez on December 23.

Both men were operating in the dark. For a while Grant was as unaware of Sherman's failure as Sherman was of his, so he still held hopes for the overall effort. The campaign, based on faulty intelligence, was ill conceived, so Grant held his favorite subordinate blameless.

Certain elements of the press were not so kind, and eagerly resumed their attacks on Sherman. Sherman counted his casualties as 208 killed, more than a thousand wounded, and 563 missing. As he wrote Ellen, "Well, we have been to Vicksburg and it was too much for us and we have backed out."[8]

Sherman did not seem to take his replacement by McClernand with any great grief. Since the order had come from Lincoln himself, through Grant, his relief did not carry with it any disapproval of his performance at Chickasaw Bluffs. Besides being McClernand's second in command, he was placed in charge of the II Corps, the other being commanded by General George W. Morgan.

Sherman never stopped planning, and he soon came up with a novel idea. He approached McClernand and suggested an attack on Arkansas Post, a Confederate base located forty miles up the Mississippi from Vicksburg. The base, where the Arkansas River flows into the Mississippi, was defended by a garrison of only five thousand bedraggled and vastly undersupplied men, but it was still important because it overlooked the Mississippi. What made the proposal odd is that it constituted a diversion, a sideshow, apart from Grant's overall plan for taking Vicksburg. This action would contribute nothing to that end.

McClernand was skeptical at first, but he eventually approved. He assembled a force to be carried by Porter's ships, with Sherman's corps in the vanguard, to debark at a point about ten miles north of the mouth of the Yazoo. By January 4, 1863, Sherman's men were ready. Five days later, on the ninth, his force was at Arkansas Post, ready for the attack.

The battle was actually conducted between Porter's three gunboats and the Confederates at Arkansas Post, more specifically Fort Hindman. For two days, as Sherman watched from the sidelines, Porter's guns bombarded those of the enemy, causing great destruction. Then, on the top of the embankment surrounding the fort, a white flag appeared. The surrender of the garrison was complete.

Sherman personally carried the news of the success back to McClernand, who had remained aboard his command ship, the *Tigress*. To Sherman's disgust, McClernand's elation was not for the cause it had furthered but for the glory that would accrue to his own name for such a victory.

Grant had been unaware of this action, and when he received word of it, he was angry. He hurried to visit McClernand at his temporary headquarters and after some conversation decided that his subordinate had to go. With the passage of time he eventually conceded the wisdom of the attack; the capture of five thousand men was a tremendous boost. But he learned that both Sherman and Porter viewed McClernand as a liability. They could not, they said, entrust the lives of men to McClernand's command.

Grant was now in a quandary. McClernand, who had received his major general rank the previous summer, was senior to any other officer in Grant's command except for Grant himself. Much as Grant would have liked to restore Sherman to his previous post, he could not so long as McClernand was on hand. Therefore, Grant made a major decision: He set McClernand aside and assumed personal command of the Army of the Mississippi himself.

With the failure of Grant's first mad dash to take Vicksburg, he settled down for what he now realized would be a long campaign. This was not to be a single day's battle such as Bull Run, nor even a two-day struggle like Shiloh. Instead it would constitute a siege, with dangers from other Confederate armies in Tennessee, Mississippi, and Louisiana. As historian Charles Bracelen Flood described the situation,

Before making any attack, points near the city would have to be approached through a cleverly defended maze of waterways, many miles of which looped through the marshland of the bayous. Grant saw that it would take an entire campaign, fighting a number of battles, simply to reach the places from which to launch a final offensive, as he put it in a letter to Julia [Grant's wife], "Heretofore I have had nothing to do but fight the enemy. This time I have to fight obstacles to reach him."[9]

Grant's gloomy predictions turned out to be correct. Historians have listed eleven separate engagements in the campaign, each of which could claim the status of a battle.

Grant now organized his Department of the Tennessee into five corps,[10] of which Sherman was to command the XV and McClernand the XIII. On January 18, 1863, Grant ordered Sherman's and McClernand's corps from Arkansas Post back to Memphis, away from Vicksburg, there to await further instructions.

For a period thereafter, Sherman's activities were varied. It can be said that Grant's entire Vicksburg campaign was ad hoc in nature—one experiment after another. So it was with Sherman. He retained command of his XV Corps but he spent the bulk of his time on other duties. One of the roles he played was that of adviser. And Grant seemed to give him missions that were necessary but on the surface did not make sense. Sherman, out of sheer loyalty, accepted the missions even though he knew they would bring on defeat for his corps and bring the press down on his back once more.

Soon after the Arkansas Post episode, Grant gave Sherman a mission that Sherman did not like but performed anyway. It involved not fighting, but digging, an effort to reopen the canal project that Banks and Farragut had abandoned the previous summer. If the canal could be expanded, from six to sixty feet wide, it might be possible to move troops and ships from the Yazoo area to the south of Vicksburg, from which its defenses were most vulnerable. The work could be done, Grant hoped, out of range of the Vicksburg guns.

Grant chose Sherman's XV Corps and McClernand's XIII Corps to do the job. Sherman was not enchanted, and he grumbled about the project he called "Banks's Ditch." It is not clear how frank he was with Grant himself, but he saw the project as useless. Soon the flooded Mississippi broke through the dam protecting the work on its northern end. The project was abandoned, much to the relief of William Tecumseh Sherman.

Meanwhile Sherman was fighting another battle in his lifelong war with the press. He had many such battles, but this one attracted unusual attention. The clash, in fact, was so serious that only President Lincoln's growing confidence in Grant saved him.

His special enemy this time was a man named Thomas W. Knox, who was the leading reporter for the *New York Herald*. Knox had surreptitiously and against Sherman's orders slipped onto one of the troop transports that had unsuccessfully attacked Chickasaw Bluffs. Though few fair-minded viewers blamed Sherman for the failure, Knox published an article in the *Herald* loaded with accusations made by individual soldiers he had interviewed. He ignored the foul weather and terrain; instead he concentrated on personal attacks against Sherman himself. Knox also accused Sherman of failing to take care of his wounded. His use of the word "unaccountable" seemed to be a resurrection of the term "insane" so widely used a year earlier, when Sherman was commanding in Kentucky.

Predictably, Sherman was furious, both at the article and at Knox's deliberate violation of his orders banning reporters from the attack. He regarded Knox as a spy—and indeed some material Knox divulged was probably of use to the enemy—and ordered him tried by court-martial. Sherman placed no limitation on the court's potential verdict; he did not even rule out execution by firing squad as a spy.[11]

The matter soon became a cause célèbre in the East, but Sherman was not deterred by public opinion. Knox attempted to make amends, and in a personal visit to Sherman he offered to issue at least a partial retraction of his article. Certain mitigating factors, Knox claimed, had been present when the attack had failed. He made an unfortunate statement, however, that the press regarded Sherman as an enemy. That did it. The trial went on.

Sherman participated personally in the trial that followed, garnering testimony from such responsible witnesses as Admiral Porter, who even praised his performance. He sent copies of pertinent documents to Ellen, to his brother John, to Grant, and to his wife's brother, an accomplished lawyer.

The court-martial dragged on for weeks, and the final verdict was gentler than Sherman had hoped for. It simply banned Knox from Grant's military department under pain of arrest if he returned. Knox returned to Washington and once there began to fight the verdict, in the process of which he secured an audience with Lincoln himself to plead his case.

Lincoln was in a spot. Much as he supported Grant, he was in an awkward position politically. Just as he bent over backward to placate McClernand, a valuable political ally, he had to avoid offending the Northern press. He promised Knox that he would rescind the verdict of the court-martial if Grant himself approved.

Grant was also in an awkward position. He wrote Knox a reasonable letter praising Sherman in lavish terms and declared that he would refer the request to Sherman. Sherman, however, never gave an inch. In a letter to Knox, he declared, "Come with a sword or musket in your hand, prepared to share with us our fate in sunshine and storm, in prosperity and adversity, in plenty and scarcity, and I will welcome you as a brother and an associate; but come as you do now, expecting me to ally the reputation and honor of my country and my fellow soldiers with you as the representative of the press which you yourself say makes so slight a difference between truth and falsehood, and my answer is Never!"[12]

Sherman had carried the day. But the Knox case was only one battle in his vendetta with the press. More lay ahead.

By early spring, after more than two months of frustration, Grant made one more effort to reduce Vicksburg from the north and avoid the risk of sending Porter's fleet south beneath the guns of Vicksburg. He still faced one serious problem, however: Porter's ships could not enter the mouth of the Yazoo because it was dominated by the fortifications that had repulsed Sherman the previous December.

Porter and Sherman therefore decided to try bypassing the mouth of the Yazoo by using a series of bayous, lakes, and streams that had once been courses of the river. The waterway they chose was winding and overgrown with vegetation, but the water was deep. Porter confirmed its navigability by making a personal reconnaissance on March 14.[13] The name of the waterway was Steele's Bayou, and it entered the Mississippi between Vicksburg and the mouth of the Yazoo.

The Steele's Bayou Expedition was a major effort. Porter's force consisted of five ironclad gunboats, followed by four towed barges carrying mortars. Behind Porter would be a division of infantry from Sherman's XV Corps, reinforced by two regiments. Sherman himself would be in command of army troops. Porter's flotilla entered Steele's Bayou on March 15, 1863.

At first all seemed to go well. Grant accompanied Porter for the first day, but then, when the flotilla had finished crossing Steele's Bayou, he departed, leaving Sherman in charge of the troops on the transports. Porter crossed Black Bayou without difficulty, likewise Deer Creek. On Rolling Fork, however, the low branches and underwater vegetation that Porter had been able to plow through previously began to close in. Forward progress was slowed to a half mile an hour, and Confederate sharpshooters began appearing in great numbers on the banks. Eventually an estimated four thousand rebels were on hand, more than Porter could handle.

In bald terms, the expedition had been ambushed. Confederate forces had discovered Porter's presence even while his ships were still on Steele's Bayou. Troops from around the area were closing in. To make matters worse, Sherman's transports, which had originally followed Porter's ships closely, became cut off. The ironclads could push their way, albeit slowly, but the tall smokestacks of Sherman's transports could not penetrate the canopy of low branches. A gap grew between the army and navy forces.

Porter now realized his predicament. He attempted to back out, but discovered that the Confederates had blocked his return passage by felling more trees. He sent Sherman an urgent plea for help and issued orders to his ships' commanders to prepare to demolish the vessels to prevent their falling into enemy hands.

Sherman received Porter's message on the evening of March 19, more than five days from the beginning of the expedition. He set out first thing the next morning, personally leading two regiments over rough terrain. After a forced march of a day and a half, he arrived at Porter's position on March 21 with enough strength to disperse the besieging Confederates. By March 27, the Steele's Bayou force was safely back on the Mississippi.[14]

The operation had failed, but it had produced two significant results: First, it further strengthened the growing bond between Sherman and Porter, and second, it finally convinced Grant that this last of his experiments to take Vicksburg from the north had to be discontinued. More direct action, despite its risks, was called for.

CHAPTER NINE

THE GUNS OF VICKSBURG

When Grant accompanied Porter up Steele's Bayou on March 17, he had along with him an unusual visitor, a forty-three-year-old gentleman of the press by the name of Charles Anderson Dana. What made Dana unusual was that, unlike most of his colleagues, he did not consider himself to be an enemy of the generals. Actually, Dana was not acting as a reporter. He bore the title of assistant secretary of war, and was anxious to contribute to the campaign against Vicksburg by utilizing whatever talents he could offer.

Understandably, Dana's presence caused much by way of conjecture around Grant's headquarters, partly because of his prominence. He had once been managing editor of Horace Greeley's *New York Herald*, and on this visit he was designated as a "special commissioner." Supposedly he was there only to evaluate procedures for the payment of troops, but nobody was fooled by that camouflage; Dana had obviously come as a sort of agent, probably to evaluate Grant for the benefit of the secretary and President Lincoln.

With today's hindsight, it seems strange that Grant, the only Union general who had won significant victories,[1] should have been in danger of losing his command. Lincoln, however, had no way of foreseeing the successful outcome of the Vicksburg campaign. What he saw was Grant's army struggling in the mud, losing one skirmish after another, his men suffering. Perhaps more important, a whispering campaign was circling around Washington about Grant's heavy drinking, rumors that were doubtless encouraged and even exaggerated by jealous men such as Mc-Clernand. Dana, however, had come with an open mind to learn the true facts, instinctively leaning in Grant's favor.

If Grant felt threatened by Dana's presence, he did not cringe. He ordered that Dana be given access to all of his papers and to his staff. Nothing, Grant had ordered, should be hidden. And after a short while Dana had come to the same evaluations as those held by Grant's associates. The general, he concluded, certainly did have a drinking problem, but the affliction appeared to come in spurts, and did not exist as a chronic condition. Granted, at times of inactivity between battles, the general would go on a drinking bout that appalled the onlooker. But such episodes were short-lived. By the next morning after a spree Grant would arise from sleep refreshed and with normal energy. His weakness had never interfered with the performance of his duties.

Dana actually noted one such incident when he accompanied Grant at Steele's Bayou. In his memoirs, Grant mentions only that he stayed with Porter one day. Dana, however, recorded something more dire in his notes:

> Grant wound up going aboard a steamer . . . and getting so stupidly drunk as the mortal nature of man would allow; but the next day he came out fresh as a rose, without any trace of the spree he had just passed through. So it was on two or three occasions of the sort and when it was all over, no outsider would have suspected such things had been.[2]

Dana pondered what to say in his report. Realizing that Grant's enemies would emphasize only the drunkenness and ignore Dana's glowing praise of Grant's overall worth, he decided to report nothing of the drinking incidents. Yet, perhaps by coincidence, Grant's wife, Julia, soon appeared on the scene, accompanied by Fred, one of their sons. Whether any connection existed between the two facts is questionable.

In the meantime Grant had realized that he could not take Vicksburg from the north, so he decided on a high-risk operation, one of the most dramatic events of the war: the movement of Porter's seven ironclads below the guns of Vicksburg southward along the Mississippi. This operation would allow Grant to launch a new battle on the dry ground to the south, which he would have preferred from the outset.

It was a necessary move. For more than three months, from December 1862 through March 1863, Grant's and Porter's forces had attempted to approach Vicksburg from the east (Corinth) and the north (Memphis) through water and mud. None of the numerous attempts had brought success. Grant had moved some troops down the west bank of the Mississippi, but the abominable weather had prevented his sending very many. The one option remaining, therefore, was to move troops and ironclads southward by water. Porter's ironclads were the critical element. Grant's soldiers alone could never attack Vicksburg without their heavy firepower. And those ships could be moved south in no other way.

It was a dangerous undertaking, and given the power of the Vicksburg defenses, Grant had delayed ordering it until he had first exhausted all other options.

Grant and Porter decided early that the operation had to be conducted at night, despite the danger of collisions between ships. The date was set for April 16, 1863. Porter had a total of seven ironclads, which he led from the bridge of his flagship, *Benton*. Three army transports loaded with supplies and troops would follow. These transports towed ten barges loaded with coal. A final, single barge, loaded with ammunition, was to follow the other ships at a distance great enough that in case of disaster, the exploding ammunition would not damage the rest of the fleet.[3]

Grant was assuming total responsibility for the risks, and he did not feel obligated to inform Washington of his plans. Washington, however, inevitably got wind of it; no operation of this size could be kept totally secret, even though all newspaper reporters with the army were being incarcerated in Memphis (much to Sherman's delight). When word of the plan reached the White House, Lincoln was concerned, as was Halleck, but neither official sent any orders forbidding Grant to undertake the movement.

Lincoln and even Stanton may have been reticent to interfere, but the secretary of the navy, Gideon Welles, was not. He was, in fact, infuriated by the zeal that Porter was putting into his support of Grant. His annoyance was heightened by his conviction that taking Vicksburg was unimportant. He freely quoted the president as believing that naval patrolling along the Mississippi between Vicksburg and Port Hudson would be of far greater value.

Porter, however, was not to be cowed by Washington. He was sorry, he informed the secretary, that "the Department is not satisfied with operations here," but he reminded Welles that he had been specifically sent to Vicksburg to support Grant. Grant, he went on, had decided on this operation, and many "sagacious officers" agreed with him. He must act, Porter declared, in accordance with his own judgment.[4] Nothing more was said, at least for the moment.

Grant and Porter could contend with Washington, but Grant was troubled by the doubts of his most trusted subordinate, Sherman. Sherman, in a cautiously worded letter to Grant, expressed those doubts. Contrary to the later contentions of critics, however, Sherman did not "protest"—so he claimed—but expressed his reservations with the request that his chief need not send any answer.[5]

Sherman's worries about moving south of Vicksburg were largely based on logistics; he questioned how Grant could supply his force once he had moved it there. A dismal fact, one that Porter also pointed out to Grant, was that the movement of the ironclads would be a one-way proposition. The current of the Mississippi was so rapid that once his ships were south of Vicksburg, it would be dangerous for them to return upstream. They would suffer from greatly reduced speed. Sherman was also concerned about the presence of Confederate boats located up tributaries of the Yazoo River, which, with Porter's fleet absent, could come out of hiding into the Mississippi and cut Grant's supply line to Memphis. Sherman suspected that Grant's moving south had an aspect other than the merely military. Pulling back to Memphis, as Sherman and Porter preferred, would give the impression of defeat, which Grant would never tolerate.[6] Nevertheless both men followed Grant's decision as stoutly as if it had been their own.

Sherman's role in this operation, like many others he played, was unconventional. Grant was concerned that if Confederate gunfire was effective, many men might find themselves blown into the water, in danger of drowning. He and Sherman came up with a scheme to minimize that danger. Sherman would leave his headquarters at Milliken's Bend and set up a line of small craft below the city, on the lookout for anyone struggling in the water. They had watched many of them sailing around beneath Vicksburg's guns, apparently considered not worth shooting at. Obtaining the small boats for the purpose was difficult, but eventually someone located some sloops at Memphis. Sherman commandeered four of them and positioned them south of Vicksburg, as planned. He also decided to check every arriving ship, whether it had been hit or not.

On the evening of April 16, 1863, according to plan, Porter's flotilla cut loose from its moorings north of Vicksburg and drifted silently down the river, hoping not to be noticed. At a little after eleven p.m., however, their presence was discovered, and guns from the Vicksburg batteries began to roar. Porter's ironclads answered, and for two hours a gun battle raged that could be heard sixty miles away. Miraculously, no Union soldiers or sailors were killed, although Porter's flagship, the *Benton*, was hit and one army transport was sunk. Julia Grant and Fred watched aboard a ship out of the line of fire. Grant and Dana went with Porter.

The town where Porter landed Grant's troops was thirty-three miles south of Vicksburg, and bore the strange name of Hard Times. Grant had chosen it because it was situated in safe territory, on the west bank of the river, thus avoiding the prospect of landing in piecemeal hunks on the Vicksburg side. Having landed without resistance, Grant organized and assembled his men. He soon realized that the territory in the vicinity could not feed his army, so on April 23, a week after landing, he sent an expedition of small craft up the river past Vicksburg for resupply.

Seven days later, Grant and Porter decided that the time had come to cross the Mississippi to the east bank. As a landing place they chose a port named Grand Gulf, directly across from Grant's assembly area. Though the spot lay beneath formidable banks, the town was thought to be unoccupied. Unfortunately, it turned out to be heavily armed, and Porter's ships were met by a heavy barrage of Confederate defenses. His guns answered back, but Porter came out second-best, losing one ship in the duel. With the Confederate guns still firing, Grant's transports were forced to withdraw.

Then came a stroke of luck. While Grant was looking for an alternative place to land, an escaped slave advised him of a small port named Bruinsburg a few miles down the river. Grant took the man at his word and ferried his men to that point, where they landed unopposed. He then moved inland and the next day fought a skirmish at a place called Port Gibson. The enemy retreated, and Grant was soon able to take the Grand Gulf position from the rear. He was now on advantageous ground from which he could mount an attack or lay a siege on Vicksburg.

Grant had a decision to make. Lincoln and Halleck, who were perhaps more interested in General Nathaniel Banks's campaign against Port Hudson to the south than they were in Vicksburg, had given orders for Grant to join up with Banks. Once they had consolidated Port Hudson they could move together against Vicksburg. Such a prospect would have been impossible while Grant's force was north of Vicksburg, but now that he was south of that obstacle the issue became feasible. Grant contacted Banks and learned, probably to his relief, that the Red River campaign was going slowly. Banks advised that he could not join forces with Grant for another month. Grant decided not to wait. He resolved to continue operations on his own and take Vicksburg from the south.

Once Grant's force had made a successful landing at Hard Times, Sherman returned to his XV Corps, which was still up north at Milliken's Bend. Grant had instructed him to remain there until about May 1, 1863, and then, leaving one division to guard Union supplies, to make the long and tedious march down the west bank of the Mississippi and join the rest of the army.[7] At that time, Grant was making his plans to land at Grand Gulf, and he made a "request" of Sherman—an unusually sheepish request—that Sherman make a diversionary attack on Haynes Bluff, near Chickasaw Bluffs on the Yazoo River. He did not issue an order; he merely "hoped" that Sherman would do so. Both men were aware that the demonstration against Haynes Bluff would be rebuffed, and that the defeat would reawaken the criticism of Sherman in the Northern press. But Grant knew his man. Sherman, aware of the consequences, did not hesitate in notifying his chief that the attack would be executed.

On April 30, Sherman made his attack, using only ten regiments in order to hold down casualties. The results were more than hoped for. In his memoirs, Sherman could not restrain himself from just a touch of self-congratulation:

> . . . I did make [the feint] most effectually. . . . We afterward learned
> that General Pemberton in Vicksburg had previously dispatched a
> large force to the assistance of General Bowen, at Grand Gulf and
> Port Gibson, . . . When he discovered our ostentatious movement
> up the Yazoo, he recalled his men, and sent them up to Haines's
> Bluff to meet us. This detachment of rebel troops must have

marched nearly sixty miles without rest, for afterward, on reaching Vicksburg, I heard that the men were perfectly exhausted, and lay along the road in groups, completely fagged out. This diversion, made with so much pomp and display, therefore completely fulfilled its purpose, by leaving General Grant to contend with a minor force, on landing at Bruinsburg, and afterward at Port Gibson and Grand Gulf.[8]

The feint at Haynes Bluff was Sherman's last action at Milliken's Bend. By May 1 he had the XV Corps, less a division, on the way to Hard Times.

Sherman's two divisions, those of Fred Steele and J. M. Tuttle, found the march down to Hard Times difficult, but the heavy equipment had gone by water, so the infantry and horses were able to make it. On reaching his destination on May 6, Sherman established his headquarters. As a curious man, he decided to take a look around the area.

To his surprise he ran across a plantation called Bowie's Plantation, owned by Thomas Fielder Bowie. Sherman had a remote connection with Mr. Bowie, as the latter was a brother-in-law of Reverdy Johnson, the attorney general in Zachary Taylor's cabinet. Sherman remembered Johnson from the days when Thomas Ewing had also been in Taylor's cabinet. The plantation house was a magnificent building, with wide lawns, a grand piano, and two handsome paintings of Reverdy Johnson and his wife, a woman acclaimed for her beauty. The house had been ransacked, with dresses and books strewn around, and seated in front of the piano, his feet on the keys, lounged a soldier who Sherman concluded was a member of Major General James B. McPherson's division. Sherman ordered the malingerer back to his post and continued his search. A short way from the house he found the slave quarters, occupied by only an old Negro and a few women. Sherman rousted them and sent them to clean up the mess in the plantation house and to prevent any further depredations. He then returned to his headquarters.

That evening Sherman reviewed the episode in his mind and became concerned. He sent a couple of soldiers with a wagon to rescue the two paintings and return them to his safekeeping. A while later the soldiers returned. The house and the paintings had all been burned to the ground. Nobody knew who had committed the act, a Union soldier or one of the former slaves.

Sherman had no time to worry about such things. Almost immediately upon his arrival he began moving his troops across the river to Bruinsburg. Despite shortages in ships, he accomplished the task in one day, May 7, and went into reserve, pending action. He reported to Grant on May 9.

CHAPTER TEN

THE BASTION FALLS

When Sherman joined Grant in the first week of May, he realized that he would be participating in a war totally different from that up at Milliken's Bend.

He also found Grant keenly aware that his army of thirty-three thousand was now in danger. For one thing, he was now deep in enemy territory. Not that the people of Memphis and northwest Tennessee had been friendly—far from it. But in that area the population had been subdued; this was territory still dominated by the Confederacy. More threatening than the populace, however, was the danger from Confederate general Joseph E. Johnston, who was known to have assembled about twenty-four thousand men in Alabama and eastern Mississippi and was planning to join the six thousand men in Jackson, Mississippi. If Johnston could join Major General John C. Pemberton's garrison of thirty thousand men in Vicksburg, Grant would be facing a very powerful force.

Grant had already determined that the way to contend with these various Confederate commands was to defeat them in detail—that is, one at a time. He therefore decided to postpone assaulting Vicksburg and to move against Jackson in hopes of capturing the Confederate force there.

Jackson held forth other lures. Besides its political importance as the capital of Mississippi, it was a major railhead. Grant had no intention of occupying the town permanently, but he intended to make it useless to Johnston in a hurry.

Grant's main vulnerability in this daring enterprise was that of supply. The distance between Port Gibson and Jackson was seventy-two miles, more than he could possibly protect, and he was unsure where Johnston or the roving Confederate cavalry were located. Even before Sherman's arrival, therefore, Grant had decided to cut his army off from his supply lines. Whatever wagons he could gather were to stay under the protection of the army and carry nothing but ammunition. The men and horses would be required to live off the land, which in that area was rough but fertile. By May he had assembled a large number of wagons of various types loaded with ordnance—"a motley assortment," he called it.[1]

Fortunately for Grant, that part of the Confederacy was currently in a state of panic over a Union cavalry force of seventeen hundred volunteers that was raiding the area under the command of Colonel Benjamin Grierson, a former music teacher who reportedly hated horses. Johnston himself joined in the general alarm. So concerned was he with the famed Grierson's raiders that he removed the six thousand men in the city and sent them to join his main force.

Grierson's troopers had actually reached their destination at Baton Rouge by the time Grant was ready to leave Port Gibson. They had begun their raids at LaGrange, in southern Tennessee, on April 17, the day after Porter and Grant had run the Confederate defenses on the Mississippi, and they had reached their destination on May 2, more than six hundred miles. Along the way, Grierson's men had torn up railroad tracks, destroyed locomotives, burned storehouses and bridges, and freed slaves. Their greatest contribution to the Union cause, however, was not the matériel destroyed, but the confusion they caused throughout that part of the

South. At Vicksburg, Confederate general John Pemberton removed a whole division from his main garrison to secure the Vicksburg–Jackson railroad while Grant had been crossing the Mississippi.[2]

Communications in the Vicksburg–Jackson area were difficult. So rough was the ground that each of Grant's corps had to operate independently. Besides the additional risk, this dispersion meant that each corps would have little by way of intelligence exchange regarding enemy movements. The route of each corps, therefore, had to be laid out in advance. Grant decided to send McPherson along the direct line between the two cities, forty-five miles apart, along which ran a railroad, a highway, and a telegraph line. Along that route, from west to east, starting at Vicksburg, were Champion's Hill, Bolton's Depot, and Clinton, all small places.

The bulk of Grant's army, however, was still located at Port Gibson, to the south. The route from there to Jackson ran through Raymond, which McPherson's corps had taken on the twelfth of May. These two nearly parallel lines were crossed by the Big Black River, an unfordable stream that flowed from the northeast to the southwest and emptied into the Mississippi some miles below. Since all of Grant's forces were below the Big Black, it provided some protection for his left flank as he moved eastward to Jackson. It would, however, constitute an obstacle to cross when he returned from Jackson to Vicksburg, as he planned to do later.

Grant's attack toward Jackson, as mentioned, was to be made by two corps: McPherson on the left along the Vicksburg–Clinton–Jackson road, and Sherman on the right, starting from Raymond, where Sherman had camped, and which was only fifteen miles from Jackson. Grant and his small staff accompanied Sherman. McClernand's XIII Corps would follow.

The operation was practically unresisted. Grant and Sherman rode into Jackson under a driving rain at about noon on May 14. Many of the inhabitants were totally surprised. Grant later reported that the two generals visited a plant where women, busy weaving blankets, did not bother to look up from their work. Grant soon sent the workers home with what cloth they could carry, and after they were gone he ordered the plant burned to the ground.

While their troops destroyed everything of military value in Jackson, Grant, Sherman, and McPherson gathered at the state courthouse to discuss what to do next. The news they received made the decision simple: Since Johnston was reported to be heading in their direction, Grant needed to get to Vicksburg before Johnston could reach it and combine with Pemberton. But the job of destruction in Jackson had to be completed, so Grant left with McPherson's corps along the direct road to Vicksburg on the morning of May 15, leaving Sherman to carry out the ruin of the city and then to follow.

———————

Johnston, in the meantime, had established communications with Pemberton at Vicksburg and had informed him of Grant's whereabouts. To these conventional thinkers, the line from Port Gibson to Jackson meant one thing: a vulnerable supply line. Pemberton therefore made a sally out of Vicksburg, crossed the Big Black, and attacked what he expected to be a supply line, but it turned out not to be there. In the meantime, Grant was already on his way back from Jackson to Vicksburg.

———————

An obstacle in Grant's path was Champion's Hill, where a battle was fought on May 16. It did not involve Sherman, but Grant delivered a near-rout of Pemberton's field army. At first Pemberton had the advantage, since Grant had on the scene only McClernand's corps plus another brigade. For a while it looked as if Grant might be defeated, especially since McClernand was so excruciatingly slow in coming up. As it was, Grant pulled through by sheer doggedness. He refused to give in and made full use of his small reserve. Eventually, Pemberton lost his nerve and retreated across the Big Black. It was not a large battle, but the Confederate losses were disproportionately heavy. By that time Sherman, but not his corps, had joined Grant, and the two sat together on a log during the evening of May 17, watching the construction of the three bridges by which Grant's army would cross the Big Black. By May 20, Grant's whole army was facing Vicksburg north of the Big Black. Sherman's corps was on the right, McPherson's in the center, and McClernand's some distance to the left.

At this time Grant made an error based on inaccurate information or excessive aggressiveness. On May 20 he ordered Sherman and McPherson to attack the Confederate parapets some seven miles east of Vicksburg. Expecting Confederate morale to be low, he believed that the attack would go easily. It did not; resistance was strong and determined, and both corps fell back with heavy losses. Two days later he ordered a second attack, hoping to take Vicksburg before Johnston could attack him from his rear. Again the attack failed.

Grant and Sherman witnessed this second failure together. At that time Grant received a handwritten note from McClernand, whose XIII Corps was holding the left flank. The wording was flowery. As Sherman recalled the note, McClernand claimed "his troops had captured the rebel parapet in his front," and "the flag of the Union waved over the stronghold of Vicksburg,"[3] and he requested reinforcement, as well as urging stronger action by McPherson and Sherman.

Grant read the note carefully. Based on McClernand's actions at Champion's Hill and other places, he had no faith in his XIII Corps commander. "I don't believe it," he said angrily. Sherman, who was with him, calmed him down. Sherman detested McClernand more than did Grant—"dirty dog," he once called him. But here was an official request for troops from a senior commander; Grant had a moral obligation to respect the request.

Grant gave in—partly. He went to a position where he believed he could see McClernand's front as well as McClernand could, and there he saw nothing to substantiate the claim. Nevertheless Grant agreed with Sherman that he had to send at least a token force, so he sent Brigadier

General Isaac Quinby's division of the XVII Corps. To no avail. Grant soon realized that his instinctive assessment of McClernand's message had been spot on. McClernand's troops were nowhere near the point he claimed he had taken, and he himself was nowhere near the area. Always reluctant to make enemies with those in his own command, and acutely aware of McClernand's powerful political connections (McClernand was a pro-Union Democrat), Grant had always hesitated to reprimand him. But Grant had reached a boiling point. Not only had Grant sacrificed troops in a futile attempt to take fortifications around Vicksburg on McClernand's word, but McClernand proceeded to issue (and publish) a laudatory note to the men of his corps—strictly against the orders of his superiors. So on June 18, he formally removed McClernand from command, and put Major General Edward O. C. Ord in control of the XIII Corps.[4]

Grant now realized that Vicksburg's fortifications could not be taken by storm. He therefore began preparing a siege, using entrenchments similar to those of Pemberton—and sometimes as close as fifty yards away—and settled down. He might not be able to carry the Confederate works, but he could seal the city off. Without supplies Vicksburg could not hold off forever. His situation, however, still entailed some risk. Pemberton had a substantial force in the city and Johnston was known to be somewhere to the east of the Big Black River. But Union reinforcements were coming in from a worried Halleck in Washington, and by the fourteenth of June Grant's army had grown to the respectable strength of seventy-one thousand.[5]

The threat from Johnston was still there, however, and by June 22, Grant decided that he had enough troops on hand that he could afford to split his force again; he could send nearly half his army to a position facing eastward to protect his rear. As was customary, he selected Sherman for the task. Sherman was to hold a line all the way between Haynes Bluff on the north and the Big Black, facing eastward. At the same time Grant began tunneling operations beneath the Confederate lines and blew at least one large crater.

———————

By early July, the Confederate situation in Vicksburg had become desperate, and Pemberton began making overtures for terms of surrender. He met no more luck in negotiating with the determined Grant than had Simon Buckner at Fort Donelson: "unconditional surrender." Pemberton's offer of a parley reached Grant's headquarters during the evening of July 3, 1863, the same day as Pickett's Charge at Gettysburg. Though Pemberton was anxious to avoid surrendering on the symbolic day of July 4, Grant refused to accommodate him. He ignored requests to appoint a commission until the witching hour of midnight had passed. Vicksburg was formally surrendered at ten a.m., July 4. The fighting over, the rebel and Yankee soldiers mingled together in friendship as if they had been fighting on the same side.

On hearing the news, Sherman began preparations for an attack on Johnston.

The end of the Vicksburg campaign found Grant's command arrangement similar to that with which it had begun: in both instances with Sherman commanding nearly half of Grant's army in a semi-independent status. The result was a team similar to others in military history: Lee and Jackson, Hindenburg and Ludendorff. The team served Lincoln and the Union well. With the fall of Vicksburg, the Confederacy was split. Future sacrifices in blood and money lay ahead, but Union victory in the Civil War was now a virtual certainty.

CHAPTER ELEVEN

CHATTANOOGA

Sherman did not bother to participate in the surrender ceremonies at Vicksburg. His focus was now on Joseph E. Johnston, whose whereabouts were uncertain. But Sherman suspected that some Confederates were located at Jackson, so on July 4, the day of Pemberton's surrender, he crossed over to the east bank of the Big Black and essentially retraced his previous steps to Jackson, determined to destroy whatever troops Johnston had there. Unfortunately, from his viewpoint, the small contingent of Confederates had evacuated before he arrived. So Sherman, ever conscious of his long line of communications, withdrew to his position on the Big Black and awaited developments.

———————

Port Hudson, at New Orleans, fell soon after Vicksburg, and the Mississippi River was now solidly in Union hands. With no further need for such a powerful force, Grant quickly dispersed his Army of the Mississippi. He personally visited New Orleans but then established his permanent headquarters in Memphis. His various corps were sent to places of strategic importance. For a while, Ord's XIII Corps (previously McClernand's) was sent to Natchez, McPherson's XVII Corps remained at Vicksburg, and Sherman's XV Corps was ordered to continue occupying his present position along the Big Black. Sherman established his headquarters in a tent near a house belonging to man named Parson Fox. Remembering that a former cadet he had known from Alexandria lived nearby, the general soon found that the young man's mother was staying at Parson Fox's farm. When Sherman called on her to pay his respects, the mother bitterly accused the general of killing her husband, the cadet's father, at Bull Run. Sherman may have not been at war with the Southern people, but they seemed to feel he was at war with them.

The Big Black River, while unfordable, was not wide, so Sherman's men were within shouting distance of the Confederates across the river. There was little by way of serious fighting. Many of the men, though officially enemies, had once been friends, and they held little or no mutual animosity. One evening a Confederate detachment carrying a flag of truce approached a bridge with a message for General Grant. Sherman accorded the detachment every courtesy. He provided forage for the animals and invited the captain commanding the detachment and his officers and men for a dinner.

It was a memorable evening. The two groups enjoyed their visit, and they seemed to differ on only one subject: the possibility of reuniting the two sections of the country after the bitterness of the Civil War, regardless of the outcome. Sherman contended that reconciliation would be easier than did the captain, who argued that friendly encounters could occur only when the participants were cultured officers such as themselves. But when Sherman took his guest to witness a group of enlisted soldiers enjoying the same conviviality as the officers, he made a point.[1]

On September 22, 1863, Sherman's period of relative peace came to an end when word arrived that Union general William Rosecrans's Army of the Cumberland had suffered a staggering defeat at the hands of Braxton

Bragg's Confederate Army of the Tennessee at Chickamauga, a place a few miles south of Chattanooga. Rosecrans had fallen back to Chattanooga and was managing to hold the city. Perhaps he was able to do so only because Bragg did not attack him; he was content to lay siege. Confederate forces held the high ground south of the Tennessee River, cutting off Rosecrans's supply lines with the intention of starving him out.

Sensing that his presence would be needed at Memphis, Sherman reported to Grant of his own volition the next day. There he learned what Grant knew about the Battle of Chickamauga, fought five days earlier. The defeat had put the authorities in Washington in a frenzy. Within a couple of days Halleck directed Grant to transfer Sherman's XV Corps from the Big Black to Chattanooga, just incidentally repairing the Memphis & Charleston Railroad as he went along. He also sent two corps from Major General George Meade's Army of the Potomac—Oliver O. Howard's XI and Henry W. Slocum's XII—under the overall command of Joseph Hooker, once commander of the Army of the Potomac. Conveniently, those were probably the three men Halleck would just as soon get out of Washington, but ironically they were destined to play a major part in the coming campaigns in the West.*

As he prepared to embark for Chattanooga, a shock hit Sherman that would have affected a lesser man's performance of duty: the death of his nine-year-old son, Willie. During this period of inactivity, Ellen Sherman had journeyed to visit her husband in Vicksburg, bringing four of their children. Their father took delight in all of them, but he took a special pride in Willie, the boy for whom he held the greatest hopes. As soon as

---

* Hooker and Howard were no mutual admiration society. When Hooker sustained his humiliating defeat at Chancellorsville the previous May, he unrealistically blamed Howard for his defeat, for it was Howard's XI Corps whose left flank was crushed. But it was four days later that Hooker withdrew across the Rappahannock. Slocum was probably the most colorless of Meade's corps commanders.

the family had arrived, Willie had adopted the 13th Regular Battalion, Sherman's bodyguard, and in turn had been adopted by them as an honorary sergeant. Willie was a precocious lad, joining in all the soldiers' activities, which included drill and riding.

Sherman, along with his troops, was to depart by steamboat for Memphis before moving overland to Chattanooga. The general's family would continue on to Cairo, Illinois, and head to Ohio. As Ellen was packing for their return home, it was noticed that Willie was missing. Soon located, he showed symptoms of typhoid fever. Despite his illness Ellen was compelled to continue with their plans. In the course of the trip, the doctors quickly gave up hope as the family steamed up the Mississippi. On October 3, 1863, Willie Sherman died in Memphis.

Sherman, burdened with organizing his corps, was overwhelmed with grief. He blamed himself for Willie's death, holding himself responsible for exposing his son to the unhealthy climate of Vicksburg. He poured out his grief in letters to those who were close to both him and Willie. One letter was directed toward a man to whom he had become especially close, Admiral David Dixon Porter.

It was the 13th Regular Battalion, however, that received Sherman's greatest expression of grief. In an unusually touching letter to Captain C. C. Smith, the commander, whom he addressed as "my dear friend," he started with a sentence that summarized it all: "I cannot sleep tonight till I record an expression of the deep feelings of my heart to you, and to the officers and soldiers of the battalion, for their kind behavior to my poor child."

He went on to review the joy that association with the battalion had given Willie, reminiscing that the boy had actually believed that he was a sergeant in that unit: "Child as he was, he had the enthusiasm, the pure love of truth, honor, and love of country, which should animate all soldiers."

In closing, Sherman went all out:

Please convey to the battalion my heartfelt thanks, and assure each and all that if in after-years they call on me or mine, and

mention that they were of the Thirteenth Regulars when Willie was
a sergeant, they will have a key to the affections of my family that
will open all it has, that we will share with them our last blanket,
our last crust! Your friend,
    W. T. Sherman, Major General[2]

Expressing his sorrow seems to have relieved Sherman's mind. He sent his family home and went about his duties. Fortunately for him, those duties were pressing, and his mind was soon occupied in his preparations for taking a ten-thousand-man corps across Tennessee from Memphis to Chattanooga. The communications from Chattanooga allowed him to keep in touch with his four divisions, each of which was following a different road or waterway. On October 11 he left Chattanooga himself.

Sherman did not expect to encounter any enemy on this trip, so when he left Memphis he took a train whose only security force was his 13th Regular Battalion; the rest of the railroad cars were loaded with clerks, office supplies, and horses for the officers. About nine miles into the journey, the train passed one of Sherman's divisions—under Brigadier General John M. Corse—that had not yet departed.

At Collierville, only twenty-six miles from Memphis, Sherman noticed that the train was slowing down, finally coming to a stop. Sherman stepped off the train to check the cause and was notified by the colonel of a volunteer regiment that he was being attacked by a large force of Confederate cavalry. Soon a flag of truce appeared and Sherman sent two aides to meet it. The Confederate commander, they reported, had demanded the surrender of the train and a nearby arms depot. Sherman refused, but instructed the aides to engage the enemy in argument and thus buy as much time in conversation as they could.

Sherman then took personal charge of the action. He directed the train's passengers to take up a defensive position on a nearby knoll, backed the train as much as he could, and awaited the attack. Fortunately the depot itself contained ammunition that he could use to arm his clerks. The enemy attacked, but were beaten back by the veteran 13th Regulars. At one point some of the attackers got to the train and stole some horses, including Sherman's favorite mare. The enemy also wrought damage to the train engine. After three or four hours of fighting, however, the Confederates withdrew, prompted by the arrival of Corse's division, to whom Sherman had sent an urgent message.

No further such difficulties were met, and at certain points along the way it was possible for Sherman to communicate with his divisions moving eastward. At Corinth, Sherman learned that Grant was heading to Chattanooga to take command of a new department that would include three armies, one of which would be the Army of the Tennessee under Sherman.

Grant had been given free rein in organizing his force. To command the Army of the Cumberland, already on hand, he decided to replace the inept and unlucky Rosecrans with George Thomas, a stolid, conservative man who had earned great accolades as the "Rock of Chickamauga" for his role in saving the Union Army, and had provided the only bright spot in the whole dismal disaster.

Grant's third army was the Army of the Ohio, commanded by the recently reassigned former commander of the Army of the Potomac, Ambrose E. Burnside. Burnside's was a small army, consisting of only one corps, the XXIII. Burnside commanded that corps himself, playing a dual role as army and corps commander. It was an odd arrangement, deemed desirable because of the additional administrative powers the title of "army commander" gave him.

Halleck, in Washington, remained frantic, ignoring such niceties as the chain of command. Bypassing Grant, he sent Sherman a message urging him to speed up the rebuilding of the Chattanooga supply line. Sherman took that in stride, and at Iuka, Mississippi, he was pleased to

learn that Admiral Porter had voluntarily sent gunboats loaded with supplies as far up the Tennessee River as possible to assist. For his part,
Sherman was careful to pick up supplies as he went along so as to avoid
taxing the tonnage going into Chattanooga by rail.

Sherman reached Chattanooga on November 14, to be greeted warmly by
Grant. Sherman's first reaction was surprise: "Why, General Grant, you
are besieged!" Grant merely responded, "Too true." Together they recon-
noitered the front, and Grant explained the situation in detail.

The town of Chattanooga nestled along the south bank of the Tennessee River, a generally meandering stream which at that point straightened
out and ran almost exactly east to west. Just to the west of the town the
river veered northward. By and large the territory south of the river was
occupied by Bragg's Confederates and the ground to the north by the
Union. The one exception was the small town of Bridgeport, Alabama, on
the river twenty-six miles by rail west of Chattanooga. Here there was a
bridgehead occupied precariously by Grant.*

The Confederate position, on the southern side of the battlefield, was
split by Chattanooga Creek, which runs northward before emptying into
the Tennessee at Chattanooga. To the west of the creek stands Lookout
Mountain, a sudden rise that reaches a height of about twenty-four hundred
feet. On the east is Missionary Ridge, a lower (eighteen hundred feet), elon-
gated rise that runs north–south. Both Lookout Mountain and the northern
tip of Missionary Ridge dominate Chattanooga. For some reason, Bragg
had chosen to deploy most of his strength (Hardee's and Breckenridge's
corps) along Missionary Ridge, holding Lookout Mountain only lightly.

---

* Technically, the commander of the Union forces in Chattanooga was George Thomas,
but since Grant was in command of the forces in the West he gave the orders. The same
situation prevailed later on in the war, when Grant accompanied George G. Meade's Army
of the Potomac in the drive from Washington to Richmond and Petersburg. For our purposes, I will refer to Grant.

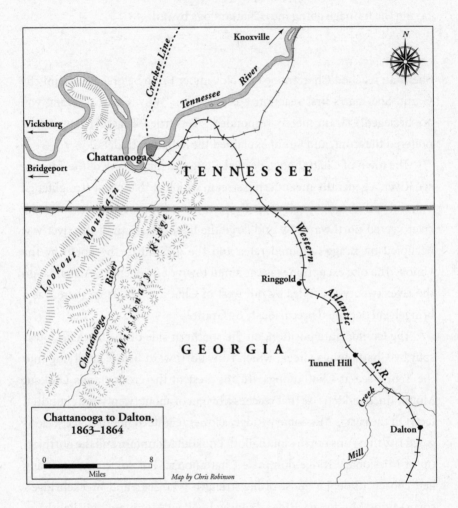

N

Knoxville

Cracker Line

Tennessee   River

Vicksburg

Chattanooga

Bridgeport

TENNESSEE

Lookout Mountain

Chattanooga River

Missionary Ridge

Western

Ringgold

Atlantic

GEORGIA

Tunnel Hill

R.R.

Creek

Dalton

Mill

Chattanooga to Dalton,
1863–1864

0   8
Miles

Map by Chris Robinson

With reinforcements pouring in, Rosecrans had fortified Chattanooga strongly, and Thomas, after replacing him, had continued to do so. Bragg's decision to lay siege rather than attack Rosecrans head-on may have made him appear timid, but the siege itself had come within a hair of success. Supplies could not reach all the way to the city on the Tennessee River, so the Union Army in Chattanooga depended on a small road that began at Bridgeport and wound its way through the hills north to a town named Anderson, thence south to his army. So little capacity had this so-called "Cracker Line" that all the army's horses in Chattanooga had died of starvation, and the men for a time had subsisted on a ration of "four cakes of hard bread and a quarter pound of pork" issued every three days.[3]

By the time Sherman arrived, Grant had already solved the supply problem. He had made use of the reinforcements Halleck had sent (Hooker, Howard, and Slocum) to enlarge the Union foothold at Bridgeport and to open enough roads on the south side of the Tennessee River to ease the supply situation.

An unwelcome complication had arisen, however. Grant had been placed in charge of all Union forces in the West, and therefore was responsible for the plight of Ambrose Burnside's IX and XXIII corps in Knoxville. There was little or no military reason for Burnside to be in that exposed position, but President Lincoln had felt an intense desire to protect the people of East Tennessee, almost all of whom had remained loyal to the Union. Burnside's corps, sent into Tennessee, learned at Knoxville that Confederate general James Longstreet's corps from Lee's army had been sent to the area and was threatening him.* Officially, Longstreet was part of Bragg's Army of the Tennessee, but Bragg commanded him with a loose rein. In addition, Bragg felt secure enough to spare him for the purpose of destroying Burnside. Grant had therefore decided to station Sherman at a point where he could move to reinforce Burnside if necessary.

Grant sent orders to Sherman, at Bridgeport, to cross his XV Corps to the north side of the Tennessee River and take station at the left (east) end

---

* A Confederate corps was about twice the size of a Union corps.

of the line, across the river from Tunnel Hill, a knob thought to be at the north end of Missionary Ridge. Then, if Burnside was seriously threatened, Grant could detach Sherman to his aid. The big question was to determine Longstreet's intentions. Though Bragg had sent him in the direction of Knoxville, Longstreet had as yet taken no positive action. By November 21, Sherman was in position to attack Tunnel Hill on Missionary Ridge or to break off and head for Knoxville.

Though Lincoln and Halleck continued to fret over Longstreet's threat to Burnside, Grant was getting impatient. By November 22 he decided to move against Bragg on Missionary Ridge, using Sherman as his main effort. Since Hooker, in the so-called Battle Above the Clouds, had taken control of Lookout Mountain, Grant planned a double envelopment: Sherman could attack southward on the left tip of Missionary Ridge and Hooker northward from the south end. Thomas, in the middle, was to hit the center of Missionary Ridge, and then turn northward to join Sherman.

Various factors delayed Grant until early in the morning of November 24. Sherman, upon crossing the Tennessee River, found that the hillock he had supposed was part of Missionary Ridge was actually not. He therefore had to reorganize before continuing beyond it. When he reached the main ridge, he found it so heavily defended that he was unable to secure a foothold. Operations ceased for the day.

Despite Sherman's disappointment, his corps had made an unexpected contribution. In order to defend the north face of Missionary Ridge, Bragg had denuded the center of his line, that facing Thomas. When Thomas had seized his limited objective, therefore, his men, of their own volition, continued on against the remaining Confederates on the ridge. They drove up the slope, and the center of Bragg's line collapsed. Bragg, who had no stomach for further defense, fled the scene. By the end of the day, the Battle of Chattanooga was history, a clear-cut, inexpensive Union victory.

Grant was allowed no time to celebrate; his mind was still on Burnside at Knoxville. But, conscious of what might have been a letdown on Sherman's part, he wrote a two-purpose order: first, to reassure Sherman, and, second, to share thoughts as to what to do next. Reassuring Sherman was not difficult, because Sherman was no glory hound. So Grant wrote, assuming that Sherman took the same pride in the recent victory as he in ". . . the handsome manner in which Thomas's troops carried Missionary Ridge this afternoon." Sherman could "feel a just pride, too, in the part taken by the forces under your command in taking first so much of the same range of hills, and then in attracting the attention of so many of the enemy as to make Thomas's part certain of success."

Grant then turned to the matter of relieving Burnside, disclosing that he had been informed on the evening of the twenty-third that the IX Corps in Knoxville had on hand from ten to twelve days' supplies. Burnside "spoke hopefully of being able to hold out that length of time. . . ."

At that point, Grant did an about-face in the same letter that would have devastated a less competent and devoted man than Sherman. Grant ended the formal letter with one idea:

> I take it for granted that Bragg's entire force has left. If not, of course, the first thing is to dispose of him. If he has gone, the only thing necessary to do to-morrow will be to send out a reconnaissance to ascertain the whereabouts of the enemy.

All well and good. But then, in a postscript, Grant completely reversed himself, now thinking out loud that he should do just the opposite:

> P.S. On reflection, I think we will push Bragg with all our strength to-morrow, and try if we cannot cut off a good portion of his rear

troops and trains. His men have manifested a strong disposition to desert for some time past, and we will now give them a chance. I will instruct Thomas accordingly. Move the advance force early, on the most easterly road taken by the enemy. U.S.G.[4]

Grant's decision to pursue Bragg required Sherman to make a drastic change in the arrangements for his next mission. He had been preparing to move eastward to Knoxville, but he had now been ordered to attack south. That meant a redeployment of troops, artillery, and trains. But by this time XV Corps was expert at adjusting to such last-minute changes, and on November 26 Sherman fell in on the left of Thomas, heading south.

The use of Sherman's force made the difference in Grant's decision, very much as Longstreet's corps made all the difference to Bragg. With Sherman's XV Corps on hand, Grant held the advantage; with Longstreet on hand, Bragg had the advantage. It had, for example, been Longstreet's absence at Missionary Ridge that made Grant's victory there a foregone conclusion. The presence or absence of either decided the outcome.

The pursuit of Bragg was soon dropped. As a result, Grant reinstated his orders for Sherman to relieve Burnside. The difficulties, as usual, were logistical. The distance from Chattanooga to Knoxville is about 130 miles, and though the countryside could provide meat, bread, and forage, it could not provide salt or ammunition. And since it was so late in the autumn, the lack of winter clothing was a cause of suffering. Thus Sherman's account of the period consists of descriptions of road conditions, blown bridges, and the like. Skirmishes were few and did not impede progress.

Sherman arrived in the vicinity of Knoxville on December 5, only to find that Longstreet, who had never reconciled himself to being detached from Lee's Army of Northern Virginia, had departed for Petersburg to rejoin Lee. That did not mean, however, that Sherman's grueling march to Knoxville was a waste of time and effort. Had it not been for his approach, Longstreet might not have lifted his threat to Knoxville, and Burnside might have been forced to surrender.

The Chattanooga campaign had been a stern ordeal for Sherman and his men. The casualties in the battle and the various skirmishes had not been heavy by the grim mathematics of war, but the endurance required of Sherman and his men had been severe. And its end saw the departure of Sherman from XV Corps.

BOOK II

SHERMAN ASSUMES COMMAND

CHAPTER TWELVE

COMMANDER IN THE WEST

On March 18, 1864, at Nashville, Tennessee, William T. Sherman assumed command of the Military Division of the Mississippi.[1] He was replacing Ulysses S. Grant, who had been promoted to the new rank of lieutenant general and called to Washington to command all the armies of the United States. It was a signal honor for both.

Considering the stellar performance of both men in the western campaigns, and the disappointing performance of Henry W. Halleck as the titular head of all the armies, the move appears logical. However, there had been many pitfalls in its coming about.

Such a move had long been in the mill. Shortly after the fall of Vicksburg in July of 1863, a bill had been introduced by Representative Elihu B. Washburne calling for the change. The bill had moved slowly in Congress, and even Lincoln himself had been cautious. Always a supporter of Grant's—a Grant man, the president called himself—he still had to ensure that Grant would not parlay future glories to political advantage. John C. Frémont had tried to do so, and George B. McClellan, whom Lincoln had relieved of command of the army for lack of aggressiveness, was now courting the Democratic nomination for president of the United States.

Lincoln had had enough political generals, and he had to make sure that Grant was not one of them.

Finally, in the light of Grant's statements denying political ambitions, and Washburne's persuasion, Lincoln had relented. In late February, Congress had reinstated the grade of lieutenant general, a title held by only two Americans: George Washington and Winfield Scott. Lincoln submitted Grant's name on March 1, 1864, and the next day he had been confirmed.

Sherman's appointment was less apparent than that of Grant. In previous moves up the chain of command, from the beginning of Vicksburg on, Sherman had always replaced Grant when the latter had stepped up, but in this case the succession was not so obvious. He could be appointed as commander of the Department of the Mississippi, of course, but he could also have gone east with Grant and assumed command of the Army of the Potomac, replacing General George G. Meade, whose victory at Gettysburg had been badly tarnished by his failure to pursue the Confederates when Lee was in a near-helpless state.

Lincoln left the decision up to Grant, and Meade, to his credit, did what he could to make the verdict easy. When Grant visited the Army of the Potomac at Brandy Station shortly after his own appointment, Meade made his case that the cause was too great for Grant to take Meade's feelings into consideration; Grant, he suggested, might desire to bring in someone from the West, meaning Sherman. But Grant had already decided to leave Meade where he was and to place Sherman in the spot Grant was leaving, the procedure that had become customary.

It was a wise decision. Grant and Sherman had never worked together directly; instead, Grant had always used Sherman to command a portion of his army while he remained with the main body. They had never occupied the same or proximate headquarters.* Sherman always considered

---

* As early as late 1862, Grant had delegated the command of nearly half his army to Sherman at Chickasaw Bluffs, even though they were out of contact. Grant sent Sherman in his place to Steele's Bayou, with Porter. Sherman's command of XV Corps on the Big Black was a semi-independent command. Finally, Grant had sent Sherman off on his own to resecure Burnside at Knoxville.

himself Grant's subordinate—which he would still be in the West—but on a very loose leash. Serving as commander of the Army of the Potomac with Grant present, looking over his shoulder and making all the real decisions, would have been stifling, even for such a devoted man as Sherman.

During the months of January and February 1864, while the command changes were brewing in Washington, Sherman and his XV Corps had been making raids against Confederate bases, principally in Mississippi. The most ambitious of these raids was conducted against a town named Meridian, near the Mississippi coastline on the Gulf of Mexico. A division under Brigadier General William Sooy Smith was attached. The raid itself was successful; the Confederate garrison was routed and the supplies destroyed or confiscated. But by some mix-up, Sherman lost contact with Smith and felt forced to abandon any plans he had to invade Alabama. He did not know for some time that Smith's force had been practically wiped out.

On the road back to his headquarters from this action, Sherman received the first word of Grant's promotion. At Memphis a message directly from Grant at Nashville was waiting for him. In his typically modest way, Grant barely mentioned his own promotion, but his tone probably accounted for his unusual warmth and informality. Instead of the usual "Major-General Sherman," he began merely with "Dear Sherman." After the briefest accounts, in which the only notable matter was a determination to keep his headquarters out of Washington, he then turned to his real purpose:

> *While I have been eminently successful in this war, in at least*
> *gaining the confidence of the public, no one feels more than I how*
> *much of this success is due to the energy, skill, and the harmonious*
> *putting forth of that energy and skill, of those whom it has been my*
> *good fortune to have occupying subordinate positions under me.*
> *There are many officers to whom these remarks are applicable to*
> *a greater or less degree, proportionate to their ability as soldiers;*

but what I want is to express my thanks to you and McPherson, as the men to whom, above all others, I feel indebted for whatever I have had of success. How far your advice and suggestions have been of assistance, you know. How far your execution of whatever has been given you to do entitles you to the reward I am receiving, you cannot know as well as I do. I feel all the gratitude this letter would express, giving it the most flattering construction.

The word you I use in the plural, intending it for McPherson also. I should write to him, and will someday, but, starting in the morning, I do not know that I will find time just now.

Your friend,

U. S. GRANT, Major-General.

Sherman's answer to Grant's letter, while just as complimentary, was far different. Though officially a subordinate, he was not above giving Grant the benefit of his assessment of his superior's characteristics. But then, showing a sentiment that Grant tended to avoid, Sherman included a sentence that has come to be regarded as an encapsulation of their relationship:

If I got in a tight place, I know you would come—if alive.[2]

Each in his own way, both men were pledging their partnership.

———————

Immediately after the change-of-command ceremony at Nashville, Grant departed for Washington on the way to the headquarters from which he would command the armies, with the Army of the Potomac on the Rappahannock. He asked Sherman to accompany him as far as Cincinnati, after which Sherman returned to Nashville to begin planning the spring campaign.

By now, Grant had decided, with Sherman's concurrence, that the time had come to start planning a major drive southward from Chattanooga into Georgia. Thus Grant and Sherman, each commanding a major army, would push south to destroy the Confederate armies—Robert E. Lee in Grant's case and Joseph E. Johnston in Sherman's. The distance between Grant's and Sherman's forces was only 550 miles, close enough that one could reinforce the other if necessary. Therefore, while the two held definitely separate commands, they were still working together.

On arrival back at Nashville on March 25, Sherman began to assess his situation. His objective in the upcoming campaign would not be a terrain feature, but rather the army of General Joseph E. Johnston. Intelligence indicated that Johnston's army consisted of only about forty thousand men, yet it was capable of rapid reinforcement. On paper Sherman's troops would be of overwhelming strength, 171,000 men, but he calculated that only about a hundred thousand were present for duty. He was, however, satisfied. One hundred thousand men, he figured, were all that he could supply. He went to work on that basis.[3]

Sherman was happy with the commanders of his subordinate armies. By all odds the largest and best supported was George Thomas's Army of the Cumberland, located at Chattanooga, with approximately ninety thousand men present for duty. James McPherson's Army of the Tennessee was back at Vicksburg with about sixty-four thousand; and John M. Schofield's Army of the Ohio, which he had taken over from Burnside, was at Knoxville with twenty-six thousand. This discrepancy in force size among the armies was not premeditated; it had come about by circumstances. Thomas was on hand where he had fought the Battle of Chattanooga, and his men had simply remained in place. Schofield's Army of the Ohio had not been at Chattanooga but maintained solid strength.[4] McPherson's Army of the Tennessee was inferior in strength to Thomas's, partly because Sherman had "loaned" two of McPherson's divisions to Nathaniel Banks, at the Red River. Sherman now sent a message to Banks requesting their return—the loan had been agreed as thirty days—but Banks and even Porter demurred, and they were never returned.

Sherman hoped to move south from Chattanooga around May 1. To support his hundred thousand men he would have to deliver about thirteen hundred tons of food and ammunition a day, considerably more than the capacity of the single-track railroad that ran from his base at Nashville and his jump-off point at Chattanooga. He therefore made use of roads and waterways as much as he could. He also specified that the men would travel on foot; roads, railroads, and waterways were reserved for supply. Based partly on his experience in living off the land in his recent Meridian campaign, he had concluded that only beef and salt needed to be supplied for sustenance of the troops. For all else, the men could live off the land, consistent with Grant's orders to destroy anything along the way that could be of use to the enemy—including food.

On arrival at their respective headquarters, Grant and Sherman began an exchange of messages that together established the details of the course they intended to follow to bring the war to an end. On April 4 Grant wrote his fundamental plan:

> It is my design, if the enemy keep quiet and allow me to take the initiative in the spring campaign, to work all parts of the army together, and somewhat toward a common centre. For your information I now write you my programme, as at present determined upon. . . .

Summarizing the orders he had issued to other commands, he then turned to Sherman's mission:

> *You I propose to move against Johnston's army, to break it up, and to get into the interior of the enemy's country as far as you can, inflicting all the damage you can against their war resources.*
>
> *I do not propose to lay down for you a plan of campaign, but*

simply to lay down the work it is desirable to have done, and leave
you free to execute it in your own way. Submit to me, however, as
early as you can, your plan of operations. . . .[5]

On April 10 Sherman answered in kind. He expressed "infinite satisfaction" with Grant's letter, and the fact that they were acting on a common
plan, converging on a common center, which he described as "enlightened
war." He pledged his cooperation and assured Grant that he would not
allow side issues to divert him from his main mission.

As to his own operation, Sherman estimated that it would take him all
of April to assemble his furloughed veterans and other groups of absentees,*
and to collect provisions and cattle on the line of the Tennessee River. Each
of the armies would guard, by detachments of its own, its rear communications.

He then explained his proposed employment of his troops. Schofield,
with twelve thousand men, was to drop down to the Hiawassee and march
against Johnston's right. George Stoneman, presently in Kentucky organizing Schofield's cavalry force, would have about two thousand cavalry
with which to protect Schofield's left flank. Thomas, with forty-five thousand men in the center, was to move straight against Johnston, wherever
the Confederate might be. McPherson, with nine divisions of the Army of
the Tennessee, would have a full thirty thousand of "the best men in
America."[†] He would cross the Tennessee River at Decatur and Whites-
burg, march toward Rome, and scout around for Thomas. If Johnston fell
behind the Coosa River, then McPherson would push for Rome; but if
Johnston fell behind the Chattahoochee River, as Sherman believed he
would, then McPherson would follow him across and join Thomas.

Much of the message was for Grant's information only, but Sherman

---

* Major General Andrew Jackson Smith had a division at Cairo that Sherman dearly
wanted. Halleck, however, sent Smith to Missouri.

† In this estimate, Sherman was counting on A. J. Smith, at Cairo. As noted above, he was
overoptimistic.

finished up with three important paragraphs that predicted the actions he would take throughout the Georgia campaign:

> *Should Johnston fall behind the Chattahoochee, I will feign [sic] to the right, but pass to the left and act against Atlanta or its eastern communications, according to developed facts.*
>
> *This is about as far ahead as I feel disposed to look, but I will ever bear in mind that Johnston is at all times to be kept so busy that he cannot in any event send any part of his command against you or Banks. . . .*
>
> *If the enemy interrupt our communications, I will be absolved from all obligations to subsist on our own resources, and will feel perfectly justified in taking whatever and wherever we can find. I will inspire my command, if successful, with the feeling that beef and salt are all that is absolutely necessary to life, and that parched corn once fed General Jackson's army on that very ground.*[6]

On April 19, Grant wrote Sherman again, offering little news but reassurance. He did, however, include one important paragraph:

> *What I now want more particularly to say is, that if the two main attacks, yours and the one from here, should promise great success, the enemy may, in a fit of desperation, abandon one part of their line of defense, and throw their whole strength upon the other, believing a single defeat without any victory to sustain them better than a defeat all along their line, and hoping too, at the same time, that the army, meeting with no resistance, will rest perfectly satisfied with their laurels, having penetrated to a given point south, thereby enabling them to throw their force first upon one and then on the other.*
>
> *With the majority of military commanders they might do this.*[7]

On April 24, Sherman wrote his last letter to Grant before the beginning of the campaign, essentially asking for as much time as possible for preparations. Acknowledging that his three armies would be separated for a while, he planned to set a point of concentration at Lafayette. He then gave a description of his supply plans that only the brain of William T. Sherman could retain in full.

This exchange of messages, sent between two men who were intimately familiar with the details, needs summation. In short their understandings were as follows:

a. The two main Confederate armies, the defeat of which would end the war, were those of Robert E. Lee, in northern Virginia and Joseph E. Johnston, in northwest Georgia.

b. Grant was to attack Lee and Sherman was to attack Johnston. The objectives of both were Lee's army and Johnston's. Terrain features such as Richmond and Atlanta, no matter how important, were secondary to the destruction of those armies.

c. Grant and Sherman were to remain in close contact. Should either Lee or Johnston send part of their forces to reinforce the other, thus attempting to defeat Grant or Lee in detail, those officers could come to the aid of each other.

d. Supply was expected to be the largest problem that Sherman, at least, would face. Normal supply means—railroads, roads and waterways—were to carry only ammunition and food. All troops were to go by foot. And if food supply went low, especially through Confederate cavalry action, Sherman was perfectly free to feed his men by forage off the countryside. The implication was that living off the land was encouraged.

e. Sherman's three armies were to be McPherson's Army of the Tennessee, at Vicksburg; Thomas's Army of the Cumberland, at Chattanooga; and Schofield's Army of the Ohio, at Knoxville. These armies were to follow routes that would converge on Dalton, Georgia, not for its invaluable communications facilities, including the Western & Atlantic Railroad, but because Confederate general Johnston had concentrated his Army of the Tennessee at that place. Johnston's army was to be destroyed.

f. The jump-off date for Sherman at Chattanooga and Grant at the wilderness along the Rapidan/Rappahannock would be as soon as possible after May 1, 1864.

On May 4, Sherman moved his small headquarters from Nashville to Chattanooga, and was on the front two days later. On May 7 all three of his armies attacked.

MAJOR GENERAL WILLIAM TECUMSEH SHERMAN

ELLEN SHERMAN

GENERAL SHERMAN IN ATLANTA, 1864

GENERAL ULYSSES S. GRANT, 1864

GENERAL
ROBERT E. LEE

CONFEDERATE GENERAL
JOSEPH E. JOHNSTON

Photos on this page courtesy of the Library of Congress

PRESIDENT
ABRAHAM LINCOLN,
1863

JEFFERSON DAVIS

Photos on this page courtesy of the National Archives

CONFEDERATE GENERAL
PIERRE GUSTAVE
TOUTANT BEAUREGARD

GENERAL
HENRY W. HALLECK

GENERAL
JOSEPH "FIGHTING
JOE" HOOKER

SENATOR
JOHN SHERMAN
OF OHIO

Photos on this page courtesy of the Library of Congress

SECRETARY OF WAR
EDWIN STANTON

GENERAL JEFF C. DAVIS

CHAPTER THIRTEEN

THE BATTLE OF KENNESAW MOUNTAIN

G rant and Sherman had done their planning well. So precise was it that both armies made their moves into position on the same day, May 4, 1864, Grant in the wilderness of Virginia and Sherman at Chattanooga, Tennessee. That evening Sherman was able to write a letter to Ellen announcing, essentially, that he was now "moving."

The first phase of Sherman's campaign involved a series of small towns on the Western & Atlantic Railroad. By the time Sherman wrote Ellen, Thomas had already taken Ringgold, about twelve miles from Chattanooga. Schofield's army was deployed on Thomas's left. McPherson's Army of the Tennessee had not yet arrived from Vicksburg, although McPherson himself was personally with Sherman. McPherson did, however, plan to leave the next day to join his command. As to his own plans, Sherman intended to join Thomas the next day at Ringgold. In his letter home Cump conceded, somewhat ruefully, that he expected heavy fighting. But on the whole, he was satisfied. "All my dispositions thus far are good."[1]

Progress at first was slower than Sherman had expected—or at least hoped. The next town along the railroad was Tunnel Hill, a noted place named after a nearby hill, through which ran the Western & Atlantic

Railroad. Schofield's Army of the Ohio was supposed to take Tunnel Hill as soon as Thomas had Ringgold, but it was May 7 before Schofield was able to capture it. Sherman was familiar with Tunnel Hill from an earlier time in his life, when it had been something of a tourist attraction. On the same day it was seized, he established his small headquarters in a previously selected hotel. He had now gone most of the twenty miles to cover his objective: Dalton, Georgia. Johnston and Sherman dined that evening within five miles of each other.

Dalton, Sherman's first objective, was the place Braxton Bragg had selected to defend the previous November after fleeing Chattanooga. Since it was a strong defensive position, Grant had decided to let Bragg be until he (later Sherman) could organize a force worthy of ensuring success. In the meantime Johnston, who had replaced Bragg, had been afforded six months to build fortifications. Johnston was a trained engineer, and the result was a position so strong that it could be taken only if the Western Atlantic railroad supplying it from Atlanta could be cut. The terrain to the south was extremely rough, especially for wagons and artillery. Sherman knew that Johnston was determined to hold out at Dalton as long as he could.

How to attack the town—which Sherman determined to do—was a problem. It was protected on the north and west by a stream, Mill Creek, that flowed in north of town from the east, ran about a mile, and then turned abruptly southward, thus shielding the position from both the north and the west. On the west side the position was further strengthened by an escarpment called Rocky Face Ridge that ran north–south about two miles behind Mill Creek. Rocky Face Ridge was exceedingly steep and, as its name implied, rocky. It was broken in only three places. On the north was Mill Creek Gap, where both Mill Creek and the Western & Atlantic Railroad broke through. About two miles to the south was Snake Creek Gap. And two miles farther south was Dug Gap. These breaks in the precipitous walls had been reinforced to Johnston's best ability.

Sherman was ready to attack the fortifications by May 8, the main effort to be made by Thomas's Army of the Cumberland. Thomas, allowed to fight his own battle, first chose to hit Dug Gap, the southern one. Besides Thomas's main effort, McPherson's Army of the Tennessee, separate for the moment, was to make its way around Johnston's left flank toward Resaca to cut the railroad. McPherson's situation, however, was an unknown factor. When he left Sherman knew only that his Army of the Tennessee had encountered delays coming from the west.

From the first, things went badly. Thomas's Union lines charged up the slopes of Rocky Face Ridge on schedule but were soundly repulsed; nothing was gained that day. The next morning Thomas attacked again, this time at Mill Creek Gap farther to the north. Again he encountered failure; the terrain was so formidable that Confederate general Carter Stevenson's men held the Yankees off even though Stevenson's forces were outnumbered ten to one.

On the ninth, news from McPherson was for a time encouraging. He reported to Sherman that he was within two miles of the Western & Atlantic Railroad at Resaca and had handily dispatched a Confederate cavalry unit, which had fled toward Dalton. Sherman hoped that if McPherson could cut the railroad, he might completely destroy Johnston's army. He sent orders to both Thomas and Schofield to be ready to pursue on a moment's notice.

It was not to be. A second message came in from McPherson declaring that the position at Resaca was "too strong," and that he was preparing a defensive position in the area. Sherman could not help feeling that McPherson had been "too cautious," and the chance to destroy Johnston had passed. And Johnston would be warned by the Confederate cavalry of his danger.[2]

The disappointment did not last long. The next evening, when Sherman sat down to dinner at Tunnel Hill, disconsolate over his rebuffs, word came in that McPherson's turning movement to the south toward Resaca had broken through. He had not yet cut the railroad, but he expected to soon. Sherman sprang from the table and without a moment's delay sent orders to Thomas to abandon the attacks on Dalton and follow McPherson to Resaca. Only enough men should be left behind at Dalton to make a demonstration against Rocky Face Ridge; his main body was to follow a hidden gulch southward. "I've got Joe Johnston dead," Sherman shouted.

He was only partially right. The alert Johnston noticed how light was Thomas's presence on Rocky Face Ridge, and a cavalry patrol to the west confirmed that the Union Army was practically gone. With no doubt in his mind, Johnston ordered the Dalton position abandoned and a retreat by the Army of the Tennessee to secure Resaca. The Battle of Dalton thus ended not with a slaughter but with an evacuation.[3]

————————

The Battle of Dalton (or Rocky Face Ridge) was not a big action as Civil War battles went—about six thousand casualties on each side—but it was significant in that it set a pattern for the campaign that followed, from position to position southward along the Western & Atlantic Railroad, which Johnston could not afford to have cut. The campaign, therefore, consisted of a number of actions where Johnston built strong positions, which Sherman flanked from the south, forcing him to evacuate to the next fortified position. The same pattern was repeated at Adairsville on May 17, Cassville on May 18–19, New Hope Church on May 25, Pickett's Mill on May 27, and Dallas on May 28, over six weeks and a distance of 110 miles.

As the campaign proceeded, a noticeable change began to develop in Sherman's mind as well as Grant's. In their exchanges of letters in the planning stage back in April, both men had emphasized that Sherman's sole objective was to shatter Johnston's Army of the Tennessee. As things progressed, however, their thinking gradually modified to include the capture of the city of Atlanta, the main center of the Confederate Southeast. The two missions were not incompatible; it was simply a matter of priority.

Toward the end of June of 1864, Joe Johnston decided to make a stand. He had wearied of occupying one fortified position after another—not the kind of action that any soldier likes, but inevitable because of Sherman's relentless drive and overpowering strength. Granted, the Army of the Tennessee was still intact and had inflicted casualties about equal to those it had received. But though Johnston had cause for personal satisfaction, his retreat did not make good reading for the newspaper headlines through the South or for Confederate president Jefferson Davis.

Johnston's reputation in Richmond was not favorable, and a summary of his career might explain why. He was a contemporary of Robert E. Lee, his fellow Virginian and West Point classmate from the class of 1829. Johnston's experiences, however, had been more checkered and variegated than Lee's. Lee had spent nearly his whole army life on the civil side of army engineering. Johnston, on the other hand, had started out as an artilleryman, but then, after a few years' service, had resigned to go into civilian life and had become a highly successful civil engineer. He had fought well during the Second Seminole War and then had decided to rejoin the army. During Winfield Scott's campaign to take Mexico City in 1847, Johnston had performed heroically as an infantryman at the battles of Contreras, Churubusco, and finally at Chapultepec. He was wounded so often that his "knack" for doing so was noted humorously by Winfield Scott himself.

In the dozen years following the war with Mexico, Johnston had held various positions in the army, and in the summer of 1860, with civil war approaching, he was appointed to the high post of quartermaster general. When the officers of the South resigned their army commissions in order to join the embryo Confederacy, Johnston was the highest-ranking officer to do so.

As a Confederate general, Joe Johnston seemed to be dogged by bad luck, receiving less than his just due for his successes, and unjustified criticism for failures not entirely his fault. Perhaps his courtesy worked to his disadvantage. At the battlefield of the first Bull Run on July 21, 1861, for example, he had declined to replace his junior, Beauregard, who had been the commander on the field before Johnston's arrival. Thus Beauregard is given credit for the Confederate victory.

Following Bull Run a rift occurred between Johnston and Confederate president Jefferson Davis, who had once been close personal friends. When Davis set out to select five full (four-star) generals, he set an order of precedence that ran Samuel Cooper,[4] Albert Sidney Johnston, Robert E. Lee, Joseph E. Johnston, and P. G. T. Beauregard. Johnston, a sensitive and proud man beneath his courtesy, had expected, because of his top position in the Union Army, to head the list. Davis was unmoved by Johnston's protests, and Johnston wrote Davis a letter so bitter that Davis read it to his cabinet.[5]

In spite of their personal hostility, Johnston commanded sufficient respect in the Confederate Army that in early 1862, Davis gave him the important command of the Army of Northern Virginia, the front between Washington and Richmond. With the coming of spring 1862, George B. McClellan, the Union commander in chief, decided that the Confederate forces between Washington and Richmond were too strong to attack directly, and in April he landed an army at Fortress Monroe, at the tip of the Northern Neck of Virginia, in an attempt to seize Richmond by a drive up the peninsula. Johnston moved to Richmond and resisted McClellan skillfully if cautiously. But if Johnston was cautious, McClellan was even more so. It therefore took the Union commander a couple of months to make his way up the peninsula to a spot near Richmond.

On May 31, 1862, Johnston made a stand at Seven Pines (or Fair Oaks), only six miles from Richmond. The results of the battle were indecisive, but most important for Johnston was another wound, so severe that Davis found it necessary to appoint Robert E. Lee in his place. Johnston's recovery took time, but even when he was eventually fit for duty once more, Davis had no intention of restoring him to his former position. Eventually he was given command of Confederate forces in the West. A reluctant Davis had offered the command to several others first.

With such a background, Joe Johnston knew that President Davis would never give him the benefit of the doubt in judging his performance. For that reason, aside from military logic, the retreat that had begun back at Dalton had to stop. To make a stand, Johnston chose a position near Marietta, Georgia, fifteen miles from Atlanta. Kennesaw Mountain and the Chattahoochee River were all that stood between Sherman and the hub of the South.

Kennesaw Mountain was a part of a rough series of ridges running north–south. Near Marietta the railroad made a sharp turn to the east, and the line of hills was astride it. The position was anchored on the north by Kennesaw Mountain itself, the first position actually in a line of three hills. With Kennesaw Mountain on the right of the Confederate line, Pine Mountain was in the middle, and on the left (south) was Lost Mountain. Johnston's army consisted of William J. Hardee's, John Bell Hood's, and Leonidas Polk's corps. In general, Johnston placed each of his corps on a single hill. And the expert engineer Johnston had joined his positions with a formidable line of trenches across a ten-mile front.

Meanwhile, Sherman was undergoing great difficulties. One of his troubles was the abominable weather that plagued him by restricting his maneuver through roads that had become quagmires. Furthermore, he could not afford to look only to his front. His rear was highly vulnerable to the depredations of the Confederate cavalry, especially that of Nathan Bedford Forrest. Forrest, Sherman feared, was capable of disrupting his supply line through Chattanooga, Nashville, and even Memphis. Sherman did what he could to protect his vulnerable points with much-needed troops. He also took with his command a supply level of twenty days.

By June 14, the rains eased, and Sherman took advantage of the letup to make a personal reconnaissance of his front lines. When he reached a place opposite Pine Mountain, he spotted a group of Confederate officers huddled in conference about eight hundred yards away. Despite his own orders to save ammunition, Sherman turned to General O. O. Howard, the commander holding that area, and ordered a nearby three-inch artillery battery to fire three volleys at the Confederates. Howard reluctantly obeyed and Sherman rode on to another position.

What Sherman did not realize at the time was that the group of rebel officers he was taking under fire consisted of generals Johnston, Hardee, and Polk—the Confederate commanding general and two of his three corps commanders. Johnston and Hardee, after the first round hit nearby, quickly took cover, but Polk, slower and perhaps a bit demonstrative, was hit and mortally wounded.

Polk's death was a big news event throughout the Confederacy. He had been a classmate of Jefferson Davis at West Point, but was known more for his position with the church as a bishop than as a combat leader. His death was observed with a great deal of ceremony. The rumor even began circling that Sherman himself had pulled the lanyard on the artillery piece that had killed the "Fighting Bishop"—which was, of course, nonsense.

Johnston did not include Pine Mountain on his final line of defense. Instead he fell back to a tighter position that included Kennesaw Mountain almost straight to Marietta. Sherman—whose armies had been deployed left to right—Schofield, Thomas, and McPherson decided to make a change and move Schofield over to the right, opposite Johnston's left flank.

Another memorable incident at about this time involved a falling-out between Sherman and Major General Joseph Hooker, commander of XX Corps under Thomas. Hooker had fought well ever since he had brought Howard's XI Corps and Slocum's XII Corps to Chattanooga. The group had received accolades, especially in the Battle Above the Clouds—Lookout Mountain. Hooker was, however, a prima donna, and he never forgot that he had once commanded the Army of the Potomac between December of 1862 and June of 1863. Though his name will always be associated with his humiliating defeat at the Battle of Chancellorsville in early May 1863, he had not been put on the shelf. His two-corps force had now been reduced to a single corps, the XX. Despite this, Hooker still seemed to consider himself a bit above his fellow corps commanders.

On June 22, after Thomas had successfully repelled a Confederate attack, Sherman received a message from Hooker, who, as noted, was one of Thomas's corps commanders.

We have repulsed two heavy attacks, and feel confident, our only apprehension being from our extreme right flank. Three entire corps are in front of us.

At first glance the message might seem innocuous enough, but to Sherman's eyes it was startling. To begin with, the reference to the right flank was a slap at Schofield, who Sherman understood was firmly entrenched on Hooker's right. In addition, Hooker's claim of three corps opposing him ran counter to all of Sherman's intelligence, which indicated that XX Corps was being faced with only one Confederate corps. And finally, Hooker's communicating directly with Sherman, bypassing Thomas, smacked of insubordination.

Sherman decided to look into the matter. He went in person to Schofield's headquarters, where he met with Hooker and Schofield together. On learning of Hooker's message, Schofield was furious. His troops, he claimed, had been out ahead of Hooker's. Hooker claimed his innocence of that fact, but to confirm it the three generals rode to the front lines to inspect the scene, where corpses from both commands still lay unburied. On inspection, they concluded that Schofield's dead were farther forward than were Hooker's.

The matter having been decided in Schofield's favor, Sherman and

Hooker rode back together for part of the trip to their respective head-quarters. It was at that time that Sherman made it clear that this type of incident must not happen again. Hooker did not respond but went into a deep sulk. Nothing more came of the incident for the moment.[6]

The time had come to attack. Because the terrain on his right appeared impassable, Sherman could no longer make use of the flanking movement that had worked so well ever since the Battle of Dalton. On June 23, he telegraphed Halleck in Washington:

> We continue to press forward on the principle of an advance against fortified positions. The whole country is one vast fort, and Johnston must have at least fifty miles of connected trenches, with abatis and finished batteries. We gain ground daily, fighting all the time. . . . As fast as we gain one position the enemy has another all ready, but I think he will soon have to let go Kenesaw, which is the key to the whole country. The weather is now better, and the roads are drying up fast. Our losses are light, and, not-withstanding the repeated breaks of the road to our rear, supplies are ample.

Sherman set the date for the attack on Kennesaw Mountain as the morning of June 27, 1864. He spent the two previous days in intensive preparation. In consultation with his three army commanders, he decided for once to attack Johnston's fortified lines head-on. He could not extend his lines any farther. Though his force was twice the size of Johnston's, he already had a front of ten miles and could stretch no more without being too thin to attack in any one place against strong trenches.

Schofield was not to be part of the main attack; he was merely to make a strong demonstration toward Marietta. Thomas, with the strongest army of the three, was to attack in the center. McPherson, on the left, was to attack eastward toward the Chattahoochee River. Sherman and his generals hoped to make one or two penetrations of Johnston's position, through which he could pour in troops. He did not like this expensive type of operation, but he felt he had no choice.

On the evening of June 26, Sherman was in a pensive mood. Contemplating war in general and his role in it, he wrote Ellen:

> Though not conscious of danger at this moment, I know the country swarms with thousands who would shoot me, and thank their God they had slain a monster; and yet I have been more kindly disposed to the people of the South than any general officer of the whole army.[7]

And four nights later, after the battle, despite great changes in the situation, he seemed to be in the same mood:

> It is enough to make the whole world start at the awful amount of death and destruction that now stalks abroad. Daily for the past two months has the work progressed and I see no signs of a remission till one or both and all the armies are destroyed, when I suppose the balance of the people will tear each other up, as Grant says, reenacting the story of the Kilkenny cats. I begin to regard the death and mangling of a couple thousand men as a small affair, a kind of morning dash. . . . [8]

When the attack was launched at nine a.m. on June 27, Sherman observed it from a knoll in Thomas's headquarters, using a huge telescope. He could view both McPherson's and Thomas's fronts, and what met his eye was not welcome. The skirmishers in both armies made it up to the top of the Confederate parapets, but both fell back with heavy losses, nothing gained. It was, Sherman later noted, the largest attack of the campaign, and it was a resounding defeat.

As at Dalton a month and a half earlier, however, the darkest hour came just before the dawn. As Sherman was counting his losses—five

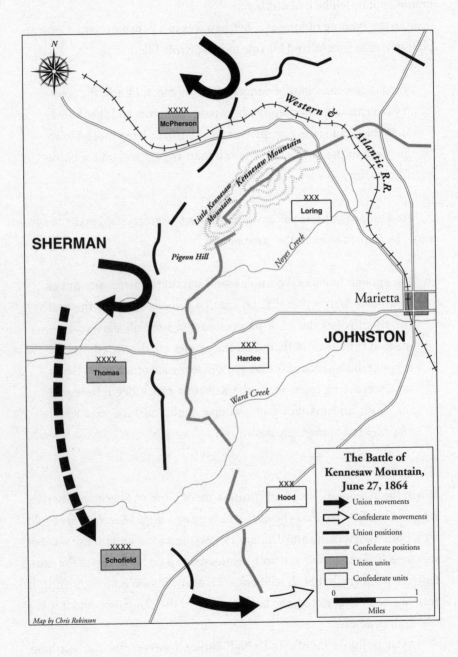

N

McPherson

Western &

Kennesaw Mountain

Little Kennesaw Mountain

Loring

Noyes Creek

Atlantic R.R.

SHERMAN

Pigeon Hill

Marietta

JOHNSTON

Thomas

Hardee

Ward Creek

Hood

Schofield

The Battle of
Kennesaw Mountain,
June 27, 1864

Union movements
Confederate movements
Union positions
Confederate positions
Union units
Confederate units

0   1

Miles

Map by Chris Robinson

hundred in McPherson's army and two thousand in Thomas's[9]—word came in that Schofield, apart from the main battle, had discovered a route around the south of Johnston's position toward Marietta. Instantly Sherman changed his plans. He could leave a cavalry screening force in McPherson's former position and move the Army of the Tennessee around to the right behind the south flank of Thomas. He could then drive to the Chattahoochee Bridge and on to Atlanta.

It was a bold move, and George Thomas, who seemed to revel in presenting opposing views, pointed out that the Western & Atlantic Railroad, which furnished Sherman's supplies, ran in from the north, whereas the general's plan called for attacking on the south side of Johnston. Sherman, however, had his mind made up. He loaded ten days' supplies in his wagons, and by the second of July he was ready.

McPherson pulled out of his lines on the evening of July 2, as planned, in hopes of going around Johnston's left in the area that Schofield had opened. Or better yet, possibly Johnston would spot the movement and attack, in which case Sherman, as he had advised Halleck, was confident that Thomas could inflict a crushing defeat once Johnston's army was in the open. Neither hope came to pass, but the movement southward continued.

On the morning of July 3, 1864, Sherman left his tent and went up to an observation post where his special telescope had been set up. Surveying Johnston's lines, Sherman could make out blue-coated soldiers swarming over unoccupied previously Confederate lines. Joe Johnston had detected McPherson's movements behind Thomas and had evacuated the position. Kennesaw Mountain was in Sherman's hands. The Chattahoochee and Atlanta still lay ahead.

CHAPTER FOURTEEN

THE FALL OF ATLANTA

Sherman, with Kennesaw Mountain seized, was now about to enter the most significant six months of his career: The capture of Atlanta and the subsequent march through Georgia to the sea constituted the achievement that has made him a major figure of history.

He had no way of foreseeing such a turn of events. His main target was Johnston's army; the capture of Atlanta, he hoped, would be easy. Such an assumption was not unreasonable. After Kennesaw he faced no serious terrain obstacles short of the Chattahoochee River. If he could catch Johnston with that formidable stream at his back, it might be possible to strike a lethal blow. In that event, Atlanta and with it the whole Deep South would be open to Union troops.

Sherman's hopes were quickly shattered. When he rode into Marietta on the morning of July 3, he found that Johnston had gotten away. The Army of the Tennessee had just evacuated the town.

Sherman was disappointed, and at first blush he tended to blame his cavalry commander, General Kenner Garrard. He soon came to realize, however, what Garrard had been up against. Over the months in the Kennesaw position, Johnston had constructed an elaborate road net over which he could evacuate his troops quickly. And McPherson, in moving around Thomas's rear, had been forced to make a ninety-degree turn left—something easier done on paper than on the ground.

On the Fourth of July, Sherman and Johnston fought a small battle at the town of Smyrna, between Marietta and the Chattahoochee. The fight was of little significance except for its date. (Sherman referred to it wryly as a "celebration of Independence Day.") Johnston then fell back, and Sherman came into view of the Chattahoochee River on the fifth. Here he met his second disappointment: his hopes of crushing Johnston against the Chattahoochee. Johnston, he discovered, had erected a defensive position, a *tête de pont*, that protected the one major crossing over the river. Sherman ruefully described it as one of the strongest he had ever seen, and he made no attempt to attack it seriously. On the favorable side, Johnston's abandoning the entire west bank of the Chattahoochee gave Sherman free rein to cross wherever he chose. He could move troops along the west bank without interference.

In the long run, Johnston's prospects were hopeless. He had only sixty thousand men, as opposed to Sherman's well-supplied hundred thousand. Nevertheless, Sherman's problem of crossing the Chattahoochee was far from insurmountable. It is a swift-running river, unfordable for most of its length. One crossing place was Turner's Creek, located a few miles south of Johnston's *tête de pont*. Eventually, however, he selected Soap Creek, about eighteen miles north, and on July 9, Schofield crossed over at that point. By July 17, Sherman had his entire army across the river.

On that same evening of July 17, 1864, Joe Johnston's dinner was interrupted by a message from Richmond informing him that he was relieved of command of the Army of the Tennessee. His successor, the message continued, was to be one of his corps commanders, Lieutenant General John Bell Hood. President Davis and the Confederate civilians had endured enough of Johnston's retreating, and Hood was a man known for his aggressiveness. Hood would attack, come what may.

The relief was doubtless influenced by the animosity between Davis and Johnston, which had never eased. But the decision was not all personal. Davis had given the action a great deal of thought. He had consulted men he trusted, and the answers were varied. Lee, for example, had advised against changing commanders in the midst of a campaign, whereas most of the men Davis consulted were less objective. Foremost among Johnston's enemies was Braxton Bragg, whom Johnston had succeeded in command of the Army of the Tennessee after the Battle of Chattanooga. Oddly, the unpopular Bragg was serving as Davis's personal adviser. In that capacity he personally visited Johnston during the weeks before Kennesaw Mountain. Supposedly Bragg had come merely to seek information, but though the atmosphere during the visit was cordial on the surface, Bragg was collecting evidence against Johnston, which he later shared generously with Davis.

Bragg's distasteful undercover activities found ample material. Johnston's worst critic was the man who stood to gain from his relief, John B. Hood. As a corps commander under Johnston, Hood owed his boss loyalty. Instead he spoke freely against him. How much influence any of these men had on President Davis is uncertain, but the time had come to replace Johnston.

Johnston, as might be expected, was not particularly surprised by this development. He bore his relief with dignity and joined his family in retirement back at Macon, Georgia. The men of the Army of the Tennessee were not so accepting; they were, in fact, enraged. Some units threatened to desert in protest over the action. But as is usual with such cases, they did not; they fought on.

Sherman's memoir does not treat the fighting around Atlanta as a single action, although one action was inaccurately given the name the Battle of Atlanta. Since Sherman considered the defenses of the city too strong to assault, he determined to squeeze it like an anaconda. To do so, he fought four separate battles as he was working his way around. By and large, each fight was fought by a different army. The first was fought north of the city along a natural obstacle named Peachtree Creek. A few days later another action, the so-called "Battle of Atlanta," was fought on the road leading east from Atlanta to Decatur. A third occurred later at Ezra Church, to the west of the city, and finally a fight at Jonesboro, to the south, almost sealed Sherman's ring. Together these actions added up to what Sherman called the "battles around Atlanta."

The first, the Battle of Peachtree Creek, was fought on July 20. On the main road leading from his Chattahoochee crossing place and Atlanta, Sherman encountered a defensive position so strong that he decided to bypass it. Farther on, he found a position and assumed the defensive, deploying his three armies along a ridge north of Peachtree Creek, with Thomas on the right (west), Schofield in the center, and McPherson on the left (east). At the same time he erected his own defenses and established his headquarters, Howard House, behind Thomas.

In essence, the Battle of Peachtree Creek was a counterattack by Hood against a crossing of the creek made at one point by Thomas. Hood's attack was poorly organized and consisted of nothing more than a headlong frontal assault. It was a one-sided affair. By Sherman's account Hood lost a whopping five thousand men as against seventeen hundred Union troops. It was difficult for Sherman to be certain as to Confederate casualties, because Hood was able to bring a good many of his wounded into his defenses.[1]

Hood withdrew, and Thomas retained his bridgehead across Peachtree Creek.

Sherman then moved eastward. From his headquarters at Howard House, he sent McPherson's Army of the Tennessee eastward to cut the railroad between Atlanta and nearby Decatur. By the twenty-first McPherson had been successful in doing that.

Sherman then looked at his lines and became concerned that a dan-

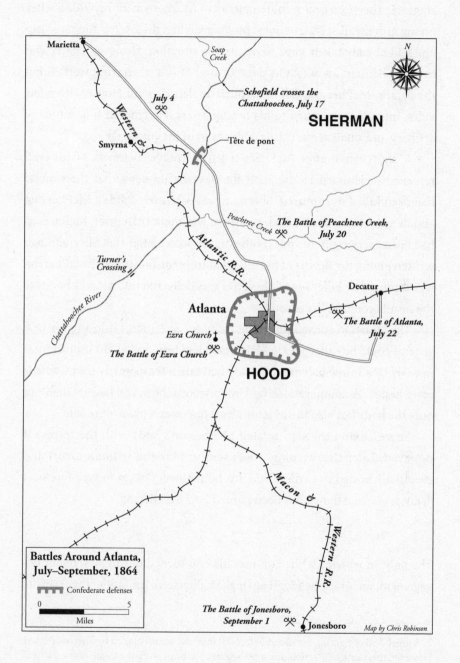

Marietta

Soap
Creek

Western

July 4

Schofield crosses the
Chattahoochee, July 17

N

SHERMAN

Smyrna

Tête de pont

Peachtree Creek

The Battle of Peachtree Creek,
July 20

Atlantic R.R.

Turner's
Crossing

Decatur

Chattahoochee River

Atlanta

The Battle of Atlanta,
July 22

Ezra Church

The Battle of Ezra Church

HOOD

Macon &

Western R.R.

Battles Around Atlanta,
July–September, 1864

Confederate defenses

0   5
Miles

The Battle of Jonesboro,
September 1

Jonesboro

Map by Chris Robinson

gerous gap was growing between Schofield's left flank and McPherson's right. He therefore sent reinforcements to McPherson along with a letter giving him detailed instructions. McPherson had discovered the same gap and had already taken steps to rectify the situation. However, he decided to visit Sherman anyway. On the morning of July 22, having worked out the details, McPherson, full of enthusiasm, left Howard House with a few aides, intending to return to his headquarters. He ignored the sounds of artillery and small arms, riding a bit ahead of his entourage.

A short while after McPherson left, a couple members of his staff returned to Howard House with the devastating news that the general had been killed or captured. Sherman was extremely fond of McPherson, and he was of course shocked. But there was more than grief. McPherson had been carrying in his pocket the highly secret letter that Sherman had written giving the details of his intended troop dispositions. If McPherson was captured or killed—and the letter was delivered into Hood's hands—the results could be disastrous.

The situation turned out to be lucky for Sherman—if losing his best general could be called lucky. McPherson had been killed almost instantaneously by a minié ball and his body had fallen temporarily into Confederate hands. A counterattack by Union troops, however, had retaken not only the body but also the letter. At least Sherman's plans were safe.*

Sherman and the staff treated McPherson's body with the respect it deserved. Later that evening it was sent to Marietta with an escort and eventually buried in Clyde, Ohio, his hometown. One of today's foremost army posts, in Atlanta, has been named Fort McPherson.

The fight in which McPherson met his end turned out to be a major engagement, an attack by Hood against McPherson's left flank. The Army of

---

* A great deal of fighting remained before Atlanta was actually taken by Sherman's men. However, this particular action, for some reason, has been given the name of the Battle of Atlanta.

the Tennessee had been taken by surprise, but since it was fighting on the defensive, the comparative losses were about equal. In the cruel mathematics of war, Hood could not afford an even trade. Sherman succinctly described it in a message to Halleck.

The previous morning, he wrote, Hood had fallen back to the entrenchments of the city of Atlanta, which he described as being "in a general circle, with a radius of one and a half miles." While the Army of the Tennessee was closing in to adjust their new position, the enemy had suddenly burst out of the woods and struck two of McPherson's corps, the XVII (Blair) and the XVI (Dodge). The movement was checked, but some Confederate cavalry was in the Union rear and had even reached Decatur, which was fairly close. For a while the Union left flank was completely enveloped. The fight went on until night, with heavy loss on both sides. Hood had launched an additional attack at about four p.m. against a division of the XV Corps and forced it back some four hundred yards, including two artillery batteries, which were immediately recovered by the same troops reinforced.

In his letter Sherman wrote that he could not estimate his losses accurately, but he put them at three thousand. He guessed that, "being on the defensive, we have inflicted equally heavy loss on the enemy."

He added a simple paragraph about the death of James McPherson, a model of suppressed emotions:

General McPherson, when arranging his troops about 11.00 A.M., and passing from one column to another, incautiously rode upon an ambuscade without apprehension, at some distance ahead of his staff and orderlies, and was shot dead.[2]

The death of McPherson meant that the Army of the Tennessee was now without a commander. Sherman's task in recommending a replacement was not easy. General John A. Logan had taken temporary command when McPherson fell, and he had performed well. He was also a popular gentleman. Sherman, however, passed him over. Logan was a political general, and Sherman foresaw much difficult fighting ahead in which the utmost professional skill would be required. So he set aside Logan's name along with that of Frank Blair—without prejudice. He sent Halleck the name of Major General Oliver O. Howard to fill the spot, and Halleck approved immediately. To replace Howard in command of the IV Corps, Sherman appointed General David S. Stanley.

Grant personally disagreed with Sherman's decision, but officially he supported the action. Grant's doubts were probably influenced by his high regard for Logan rather than any feelings against Howard, who was a distinguished soldier. Howard had sustained hard knocks at Chancellorsville and on the streets of Gettysburg, but it was he, in conjunction with Winfield Scott Hancock, who had selected the critical Union position of Cemetery Hill at the end of the first day's battle, July 1, 1863.* Most important, however, was the fact that Sherman had been observing Howard from the first days of Chattanooga through the crossing of the Chattahoochee, and he had liked what he'd seen of Howard's qualities.

Logan was disappointed by Sherman's decision, of course, but he accepted it gracefully. One officer who did not accept it, however, was Joe Hooker, who tendered his resignation from command of XX Corps in protest. Hooker had previously made it no secret that he felt he deserved McPherson's command, and when it was given to Howard, Hooker's pride could not tolerate the rebuff.

To be fair, Hooker had reasonable arguments on his side. He was the senior officer available, and he had received accolades for his performance at Chattanooga on Lookout Mountain. Never mind his failure more than a year before at Chancellorsville when in command of the Army of the Potomac. To make matters worse, it had been Howard's corps that had taken the brunt of Stonewall Jackson's attack on May 2, 1862. Hooker had always

---

* There had been controversy as to where the credit for selecting the position belonged, but Congress voted its thanks to Howard. The controversy may have influenced Halleck's selection of Howard as one of the three men to send to Chattanooga.

held Howard at least partially responsible for his own defeat at Chancellorsville.

Sherman, however, was unmoved by Hooker's protest and subsequent resignation. "Fighting Joe" had never been on his list of possibilities. Hooker's attitude in the confrontation with Schofield at Kennesaw Mountain was a factor in Sherman's estimation of him. Hooker was reassigned to an innocuous post in the North. Sherman was not a man who liked vainglorious subordinates.

To succeed Hooker at XX Corps, Sherman chose Henry W. Slocum, who had lost his corps command (without prejudice) when his and Howard's two corps had been consolidated under Hooker in the reorganization of a couple of months back.

Following the "Battle of Atlanta," Sherman decided that he had isolated the city from Decatur sufficiently. He had destroyed the railroad and believed that his cavalry could keep that avenue safe from Confederate reinforcement. He therefore decided to move Howard's Army of the Tennessee all the way to his right flank, where he could drive down the west side of Atlanta and cut it off from Columbus. Howard moved out on July 27.

This move was a major action for Sherman's force, and it required his supervision. He left his base headquarters at Howard House on July 28, followed Howard, and caught up with him and Logan at a spot near Ezra Church, between Atlanta and Turner's Ferry. An unfriendly Confederate artillery piece had his road under enfilade and caused him to dive into a ditch for cover, where he found both Howard and Logan together in the same predicament. As the three generals were discussing the whereabouts of General Jeff C. Davis's division, the sounds of fire from the left front indicated that a major battle was in progress.

And so it was. Hood, having hit Sherman at Peachtree Creek and at the Battle of Atlanta, was now attacking his right at Ezra Church. Howard's men, though surprised, were able to throw up defenses, with the result of another bloody repulse for Hood.

Sherman had now fought four battles around Atlanta during the month of July 1864: on the fourth at Smyrna, the twentieth at Peachtree Creek, the twenty-second at the Battle of Atlanta, and now, on the twenty-eighth, at Ezra Church. Losses had been heavy, but so were those of Hood. Sherman, however, had seen enough blood, so at the beginning of August he settled down to a siege. Hood, he estimated, probably lacked the strength to make another major attack, so Sherman set out to pound the city with artillery. Always conscious of ammunition supply, he regulated the rate of fire meticulously. To Schofield, he admonished,

> You may fire 10 to 15 shots from every gun you have in position into Atlanta that will reach any of the houses. Fire slowly and with deliberation between 4 p.m. and dark.

Sherman later issued a similar order to Thomas.[3]

As early August rolled around, Sherman was by and large satisfied with the condition of his command. As he described the situation, the weather was hot and sultry, but the men were healthy. The army had an ample supply of wood, water, and provisions. He noted that the troops had become habituated to the slow and steady progress of the siege. He kept his skirmish lines up close to the Confederate defenses, holding the main line farther back. The men loitered about the trenches carelessly and constructed huts of the abundant timber. Perhaps a bit overoptimistic, he described his troops as "snug, comfortable, and happy, as though they were at home."

As to his dispositions, he had Schofield on the extreme left, Thomas in the center, and Howard on the right. He held two divisions of the XIV Corps in reserve.[4]

There was one weakness to this position: He had not completely blocked the city's south side. In order to avoid further infantry fighting, he placed his hopes on the ability of cavalry to cut the city off from the south. In this effort, however, he was disappointed. On August 1, reports came in that a whole Union cavalry division, that of Edward McCook, had been ambushed and captured. Sherman did not entirely believe the report, and on August 2 he was relieved when the division commander himself arrived. Actually, McCook had inflicted a great deal of damage on Confederate railroads and locomotives, but the unit had been badly mauled. On August 4 a similar report came in, this time involving Stoneman's cavalry division. Once more Sherman admitted to himself the superiority of the Confederate cavalry. He was now convinced that his own cavalry would not suffice to close the gap; he would have to encircle the city with his stretched-out infantry.

On August 28, Sherman's armies, making a general left wheel, pivoting on Schofield, reached the West Point Railroad on the south side of town. There they spent an entire day tearing up the tracks. It was not a simple or easy procedure. As Sherman describes it,

> The track was heaved up in sections the length of a regiment, then separated rail by rail; bonfires were made of the ties and of fence-rails on which the rails were heated, carried to trees or telegraph-poles, wrapped around and left to cool. Such rails could not be used again; and, to be still more certain, we filled up many deep cuts with trees, brush, and earth, and commingled with them loaded shells, so arranged that they would explode on an attempt to haul out the bushes. The explosion of one such shell would have demoralized a gang of negroes, and thus would have prevented even the attempt to clear the road.[5]

Sherman's attention now turned to the small town of Jonesboro, a communications center within the defenses of Atlanta, occupied by

Hardee's corps. On August 30, Schofield reported that he was now within a couple of miles of the hamlet. The next morning Schofield and Thomas reached it, tearing up the railroad track as they advanced. About three p.m. on August 31, Hardee sallied from Jonesboro to attack the XV Corps, but was easily repulsed, so easily that few of Sherman's men were taken off their vital task of tearing up the railroad.

On the evening of September 1, Sherman launched an attack against Jonesboro. Some of his men formed up at about four p.m. and went over the rebel parapet handsomely, capturing a whole brigade, with two field batteries of ten guns. Sherman, being present, checked the movement. He was not yet ready for a final attack. Desiring that the major attack should be made with all his troops at once, he ordered Howard to send two divisions around by his right rear, to get below Jonesboro to cut off a Confederate retreat in that direction. Since night was approaching, and the country was densely wooded, two divisions were all Sherman could manage to prevent a Confederate retreat.

In addition to the fighting around Jonesboro, Sherman was making another probe. He had sent Slocum to the Chattahoochee Bridge with orders to feel forward occasionally toward Atlanta. That night was tense. At about midnight Sherman, who described himself as "so restless and impatient that I could not sleep," heard the sounds of shells exploding from the direction of Atlanta. Then, at about four a.m., another set of similar explosions began. Sherman had no idea whether Hood was blowing up his own magazines or whether Slocum had made contact and begun a real battle.

The next morning Sherman's men found that Hardee's men had left Jonesboro. The Union troops pushed along the railroad south in close pursuit until they encountered a strong fortification at Lovejoy's Station. At that point Sherman received rumors that the enemy had evacuated Atlanta, and that General Slocum was in the city.

Sherman was frantic to verify this report, and fortunately it turned out to be accurate. The news seemed too good to be true.

Sherman was not alone in feeling the tension. He was amused by the way General George Thomas received the confirmation:

He snapped his fingers, whistled, and almost danced, and, as the news spread to the army, the shouts that arose from our men, the wild hallooing and glorious laughter, were to us a full recompense for the labor and toils and hardships through which we had passed in the previous three months.

Sherman lost no time in sending a message to Washington: "Atlanta is ours, and fairly won."

Congratulations poured in. The most important were those of President Lincoln and General Grant:

EXECUTIVE MANSION
WASHINGTON, D.C.

September 3, 1864.
The national thanks are rendered by the President to Major-General W. T. Sherman and the gallant officers and soldiers of his command before Atlanta, for the distinguished ability and perseverance displayed in the campaign in Georgia, which, under Divine favor, has resulted in the capture of Atlanta. The marches, battles, sieges, and other military operations, that have signalized the campaign, must render it famous in the annals of war, and have entitled those who have participated therein to the applause and thanks of the nation.
ABRAHAM LINCOLN
President of the United States

CITY POINT VIRGINIA,

September 4, 1864—9 P.M.

Major-General SHERMAN:

I have just received your dispatch announcing the capture of Atlanta. In honor of your great victory, I have ordered a salute to be fired with shotted guns from every battery bearing upon the enemy. The salute will be fired within an hour, amid great rejoicing.

U. S. GRANT, Lieutenant-General.

CHAPTER FIFTEEN

MARCHING THROUGH GEORGIA

Around noon on September 2, 1864, Major General Henry W. Slocum, designated by Sherman to be military governor of Atlanta, entered the city in triumph. The general pulled out all the stops; he put on a full-fledged parade, with the band playing "Yankee Doodle."[1]

Four days later Sherman entered Atlanta in an entirely different style: dressed inconspicuously, wearing a plain suit, even though he was accompanied by a bodyguard of a hundred men. Granted, his few staff officers were resplendent in their full dress uniforms, but Sherman showed no interest in any fanfare.

Sherman was far from a cruel man; his nature ran to the sentimental, which included the people of the South. He did, however, possess a remarkable ability to reconcile his humanitarian feelings with his hardheaded assessment of what was necessary from a military viewpoint.

His treatment of Atlanta was possibly the most famous case in point. Upon taking the city, he ordered its population of ten thousand people to be evacuated and turned out in the surrounding countryside, thus converting a civilian metropolis into an army post. This was the first time he had taken such action, and in his mind it was necessary from a military viewpoint. His previous experience in occupying much friendlier areas had shown him that maintaining order in places like Chattanooga forced him to assign a tactical unit, as much as a division, to keep the populace subdued. He could no longer afford that luxury. He did not regard sending civilians out into the wilderness as excessively cruel. It was, after all, late summer in Georgia, and Sherman was not worried about the abilities of the population to find relatives in nearby communities. Atlanta thus became a wholly military installation, with no combat troops to maintain security.

Neither Sherman nor Grant regarded Atlanta as the final destination of his current campaign. Once settled down in the city, therefore, Sherman lost no time beginning plans to move deeper into the South. His eventual

destination was a matter to be settled later, but he was going somewhere. So the two generals, as in times past, began exchanging views as to what further actions he might take. They did not always agree as to what his mission should be, and though Grant was disposed to give Sherman almost complete latitude, it took them a while to formulate plans.

———

Despite Sherman's itch to move on, it appeared for a while that his occupying Atlanta might in itself bring about an end to the Civil War. About a week after Sherman had entered Atlanta, two citizens of Georgia approached one of his outposts at Decatur and asked for an audience, which Sherman readily granted. Mr. Hill and Mr. Foster had good credentials. Both had been congressmen in the United States House of Representatives, and both claimed plausibly to be friends with Sherman's brother Senator John Sherman.

The two men were on a humanitarian mission. Mr. Hill's son, a soldier in Johnston's Army of the Tennessee, had been killed at Cassville, a place nearby. A witness had provided the bereaved father with the location of the boy's grave, and they had come to retrieve the body. Sherman immediately arranged for the men to be escorted and aided in their grim mission. He also invited them for dinner.

Sherman was encouraged by the attitudes of his visitors. Mr. Hill had come from his home in Madison, located on the road between Atlanta and Augusta, and on their way the two men had witnessed the devastation from the fighting around the countryside. They had no desire to see similar devastation spread throughout the Confederacy. Sherman was much encouraged by their outlook.

Sherman decided to make whatever use he could of his new friends' attitude. It so happened that the governor of Georgia, Joseph E. Brown, had taken the term "confederacy" literally, defining it as an alliance between independent states, not a single nation. He had made moves in that direction. On September 10, 1864, for example, Brown had temporarily withdrawn all of Georgia's militiamen who were serving in Hood's army so they could go home for the harvest of corn and sorghum, which was ripe at that time.

Sherman saw an opportunity. He advised Mr. Hill that one of the possible objectives in his Georgia campaign might be Augusta, in which case Madison would be in his path. He therefore asked his guest to use his influence with Governor Brown. If Brown would withdraw all Georgia troops from Hood's command, then, as a reward, Sherman would spare the entire state from the depredations that Hill had witnessed on the way from Madison. Further, he would order all Union troops to stay on the main roads and pay for any food and forage.*

The effort, while a worthy try, did not work out. Sherman later learned that Governor Brown had seriously considered his proposal and had even attempted to call a meeting of Confederate governors at Milledgeville. But he went no further. The governor was afraid to act against Jefferson Davis on his own; he needed much support, if not unanimity, to take such a drastic action as removing state troops from Confederate command.

———————————

Sherman's capture of Atlanta had a shocking effect throughout the South, and most of all on Jefferson Davis. On September 20 the Confederate president turned up at Palmetto, Georgia, where he gave a scathing speech denouncing not only Johnston but Brown as well, coming close to calling them traitors. He then predicted disaster for Sherman, claiming that the invader could never supply himself so deep into the South. Sherman could not move forward, Davis asserted, and if he attempted to retreat from Atlanta to Chattanooga the result would be as disastrous as the fate that had befallen Napoleon at Moscow in 1812. Davis finished by promising the citizens of Tennessee and Kentucky that their soil would soon be cleared of the invaders. Two days later Davis gave the same message at Macon.[2]

———————————

* Sherman reported the meeting to President Lincoln himself. For some reason Lincoln was especially interested that corn and sorghum were the principal crops of the region.

Davis's bombast sounded desperate, but his threats were serious. Shortly after he uttered them Hood broke contact at Atlanta and was soon heading northwestward through Rome, presumably headed for Chattanooga and Nashville. Along the way he tore up Sherman's railroads, aided by Forrest's cavalry.

When Sherman received the text of Davis's remarks, his reaction was not one of fright. On September 26 he telegraphed a full account to Halleck, describing Davis's speech at Palmetto and other places. He was not impressed:

> Davis seemed to be perfectly upset by the fall of Atlanta, and to have lost all sense and reason. He denounced General Jos. Johnston and Governor Brown as little better than traitors; attributed to them personally the many misfortunes which had befallen their cause, and informed the soldiers that now the tables were to be turned; that General Forrest was already on our roads in Middle Tennessee; and that Hood's army would soon be there. He asserted that the Yankee army would have to retreat or starve, and that the retreat would prove more disastrous than was that of Napoleon from Moscow. . . . To be forewarned was to be forearmed, and I think we took full advantage of the occasion.[3]

While Davis was making his foray into Georgia, Sherman soon came to realize that things were already happening. He detected a thinning out of Hood's position at Palmetto, and on follow-up confirmed that Hood had already slipped off to the west, leaving no significant troops on Sherman's front. From that he concluded that the Confederate was bent on cutting the Union supply line, especially the Western & Atlantic Railroad. That would be a significant development. Hood had left garrisons at all the important points along the line, but the long stretches of railroad between them were vulnerable.

Actually Sherman saw the evacuation of the enemy before him as an opportunity, and he began to think in terms of marching his force to the seacoast. But in what direction? He could go eastward through Augusta or southeast through Milledgeville. When he broached the idea to Grant, however, his chief was at first dubious. Grant did not deny the possibility, but he specified that no move south should be made until ordered by him. Sherman was willing to wait. The fact is that he had by this time given up the idea of destroying Hood's army; that being the case, he was now thinking of the political value of destroying the Confederate will to fight by devastating her cities.

Hood, meanwhile, was beginning efforts to destroy Sherman's supply lines. Forrest's cavalrymen hit the railroad in his rear and tore up a full ten miles of track, damage that would take weeks to repair. He then headed for a town named Allatoona, on the way to retaking Chattanooga and Nashville. To stop Hood, Sherman sent two divisions toward Kennesaw Mountain, which was only fifteen miles from Allatoona, and followed in person. He arrived at his former headquarters at Kennesaw Mountain on October 5.

The resulting Battle of Allatoona Pass was small in the number of men involved—one Confederate division against a couple of Union brigades—but it was important for protecting Sherman's flank. It is remembered largely for the heroism of the Union brigade commander, Brigadier General John Corse, a volunteer officer with unusual military ability. Painfully wounded, Corse remained at his post in command despite the loss of a cheekbone and an ear.

Though Hood had been turned back, he had not been destroyed, and Sherman was now even more convinced that chasing him would be futile. He therefore abandoned his policy of defending his supply line. With Grant's approval, he sent Thomas with his Army of the Cumberland to "watch" Hood while he, with the rest of his army, prepared to march deep into Georgia. Slocum's XX Corps was designated to hold Atlanta temporarily, and Schofield was to join Thomas as an individual, where he would build a new corps from the reinforcements that Grant was sending to Nashville from the west and from Ohio. Sherman's remaining force would now be down to an estimated sixty thousand men, but they were tough, as tough as any soldiers in the world.

Sherman's concept of a march to the sea was revolutionary in military thinking. It did not erase the time-honored concept that the object of a campaign was the enemy's armed forces, but it added a secondary target: the entire population of the Confederacy. It was not an easy notion to sell to the Union leaders—Lincoln, Grant, and Halleck—who still thought in terms of reconciliation between the Union and Confederate sides. Sherman's new idea of punishing the Confederate population virtually invented total war. On October 1, 1864, Sherman expressed his views clearly in a message to Grant:

> Why will it not do to leave Tennessee to the forces Thomas has, and the reserves soon to come to Nashville, and for me to destroy Atlanta and march across Georgia to Savannah or Charleston, breaking roads and doing irreparable damage? . . . The possession of the Savannah River is more fatal to the possibility of Southern independence. They may stand the fall of Richmond but not all of Georgia.[4]

Sherman had made his point, but being Sherman, he could not resist a bit of irreverence. "If you can whip Lee and I can march to the Atlantic, I think that Uncle Abe will give us twenty days' leave of absence to visit the young folks."

It took a full month for Grant to give his approval to this radical approach. When he finally agreed, he described it in routine terms:

> On the 2d of November . . . I approved definitely [Sherman's] making his proposed campaign through Georgia, leaving Hood

behind to the tender mercy of Thomas and the troops in his command. Sherman fixed the 10th of November as the day of starting.[5]

In later evaluations, when the success of Sherman's march came to be almost universally recognized as a stroke of genius, Grant was typically generous; he took no credit for the concept. The whole idea, he insisted, was Sherman's own.

Though Sherman had initially set November 10 as the date for his departure from Atlanta, he experienced some delay. Nevertheless, he had his plans all worked out, but only so far as Milledgeville, the capital of Georgia. Beyond Milledgeville he was not certain which city on the coast he would make his destination. Options were Charleston, Savannah, or even someplace as far south as Mobile. The important purpose of marching across Georgia was to demonstrate to the Confederates—indeed, to the whole world—that the Confederacy was a shell.

To reach Milledgeville, Sherman decided to go in two columns. The right wing he put under the command of O. O. Howard, who was to pass through Jonesboro and Macon. The left wing he assigned to Henry Slocum, who was to proceed by way of Decatur and Madison, threatening but actually bypassing Augusta. Sherman planned to accompany the left wing. He had confidence in both commanders, but he seemed to consider Howard the more capable of independent command.

Before his departure, Sherman ordered that the city of Atlanta be destroyed—at least all parts that could contribute to the Confederate war effort. That task he placed under the immediate supervision of his army engineer, Colonel Orlando M. Poe, who did a thorough job. During Sherman's last night in the city, a minor disaster occurred. As Poe was burning the railroad depot, it turned out that one of the buildings had been used by the Confederates as an ammunition storage depot. When the fire reached the hidden artillery shells, they exploded, sending shell fragments through the air. Some of them came close to the house where Sherman was spending the night. He professed to be uncomfortable, but mentions no casualties.

The next morning, accompanied by a detachment of infantry, Sherman left Atlanta by way of the Decatur road at about seven a.m., never to return. At the top of the ridge where the so-called Battle of Atlanta had taken place the previous June, Sherman took a moment to note the copse of trees where McPherson had fallen. After a short pause he then went on.

———————

Sherman was struck by the spirit of all the men as they started out on this last long adventure. "Uncle Billy," he quoted them as shouting, "I guess Grant is waiting for us at Richmond!"[6] Sherman was amused by the fact that his troops gave little thought to the thousand miles of marching they would have to cover before meeting Grant. All they knew was that they were under way.

With his rear to Atlanta and Chattanooga cut off, Sherman now recognized that his army would have to live off the land in his coming march. The collection of forage for men and animals was to be no haphazard affair, however; it was to be done strictly to Sherman's specifications. The commander of each brigade (about a thousand men) was to detail a company of foragers, usually about fifty men, commanded by a commissioned officer, with a lieutenant, to be sent out before daylight, thoroughly briefed on the route of the day's march and camp. At a specified point along the route, the foraging company would leave the main route and proceed on foot five or six miles from the main route. They would then visit every plantation and farm on that piece of road and commandeer "a wagon or family carriage, load it with bacon, corn-meal, turkeys, chickens, ducks, and everything that could be used as food or forage, and would then regain the main road, usually in advance of their train. When this [train] came up, they [the foragers] would deliver to the brigade commissary the supplies thus gathered by the way."[7] The same procedure was followed day after day.

Sherman found some amusement at the sight of foraging parties on the route waiting for their main bodies of troops to join them. He noted their "strange collections—mules, horses, even cattle, packed with old saddles and loaded with hams, bacon, bags of cornmeal, and poultry of every character and description." He also remarked that despite the hard labor and even danger in this sort of business, the men found a certain excitement in it, and it was considered a "privilege" to be detailed as a forager.

Forage had a double purpose. The first and most important was to feed his troops, necessary since his rear was cut off by Confederate cavalry. The other was to confiscate items essential to the enemy's cause. But robbery of personal property was forbidden. Sherman realized that his orders were not always followed. "No doubt," he wrote later, "many acts of pillage, robbery, and violence were committed by these parties of foragers, usually called 'bummers'; for I have since heard of jewelry taken from women, and the plunder of articles that never reached the commissary." He claimed, however, that such acts were "exceptional and incidental."

By and large, Sherman was well satisfied. The system ensured that his men were well supplied, with enough reserve in his wagons to cope with any unexpected delay. "Indeed," he wrote with a touch of smugness, "when we reached Savannah, the trains were pronounced by experts to be the finest in flesh and appearance ever seen with any army."

———

On November 20, Sherman, still with Slocum's left wing, reached a point near Eatonton Factory, where he received word of Howard and the right wing. Satisfied, he moved his camp forward the next day to a wooded ridge about ten miles short of Milledgeville. It was a raw day, and Sherman went ahead of the spot selected by his staff and rode on some distance to the border of a plantation. He there instructed the staff to pick out the place for the camp.

Soon his orderly arrived with his saddlebags, which contained a change of underclothing, maps, a flask of whiskey, and a bunch of cigars.

Taking a drink and lighting a cigar, Sherman walked over to a slave hut, where he joined a couple of soldiers warming themselves by a wood fire. His plans changed, however, when someone reported that better quarters were down the road. He left on foot and soon found a fine double-hewn log house. He immediately sent orders to move the headquarters up to that place. Once inside he looked around the room and noticed a candle box marked "Howell Cobb." He soon confirmed that this was the plantation of General Howell Cobb, whom Sherman regarded as one of the leading rebels of the South, currently serving as a general in the Confederate army. Sherman also recalled that Cobb had once been secretary of the treasury in the administration of President James Buchanan. In Sherman's words, "Of course, we confiscated his property, and found it rich in corn, beans, peanuts, and sorghum-molasses. Extensive fields were all round the house; I sent word back . . . to spare nothing. That night huge bonfires consumed the fence-rails, kept our soldiers warm, and the teamsters and men, as well as the slaves, carried off an immense quantity of corn and provisions of all sorts."

Shortly after Sherman had changed location, the headquarters wagons came up, and Sherman and his staff had supper. Then a memorable incident occurred:

After supper I sat on a chair astride, with my back to a good fire, musing, and became conscious that an old negro, with a tallow-candle in his hand, was scanning my face closely. I inquired, "What do you want, old man?" He answered, "Dey say you is Massa Sherman." I answered that such was the case, and inquired what he wanted. He only wanted to look at me, and kept muttering, "Dis nigger can't sleep dis night." I asked him why he trembled so, and he said that he wanted to be sure that we were in fact "Yankees," for on a former occasion some rebel cavalry had put on light-blue overcoats, personating Yankee troops, and many of the negroes were deceived thereby, himself among the number—had shown them sympathy, and had in consequence been unmercifully beaten therefor. This time he wanted to be certain before committing himself; so I told him to go out on the porch, from which he could see the whole horizon lit up with camp-fires, and he could then judge whether he had ever seen any thing like it before. The old man became convinced that the "Yankees" had come at last, about whom he had been dreaming all his life; and some of the staff officers gave him a strong drink of whiskey, which set his tongue going.[8]

The odd story did not end there. Lieutenant George Spelling, the commander of Sherman's escort, was a native of that area, and he recognized this old man, who happened to be a favorite slave of his uncle, who resided about six miles away. The old man did not at first recognize the lieutenant, because the young officer was wearing a Union uniform. On inquiry, he said that he had lost track of young George, except that he had gone off to the war. He supposed him killed. Finally the old slave recognized young George, and he fell on his knees and thanked God that he had found him alive and fighting along with the Yankees. Learning that his uncle was nearby, Spelling secured Sherman's permission to go and pay him a visit. On the next morning Spelling described his uncle as "not cordial, by any means, to find his nephew in the ranks of the host that was desolating the land." Spelling soon left, having exchanged his tired horse for a fresher one out of his uncle's stables. Surely some of the "bummers," he explained, would have gotten the horse had he not.

The next day, Sherman rode into Milledgeville. Most of the inhabitants had stayed in their homes, the principal exceptions being Governor Brown, the state officers, and the legislature. A remarkable aspect of their flight was the amount of material the governor had removed from the governor's mansion. It included carpets, curtains, and furniture, all transported on freight cars. Still, Sherman decided to use the mansion as his headquarters. The ignominious retreat of the governor and others stood in stark contrast to the Confederate newspapers that Sherman's men found in the town. One of the messages was from General Beauregard:

Corinth, Mississippi, November 18, 1884.

To the People of Georgia:
Arise for the defense of your native soil! Rally around your patriotic Governor and gallant soldiers! Obstruct and destroy all the roads in Sherman's front, flank, and rear, and his army will soon starve in your midst. Be confident. Be resolute. Trust in an overruling Providence, and success will soon crown your efforts. I hasten to join you in the defense of your homes and firesides.
G. T. BEAUREGARD.[9]

There were others, equally desperate in tone. Sherman found these messages amusing rather than alarming. From the perspective of later years, it is difficult to visualize what else Beauregard could do.

———————

Sherman stayed only a short time in Georgia's capital; his next chore was to make contact with Howard's right wing, which he did, and found it in good condition.

By the time Sherman reached the town of Millen, he estimated that he had completed about two-thirds of his march. He had sustained almost no casualties, and his wagons were full of ammunition, food, and forage. He knew, however, that from then on the land would be sandy and less productive than the territory he had crossed. Nevertheless, he determined to continue with the supplies he had on hand.

At this point an incident occurred that prompted Sherman to issue a threat, something he did not often do. Having spotted Confederate cavalry in the distance burning forage, he sent for some citizens of Millen who he knew would spread the word. He reminded them of the "conditions" he had laid down before leaving Atlanta. Since the railroad leading to his rear had been torn up by Hood and his cavalry, he reminded those citizens that he would now be forced to live off the land. Granted, he had promised not to molest the populace nor destroy personal property unnecessarily. If the Confederates assumed a "scorched earth" policy, however, he declared that he would destroy all the villages in his path, leaving the people homeless. The rebel destruction of food and forage ceased immediately.

That was not the only incident in which Sherman found it necessary to exercise an iron fist. On December 8 one of his lieutenants was wounded so severely that his leg had to be amputated. The wound was caused by his stepping on a buried artillery shell, known as a "torpedo" at that time. As Sherman describes it, "I immediately ordered a lot of rebel prisoners to be brought from the provost guard, armed with picks and spades, and made them march in close order along the road, so as to explode their own torpedoes, or to discover and dig them up. They begged hard, but I reiterated the order, and could hardly help laughing at their stepping so gingerly along the road, where it was supposed sunken torpedoes might explode at each step, but they found no other torpedoes."

When Sherman arrived at the defenses of Savannah on December 10, 1864, he could see at once that the Confederate position was strong. It consisted of an estimated ten thousand men, well entrenched. Furthermore, he respected the Confederate commander, William Hardee, as a competent officer.[10] He therefore decided that a direct assault on the city would be too costly; instead he would lay a siege.

That decision brought the old bugaboo of supply once more to the forefront. In the last few miles of the march from Atlanta, forage from the surrounding land had become sparse—so sparse that Sherman realized that he could not, without help, continue a siege indefinitely.

Sherman was too good a planner to be surprised. He had always counted on the navy to sustain him once he had reached the coast. To that end, he had previously made arrangements with Admiral John A. Dahlgren, one of whose squadrons was blockading the Confederate coast some miles to the south. One of Dahlgren's ships had made contact with Sherman's headquarters, and together they had planned to transfer supplies at the Ogeechee River, fifteen miles south of Savannah. One problem had to be dealt with, however: The mouth of the river was guarded by Fort McAllister, a Confederate position on the right (south) bank. The reduction of that fort therefore became Sherman's main effort. He sent word to General Howard to prepare an attack, delegated the siege of Savannah to Slocum, and joined Howard on December 12.

Fort McAllister was not expected to present much difficulty, because its heavy guns were all pointed seaward, leaving it vulnerable to attack from the land. The fort could drive off any Union naval vessels, but the garrison consisted of only about a hundred and twenty men. The division that Howard selected for the assault, that of General William B. Hazen, consisted of about four thousand men.[11]

Sherman and Howard witnessed the attack from the top of a rice mill on the south bank of the Ogeechee, where they could see both Fort McAllister and the river mouth. After some time they eventually spotted wisps of smoke, indicating the approach of a naval vessel. Because of the heavy foliage, neither Dahlgren's ship nor Hazen's troops knew of the existence of the other. At Sherman's prodding, therefore, Hazen's men went into position and attacked the fort. The fighting was over in a few minutes. Hazen's men swarmed over the parapets and killed or captured all of the garrison. A delighted Sherman dined with General Hazen that evening, and one of their guests was the former commander of Fort McAllister, Confederate major George W. Anderson.

The next day Sherman took a small boat out to meet his naval counterparts. With the supply by sea open, Sherman sent a message back to Washington saying that he considered Savannah already taken.

When Grant received Sherman's optimistic message at City Point, Virginia, he took it too seriously, at least from Sherman's viewpoint. With his mind always focused on Lee—and with Savannah no longer of interest—

Grant came up with a plan that could not help but cause concern. By Grant's new scheme, Sherman should leave a force at Savannah sufficient only to keep the city contained. He would move his army—still sixty thousand men—by ship to join Grant at Petersburg, which Grant had under siege. This arrangement would deprive Sherman of his independent command and would leave unfinished the much-touted march from Atlanta to Savannah. But these were merely personal considerations. Sherman offered no complaint and began making preparations to carry out Grant's idea.

Fortunately for Sherman, Confederate general William Hardee solved his problem. On the morning of December 21, 1864, Sherman's pickets discovered that the Confederate positions in Savannah were empty. Hardee had used the only causeway still in his hands and evacuated during the night, moving across the Savannah River to the north. Hardee had lost Savannah, but he had saved his troops from certain capture.

An elated William T. Sherman sent a message back to President Lincoln:

SAVANNAH GEORGIA, December 22, 1884.

His Excellency President Lincoln, Washington, D.C.:
    I beg to present you as a Christmas-gift the city of Savannah,
with one hundred and fifty heavy guns and plenty of ammunition,
also about twenty five thousand bales of cotton.
    W. T. SHERMAN, Major-General.[12]

CHAPTER SIXTEEN

SAVANNAH

When word of Sherman's capture of Savannah was blazoned across the headlines of the North, his star was at its zenith. His letter to Lincoln arrived in Washington on Christmas Eve—perfect timing. With congratulations pouring in from all quarters, Cump would not have been human had he not relished them. The fact that he had been pictured as a monster in the Southern press only seemed to amuse him. He was, however, aware that his bubble of fame could burst. On January 15, 1865, he wrote Ellen,

> . . . and yet I dread the elevation to which they have got me. A single mistake or accident, my pile, though well founded, would tumble; but I base my hopes of fair fame on the opinion of my own army, and my associates. . . .[1]

A trifle that perplexed him, however, was the faith that the members of the Southern gentry placed in him. One day, for example, the wife of Confederate general Gustavus W. Smith, whom Sherman had known rather casually some years earlier at West Point, was ushered into his headquarters, anxious to see him, bearing a letter of introduction from her husband. She was complaining about the accommodations she was occupying. Sherman described her as a "handsome" woman, and he cheerfully agreed to visit her apartment to see for himself the hardships she was undergoing. Possibly to his surprise, he found her boardinghouse quite suitable. Her complaints boiled down to the fact that some Union soldiers were quartered in the same house. Mrs. Smith was worried that the noise they made might disturb her landlady, who was in her "confinement." That complaint fell out of Sherman's area of concern and the matter ended there. A later request for "protection" from the brother of the departed Confederate general William Hardee caused him to comment in his memoirs on the trust that former friends put in him:

> Before I had reached Savannah, and during our stay there, the rebel officers and newspapers represented the conduct of the men of our army as simply infamous; that we respected neither age nor sex; that we burned every thing we came across—barns, stables, cotton-gins, and even dwelling-houses; that we ravished the women and killed the men, and perpetrated all manner of outrages on the inhabitants. Therefore it struck me as strange that Generals Hardee and Smith should commit their families to our custody, and even bespeak our personal care and attention. These officers knew well that these reports were exaggerated in the extreme, and yet tacitly assented to these publications, to arouse the drooping energies of the people of the South.[2]

Sherman did not find the city of Savannah particularly attractive, though he found its orderly layout interesting. The one aspect that he appreciated was the foliage.[3] But like it or not, he knew that for better or worse he would have to remain there for some time, so he set out to find lodging. He soon received an offer from a citizen of Savannah with Union proclivities named

Charles Green, the owner of a sumptuous home capable of housing both Sherman and his staff. At first Sherman was hesitant, concerned over the possibility of unwitting damage to the premises, visualizing future damage claims against the government. However, once he had made an extensive survey of what else was available, he gladly accepted Green's offer.

Sherman was now more than a military commander. He was also a temporary governor of the twenty thousand civilians of a major city, a type of job he was particularly good at. His policy, coordinated with Grant, was strictly practical: He would treat the citizenry with all the kindness possible in a wartime situation. He allowed those who opted to leave the city to do so, though he took the precaution of making a record of their names. As to those who chose to stay in their homes, he defined the conditions in Special Field Order Number 143:

> . . . The Mayor and City Council of Savannah will continue to exercise their functions . . . They will ascertain and report to the chief commissary of subsistence, as soon as possible, the names and number of worthy families that need assistance and support. The mayor will forth with give public notice that the time has come when all must choose their course, viz., remain within our lines, and conduct themselves as good citizens, or depart in peace. He will ascertain the names of all who choose to leave Savannah, and report their names and residence to the chief-quartermaster, that measures may be taken to transport them beyond our lines. . . .[4]

During his stay in Savannah, Sherman received many visitors, some of them on serious business and some only curiosity seekers. Most of them came from Washington. The most prominent group of visiting dignitaries was headed by Secretary of War Edwin Stanton, whose ostensible purpose was to decide the future disposition of the twenty-five thousand bales of cotton that General Hardee had been forced to leave behind. A certain degree of competition existed between the various departments of the federal government over this cotton. The matter gave Sherman little difficulty, however. He simply followed the orders of his direct bosses, the war department.

The cotton problem, however, was obviously only a sort of camouflage. Sherman soon realized that Stanton had other things on his mind, foremost of which was to investigate rumors that Sherman's men were treating the newly freed slaves in a cruel manner. Sherman may have been half suspecting that Stanton would bring the matter up, because he had received a letter from Halleck warning him that there were certain political sycophants around President Lincoln who were after Sherman's scalp, and rumors of this cruelty were the weapon they were using.

Sherman was inevitably somewhat vulnerable on this point, because regardless of his desires he lacked the means to meet the needs of freed slaves as he would like. Though many of these so-called "freedmen" had remained at their old homes after becoming legally free, most had left without destinations and had trailed after Sherman's army, seeking protection and food, which he was unable to supply.

Stanton was particularly interested in one of Sherman's division commanders, Brigadier General Jeff C. Davis, who by birth was a Southerner and was therefore a target for some Washington rumormongers as harboring a hatred for blacks. It was reported that he had deliberately destroyed a bridge that a group of freedmen were attempting to use in their flight from Forrest's cavalry. The result had been a slaughter, so the rumors went. Sherman did not deny the allegation, but he defended Davis as a top-notch soldier, and though Davis was not noticeable as a lover of the ex-slaves, he was not deliberately cruel to them. Davis's actions, difficult as they were, stemmed from the need to ensure that the welfare of his troops came first.[5]

Without doubt, Stanton was serious in his investigation, though Sherman suspected that his motives had more to do with Washington politics than with concern for the freedmen. At his request, Sherman cheerfully sent for General Davis for Stanton to interview. Apparently the general did well, for nothing more came of his case. That was fine. But Sherman was resentful when Stanton ordered him to call in twenty freedmen for an interview. The former slaves actually gave Sherman great accolades that seemed to satisfy Stanton. What Sherman resented was that Stanton ordered him to leave the room while the interview was being held. The leader of the group, a clergyman, seemed to regard Sherman as a savior. But Sherman could not overlook the fact that he was, after all of his accomplishments, being judged by those he had freed.

All these decisions were conducted with an aura of surface congeniality. Stanton lived on his ship for the days he was at Savannah, but he spent a great deal of time with Sherman at the Green house. He was frank in describing the terrible state of affairs in the nation's capital. He went into detail regarding the backbiting and petty politics. He was concerned, he said, about the fiscal state of the nation. The expenses of the war were such that he feared a national bankruptcy. The war must be won as quickly as possible, he said, and he admonished that it was up to the soldiers to bring that about. Sherman took those conversations as a sign of mutual confidence.

The Sherman–Stanton talks were the most important events in Sherman's stay in Savannah. They were also tragic because Sherman read Stanton wrong when the secretary declared that the war had to be won quickly. Sherman apparently assumed that Stanton viewed the war in the same light as Lincoln. Whereas Lincoln was the soul of magnanimity, Stanton was actually a passionate Radical Republican who believed that the South should be direly punished for what he conceived as its guilt in starting the war.

When Stanton left Savannah on January 15, 1865, Sherman was not sorry to see him go. He had stood up to the secretary in their discussions, but he had had enough of Washington politics and was anxious to get back to his military duties.

CHAPTER SEVENTEEN

MEETING AT CITY POINT

While Sherman was governing the city of Savannah and fencing with Secretary of War Edwin Stanton, he was also exchanging messages with Grant, planning the next move northward to end the war.

Happily for Sherman, a historic development eased his planning problems tremendously. On December 15 and 16, 1864, General George Thomas's Army of the Cumberland and William Schofield's Army of the Ohio had burst out of their defenses at Nashville and had inflicted on John B. Hood's Army of the Tennessee practically the only battle of annihilation of the entire Civil War. For the moment, at least, Hood's army had ceased to exist, and Sherman no longer had to look over his shoulder as he planned to join Grant. Both Sherman and Grant hoped that the Confederates would be unable to put the pieces back together again. Even were they able to do so, the Army of the Tennessee would no longer be the same professional fighting force that had resisted Sherman all the way from Chattanooga to Atlanta.

On December 27, 1864, Grant wrote Sherman a message explaining his plans for his future actions. He began by approving Sherman's idea to march overland to join him at Petersburg. "The effect of such a campaign," he wrote, "will be to disorganize the South, and prevent the organization of new armies from their broken fragments."[1] He went on to observe that Hood's army was "broken and demoralized," having lost an estimated twenty thousand men. The fragments might eventually be collected, he admitted, and "we should act to prevent this." He hoped that Schofield, still with Thomas in the area of Nashville, could see to that.

Grant visualized another possibility, admittedly remote: Lee might possibly abandon the trenches defending Petersburg and make his way to North Carolina and attack Sherman. "In the event you should meet Lee's army," Grant wrote, "you would be compelled to beat it or find the seacoast. Of course, I shall not let Lee's army escape if I can help it, and will not let it go without following to the best of my ability."[2]

The matter of an overland march settled, Sherman began making detailed plans. He decided to move on Columbia, South Carolina, in two columns. The left column would march directly, but he had one other consideration in mind: The coastal railroad between Savannah and Charleston was important, and must not only be cut, but kept cut. He therefore planned to send his right wing (Howard) along that railroad for some twenty miles and establish a firm base, strong enough to ensure that the railroad would not be repaired. The town of Pocotaligo would be an excellent place for such a base. Howard's right wing could march from Savannah to Pocotaligo, set up a permanent base, and then turn north on the Salkehatchie River.

In the middle of January 1865, an event occurred that promised to make Sherman's march through the Carolinas even more significant. Union forces finally managed to capture Fort Fisher, North Carolina, a bastion that dominated the mouth of the Cape Fear River that leads up to Wilmington, the last important seaport remaining to the Confederacy. Previous Union attempts had been made to take the fort from both land and sea, but up to this time its large guns had been able to stave off all such attacks.[3] But now a new division, under Major General Alfred Terry, had succeeded. On

January 15, Terry's men had crossed the Cape Fear River at a point north of the fort, turned south, and taken it. A couple of weeks later the city of Wilmington itself also fell. The noose around Lee's army, which all active Union forces were engaged in tightening, was practically complete.

———

Sherman left Savannah on February 1, 1865, following Howard's right wing for the twenty-some miles to the already established base at Pocotaligo. He was pleasantly surprised to learn from Howard of the haste with which the Confederates had evacuated the position. In a letter to Ellen, he happily conjectured that possibly his own terrible reputation had influenced their action.

At Pocotaligo, Sherman turned inland and followed Howard's right wing northward to join Slocum at Columbia. As in his march through Georgia, Howard's wing traveled by several parallel roads, and on Sherman's order followed the same foraging policies as those he had exercised in his march to Savannah. On meeting at Columbia they would again march separately but in fairly close proximity to each other. Fayetteville would be the first objective, and then both wings would continue to Goldsboro. There Sherman hoped to pick up Schofield's Army of the Ohio, en route from Nashville. That was as far as Sherman could foresee when he left Savannah. From then on, he and Grant would have to make new plans.

Before Sherman left Columbia, somebody set fire to the city. Sherman then and later disclaimed responsibility. Columbia was not Atlanta. The truth of the matter has never been settled.

———

It was at the Battle of Monroe's Crossroads, on the site of present-day Fort Bragg, that a battle was fought that gave Sherman's men a much-needed chuckle. It was strictly a cavalry affair, and the results were indecisive. A special animosity existed between Sherman and Confederate cavalry commander Wade Hampton, who accused the Yankees of deliberately burning down private homes while on the march. Hampton reputedly had gone so far as to hang eight Union soldiers who had allegedly committed such acts. Sherman made a counterthreat. None of the threats were carried out.

One Union general, Brigadier General Hugh Judson Kilpatrick, was certainly guilty. Kilpatrick was a good cavalryman and had performed well in battle, including Gettysburg. But he was uncouth, corrupt, and downright cruel, both to his men and to civilians. He was as unpopular among the soldiers of Sherman's army as he was elsewhere. Sherman kept him for his fighting qualities.

Wade Hampton decided to take revenge on Kilpatrick. On March 10, 1865, he moved on the Union troops at Monroe's Crossroads, and by some luck knew of his target's whereabouts. He organized a handpicked patrol and sent them toward Kilpatrick's tent at first dawn.

Kilpatrick's security was poor and he was caught asleep. Hastily aroused, he deserted his female companion and dashed out of camp in his nightshirt. Taking safety in a swamp, he was soon retrieved and succeeded in organizing his men to the point that the battle was meaningless.

But from then on the Battle of Monroe's Crossroads was known as the Battle of Kilpatrick's Nightshirt Skedaddle.

Though the cause of the Confederacy was rapidly degenerating, Grant and Sherman were in for one disappointment. Word came in that Hood had been successful in gathering the fragments of his shattered Army of the Tennessee to form a force of twenty-six thousand men, which he was bringing eastward to oppose Sherman.[4] Hood himself, however, was finished. He was relieved of command and replaced by Johnston. But the balance of strength was still lopsided. Sherman's force was more than three times the size of Johnston's.[5]

Jefferson Davis had brought Joe Johnston back to duty very reluctantly. In doing so, he was much influenced by Lee, whom he had placed for the first time in command of all the armies of the Confederacy. One of Lee's first acts had been to recommend Johnston's recall to duty. Though that change did not come easily for Davis, so prestigious was Lee that

Johnston's supporters—of whom there were many—urged Lee to make the change unilaterally, without consulting the president. Lee was too discreet for that insubordinate act, however, and he was able, through sheer persuasion, to secure Davis's approval.

For his part, Johnston himself was not exuberant over his reappointment to command the rebuilt Army of the Tennessee. He resented serving under Davis even more than Davis resented having him as a subordinate. Nevertheless, Johnston accepted the position but did so in what one historian calls "vintage Johnston" style:

> It is too late to expect me to concentrate troops capable of driving back Sherman. The remnant of the Army of Tennessee is much divided. So are other troops. I will get information from General Beauregard as soon as practicable. Is any discretion allowed me? I have no staff.[6]

Johnston was nevertheless concerned about his own reputation. In the past he had been accused of being too unwilling to incur casualties among his men, and he felt that he was still under a cloud for that reason. Therefore, he now concluded that he must at least try to win a battle. The place he chose to make a stand was a field near the small town of Bentonville, North Carolina, more or less halfway between Fayetteville and Goldsboro.

With only twenty thousand men, Johnston's only hope for even a partial success was to catch one of Sherman's wings while it was separated from the other. He chose Sherman's left wing, Slocum's.

Johnston struck in the middle of the afternoon, March 19, with his left commanded by Braxton Bragg and his right by Hardee. For a short period of time he achieved success. To the north of the Fayetteville road, Slocum's left, the Union division under William P. Carlin quickly gave way and broke. Slocum's right, under James D. Morgan, nearly did the same. Morgan, however, managed to survive, if only barely. Neither Johnston nor Sherman was certain where Howard was. His wing actually began arriving on the field of Bentonville that evening.

Sherman had apparently never expected this battle. He seemed, in fact, convinced that serious fighting was finished for the duration of the war—certainly he hoped so. But when this attack occurred he reacted immediately, instructing Howard, who was converging on Goldsboro from the south, to come with all speed. Still, even after Howard's arrival, Sherman was in no hurry for a slaughter. He spent the entire day of March 20 on the defensive, facing Johnston and building up his force. Johnston, realizing what was facing him, slipped away on March 21, after Sherman had made a small, one-division attack on his position.

Sherman always regretted this action as a tragic and unnecessary battle, and he did not change plans. Rather than pursue Johnston, he continued his concentration on Goldsboro. His choice not to pursue has brought him some criticism for failing to "finish Johnston off." Whatever merit that viewpoint may have, allowing Johnston to escape avoided any further heavy fighting and its loss of lives. As it turned out, Bentonville was the last pitched battle that the Military Division of the Mississippi would fight.

As of March 25, 1865, Sherman was feeling secure. His armies were consolidated at Goldsboro, and Johnston had withdrawn beyond reach. His concern—and that of Grant—was now concentrated on two objectives: to prevent Lee from pulling his army out of his fortifications at Petersburg and joining with Johnston, and to bring the war to a close without another bloody battle. A message from Grant confirmed all this.

At this point, Sherman had developed an itch to see his boss, and he determined to visit Grant's headquarters at City Point. Accordingly he left Goldsboro on the afternoon of March 25, perfectly confident that Schofield, whom he left in charge, could handle any problems that might arise during his absence. By the morning of March 27 he arrived at the town of City Point, just east of Petersburg.

City Point, a town founded only a few years after Jamestown, was a spectacular sight. It was located on a height above the James River on the north and the Appomattox River on the south. The harbor was jam-packed with vessels carrying supplies to Grant's troops besieging Lee at nearby Petersburg. The area included seven hospitals that cared for an estimated six thousand wounded or sick a day. Its dock facilities constituted one of the busiest seaports in the world, as Grant's hundred thousand men were consuming food and ammunition at a fast rate. Grant kept his headquarters in a mansion called Appomattox Manor, which had formerly belonged to a wealthy man named Eppes, the possessor of a hundred and thirty slaves—who had elected to depart the scene with the approach of the Yankees. Immediately on arrival Sherman sent a message to his brother John, inviting him to visit Goldsboro on his own return, and he then went in to see Grant.

Grant, as usual, greeted Sherman effusively, and for at least an hour the two men talked alone. At the end of that time Grant mentioned that President Lincoln was on a two-week visit to City Point and was staying on a small ship, the *River Queen*, anchored out in the harbor. It would be proper, Grant said, for the two of them to pay a call on the chief executive. They walked down the hill to a dock and were delivered to the president's vessel.

On boarding the *River Queen*, Grant and Sherman found Lincoln relaxing on the rear afterdeck. To Sherman's pleasure, the president remembered him well from the days nearly four years earlier when the then–brigadier general Sherman had demanded, on leaving for the West, to be spared the responsibility of overall command. And since Lincoln had been Grant's guest for days, the president focused his attention on Sherman, keen to obtain what information he could glean; Grant hardly participated.

One of Lincoln's concerns was a bit surprising to his guest: his worry about Sherman's absence from his army at Goldsboro. This despite Sherman's touting the great number of troops he had amassed at that town and the abilities of Schofield to handle any emergency. In the course of a two-day visit, Sherman later noted, Lincoln mentioned the matter several times. But not all the conversation was serious. Lincoln particularly enjoyed stories of Sherman's "bummers," who had experienced humorous confrontations with the country folk between Atlanta and Savannah. The first day's visit was chiefly a get-acquainted affair, and the two generals soon returned to Grant's headquarters.

The atmosphere at City Point was hardly the usual all-male camp, for Julia Grant was present. Thus when Grant and Sherman returned to Appomattox Manor, Mrs. Grant's first question was after Mrs. Mary Todd Lincoln. Grant admitted that she had not been present at the meeting, and Sherman's defense went even further: He claimed he did not even know of her presence at City Point. Grant hastily promised his wife that an inquiry after Mrs. Lincoln would have first priority on their next visit.

The next day, Grant and Sherman paid another visit to the *River Queen*, this time accompanied by Admiral David Porter, their old comrade from the days of Vicksburg. The talk was all business. The main topic for discussion was the endgame: how to bring the war to its inevitable conclusion. Here Sherman, always blunt, seems to have taken the initiative. He asked the president, "Have you thought of the peace that will reign after the end of the fighting?" Lincoln assured him that plans for peace were in hand and that it was the job of these generals and this admiral to tend to the fighting.

Sherman, however, persisted, and he asked for instructions as to how to handle Confederate president Jefferson Davis if that unfortunate should fall into his hands. Here Lincoln made a strange admission. He would not say such a thing in public, he said, but he hinted that he would not be unhappy if Davis should make a clean escape. In his memoir Sherman used these words:

> *Should we allow them to escape, etc.? He said he was all ready;*
> *all he wanted of us was to defeat the opposing armies, and to get*
> *the men composing the Confederate armies back to their homes,*
> *at work on their farms and in their shops. As to Jeff. Davis, he was*
> *hardly at liberty to speak his mind fully, but intimated that he ought*
> *to clear out, "escape the country," only it would not do for him to*
> *say so openly. As usual, he illustrated his meaning by a story:*

"A man once had taken the total-abstinence pledge. When visiting a friend, he was invited to take a drink, but declined, on the score of his pledge; when his friend suggested lemonade, which was accepted. In preparing the lemonade, the friend pointed to the brandy-bottle, and said the lemonade would be more palatable if he were to pour in a little brandy; when his guest said, if he could do so 'unbeknown' to him, he would not object." From which illustration I inferred that Mr. Lincoln wanted Davis to escape, "unbeknown" to him.[7]

This lighthearted treatment of a serious subject was part of a broader, more all-encompassing one. Both Grant and Sherman expected one more bloody battle to be fought against Lee before the Confederacy would admit defeat and surrender; Lincoln did not. The president seemed ready to grant almost any concessions to bring the war to an end. Certainly that is the impression that Sherman received before he departed for Goldsboro later in the day of March 28, 1865.

Sherman regarded the visit at City Point with a feeling of intense satisfaction. Grant had given him permission to reorganize his army,[8] and they had agreed on his next move. He was even more elated by his conferences with President Lincoln, which were practically one-on-one. In typical Sherman hyperbole, he later wrote of Lincoln that

Of all the men I ever met, he seemed to possess more of the elements of greatness, combined with goodness, than any other.[9]

He was most impressed by Lincoln's statement that "all he wanted of us was to defeat the opposing armies, and to get the men composing the Confederate armies back to their homes, at work on their farms and in their shops." To Sherman that meant an order: take all measures necessary to avoid another major battle.[10]

CHAPTER EIGHTEEN

SURRENDER

Sherman's return to Goldsboro was uneventful. He took a small boat from City Point to Old Point Comfort, where he picked up his brother John and Edwin L. Stanton Jr., son of Secretary Stanton. They arrived back at Sherman's headquarters on March 30.

Sherman had every reason to be confident in his situation. His army had now swelled to a strength of nearly ninety thousand troops—eighty thousand infantry, twenty-five hundred artillery, and fifty-five hundred cavalry, well supplied from the North Carolina seaports by numerous railroads over flat terrain. Even if Lee should succeed in evading Grant at Petersburg and joining Johnston, he was certain, he wrote Grant, that his Military Department of the Mississippi could handle the situation easily until Grant, in pursuit of Lee, could catch up. If such were the case, he expected Lee to head westward to Danville and then turn southward to join Johnston, currently at Smithfield, North Carolina. To prevent such a development, Sherman decided to ignore Johnston for the moment and take a position to block Lee's path. He chose to deploy his army in an east–west position at Warrenton, a small community located almost on the boundary between North Carolina and Virginia.

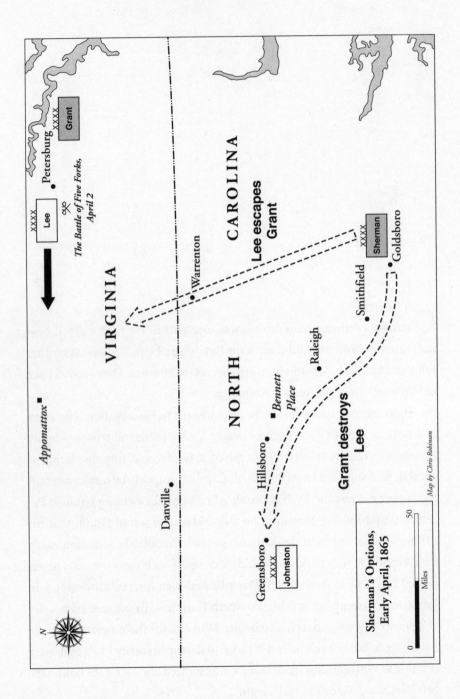

N

VIRGINIA

NORTH CAROLINA

Petersburg

XXXX
Grant

XXXX
Lee

The Battle of Five Forks,
April 2

Appomattox

Danville

Hillsboro

Bennett
Place

Warrenton

Lee escapes
Grant

Raleigh

Smithfield

XXXX
Sherman

Goldsboro

Grant destroys
Lee

Greensboro

XXXX
Johnston

Sherman's Options,
Early April, 1865

0   Miles   50

Map by Chris Robinson

As usual, Sherman planned to advance to Warrenton with three armies abreast: Slocum's newly named Army of Georgia on the left, Schofield's enlarged Army of the Ohio in the center, and Howard's Army of the Tennessee on the right.[1] He attached Kilpatrick's fifty-five hundred cavalrymen to Howard, as he expected Lee to approach him by way of the right. He set the date for his forward move at April 10, 1865. All of the operations were to be conducted north of the Neuse River.[2]

On April 6, the situation changed dramatically. A message arrived from Grant advising that the Confederate lines at Petersburg had broken on April 2 and that Lee had begun to withdraw westward. All indications were, Grant wrote, that Lee would attempt to reach Danville with what was left of his once-proud Army of Northern Virginia. Major General Philip Sheridan, whose cavalry was following Lee closely, estimated the Confederate force at twenty thousand, "much demoralized." Grant planned to follow closely, and if Lee made a stand at Danville, he would attack there. He now directed Sherman to turn back to Johnston. "If you can possibly do so," he wrote, "push on from where you are, and let us see if we cannot finish the job with Lee's and Johnston's armies. Rebel armies now are the only strategic points to strike at."[3]

Based on these orders, Sherman abandoned his plans to drive to Warrenton and headed almost due westward, intending to hit Johnston at Smithfield, where he believed Johnston was still located. He kept the date for departure at April 10.

Sherman arrived at Smithfield on the eleventh, and to his surprise he found the town empty: Johnston had retreated to Raleigh. Continuing in hot pursuit, Sherman received the welcome message from Grant telling of Lee's surrender at Appomattox on April 9, 1865. An elated Sherman put out the following order:

The general commanding announces to the army that he has official notice from General Grant that General Lee surrendered to him his entire army, on the 9th inst., at Appomattox Court-House, Virginia.

Glory to God and our country, and all honor to our comrades in arms, toward whom we are marching!

A little more labor, a little more toil on our part, the great race is won, and our Government stands regenerated, after four long years of war.

The troops were understandably exuberant to learn that the long and bloody war was almost over. Sherman, though likewise elated, was still required to face what problems might arise from this development. He had no concern over the prospect of a battle with Johnston; the latter's force was pitiable. But if Johnston decided to flee, Sherman had no way to catch him. Both armies were located in Confederate territory, and Sherman feared that whatever remained of the Army of the Tennessee might break up in small pieces and reassemble somewhere else—or resort to guerrilla warfare. The answer, as Sherman saw it, was to exact a quick surrender from Johnston, on terms similar to those Grant had offered Lee.

Fortune seemed to smile on him. Almost immediately after he entered Raleigh, a Confederate locomotive entered town from the west, and Sherman soon learned that a courier was carrying a message addressed to him. It was from Johnston himself:

The results of the recent campaign in Virginia have changed the relative military condition of the belligerents. I am, therefore, induced to address you in this form the inquiry whether, to stop the further effusion of blood and devastation of property, you are willing to make a temporary suspension of active operations, and to communicate to Lieutenant-General Grant, commanding the armies of the United States, the request that he will take like action in regard to other armies, the object being to permit the civil authorities to enter into the needful arrangements to terminate the existing war.

This was exactly what Sherman had been hoping for, and he replied with no hesitation. He was empowered to negotiate, he said, and was willing to do so. To facilitate negotiations he was stopping the forward movement of his army. He further volunteered that his demands would be based on those that Grant laid on Lee.

It took two days for an answer to arrive. But again, when a courier came in on the sixteenth, it was exactly what Sherman wanted: Johnston would meet him, at a place to be determined, the next morning, April 17.

Sherman left his headquarters early and at ten a.m. he arrived at the Raleigh/Durham railroad station. The arrangements were crafted very carefully, each side careful to ensure safety for its commanding general but to do so with courtesy. The staffs jointly settled on a farmhouse located between Durham Station and Hillsboro. Its owner, a man named Bennett, readily made it available.

Though Sherman and Johnston were all too aware of each other's reputation—they had been fighting each other for months—they had never met before in person. Physically, they could hardly have been more different. Sherman was tall, gaunt, and rough-hewn; Johnston was tiny, smooth, and dapper, fourteen years older than Sherman. Their relations with their respective superiors were far different. Sherman was on the warmest terms with both Grant and Lincoln; Johnston, while he enjoyed a mutual respect with his immediate boss, Lee, shared a mutual animosity with President Jefferson Davis that has become legendary. Most important, the two generals took an instant liking to each other.

They also discovered that their views were very much the same. They shared a hatred of war, and looked on any further bloodshed as sheer waste of human life. Johnston readily agreed that his army was no match for

Sherman's, and to Sherman's relief had no stomach for reverting to guer-rilla warfare if peace negotiations failed. However, in addition to the gen-erous terms that Grant had rendered to Lee at Appomattox, Johnston had an additional request. Rather than confine his surrender to his own army, he proposed a day's delay in hopes that he could attain authority to sur-render all the other Confederate armies in the field. Sherman agreed, and the two friendly antagonists returned to their respective headquarters, agreeing to meet again at the Bennett House at noon the next day.

All seemed to be going well, and Sherman set out to board his locomotive, as planned, on the morning of April 18. As he was about to leave, however, he received an urgent message from his telegraph operator to hold up a bit. An important message had come in, the man advised, and he strongly recommended that Sherman wait for whatever time it took to decode it. Sherman trusted his operator and complied.

It was well that Sherman waited, because the message was devastating. It was from Secretary of War Stanton, and it bore the crushing news that President Abraham Lincoln had been assassinated while viewing a theat-rical production in Washington on the night of the fourteenth. Vice Pres-ident Andrew Johnson, a little-known Union Democrat from Tennessee, had assumed the reins of office.

Sherman was stunned and aggrieved, but he typically recovered his senses and began to weigh how this news might affect military-civilian relations and the ongoing peace negotiations. First he confirmed that the telegraph operator had given nobody else the message. He then ordered the man in strong terms that the message must be kept absolutely secret from everyone pending his return. He told nobody on his staff, and when he stopped in Raleigh for a short visit with his XV Corps commander, General Blair, he did not mention it.

Oddly, the first person to whom Sherman divulged the news of Lin-coln's death was Joseph Johnston. As Sherman recounted the story, he carefully observed Johnston's reaction, noting that sweat had broken out on his forehead. Johnston seemed most concerned that such a crime would reflect on Southern society as a whole. But he and Sherman agreed that the tragedy should not affect the surrender negotiations. Johnston asked Sherman's permission, however, to bring in a third member to the conference, Confederate vice president John Breckenridge, who was in the vicinity. At first Sherman balked, on the basis that Breckenridge, as a politician, had no place in a military surrender. When Johnston informed him that Breckenridge was also serving as a major general in the Confederate Army, however, Sherman reluctantly relented. Even then he personally warned Breckenridge that he had better flee the country, because public feeling in the North was unforgiving toward him, along with Jefferson Davis.

Sherman then wrote out his terms of surrender. As guidance for drafting them, he had a copy of those signed by Grant and Lee at Appomattox. That document placed all the officers and men of Lee's army on parole and made provision for keeping records of their names. All Confederate arms, artillery, and public property were ordered to be stacked on the spot, where they were to be picked up by Grant's men. The most generous provision was that it allowed officers to keep their horses and even their sidearms. That was all.

Incredibly, Sherman's terms bore little resemblance to those signed at Appomattox. Apparently inspired by his visit with Lincoln and a determination that Lincoln's philosophy be the guide, his provisions hardly made a nod to such military details as administration of paroles, retention of horses and sidearms, and the like. Instead of stacking arms it proposed that Johnston's men could keep their arms until they arrived back at their homes. Their state governments' capitals would then turn them over at a later date to the chief of ordnance. The terms then turned to strictly political matters:

3. The recognition, by the Executive of the United States, of the several State governments, on their officers and Legislatures taking the oaths prescribed by the Constitution of the United States, and, where conflicting State governments have resulted

from the war, the legitimacy of all shall be submitted to the Supreme Court of the United States.

4. The reestablishment of all the Federal Courts in the several States, with powers as defined by the Constitution of the United States and of the States respectively.

5. The people and inhabitants of all the States to be guaranteed, so far as the Executive can, their political rights and franchises, as well as their rights of person and property, as defined by the Constitution of the United States and of the States respectively.

6. The Executive authority of the Government of the United States not to disturb any of the people by reason of the late war, so long as they live in peace and quiet, abstain from acts of armed hostility, and obey the laws in existence at the place of their residence.

7. In general terms—the war to cease; a general amnesty, so far as the Executive of the United States can command, on condition of the disbandment of the Confederate armies, the distribution of the arms, and the resumption of peaceful pursuits by the officers and men hitherto composing said armies.

Sherman was well aware of how far he had strayed from Grant's strictly military terms, so he added a strong caveat:

Not being fully empowered by our respective principals to fulfill these terms, we individually and officially pledge ourselves to promptly obtain the necessary authority, and to carry out the above programme.[4]

———

Sherman knew that these terms went far beyond military matters, but he believed that the tentative nature of the agreement of his recommendations would justify his decisions. He sent a copy to Grant and Stanton and went on to other things. The war was over—or so he thought.

CHAPTER NINETEEN

TROUBLED PEACE

At his headquarters in Raleigh, North Carolina, Sherman was puzzled to receive a message notifying him that Grant was about to pay him a visit. Though he gave the matter little thought, he looked forward to seeing his friend. He made no connection between the visit and the recommended peace terms he had signed with Joseph Johnston. Be that as it may, Grant was scheduled to arrive on April 23.

Grant arrived as planned, but he was not bringing good news; the authorities in Washington, he said, had disapproved Sherman's proposed surrender terms with Johnston, and furthermore they were holding Sherman responsible for exceeding his authority as a military commander in the surrender terms he had submitted. He cited a paragraph containing Lincoln's instructions to Grant from March 3:

> The president directs me to say to you that he wishes you to have
> no conference with General Lee, unless it be for the capitulation of
> Lee's army, or on some minor or purely military matter. . . . [Y]ou
> are not to decide, discuss, or confer upon any political question.
> Such questions the President holds in his own hands, and will

submit them to no military conferences or conventions. Meantime you are to press to your utmost your military advantages. EDWIN M. STANTON, Secretary of War.[1]

Upon learning of Sherman's surrender negotiations with Johnston, Lincoln immediately fired off a missive to Grant, instructing him to "give notice of the disapproval to General Sherman, and direct him to resume hostilities at the earliest moment."[2] Sherman had been treated unfairly, because he had not been informed of Lincoln's instructions to Grant regarding terms of surrender. For now, however, he had an immediate task: to notify Johnston of the disapproval and advise him that hostilities would recommence at the end of a forty-eight-hour period. He immediately sent two separate messages. One was stiff and proper, notifying Johnston of the Washington action; the other was a short, blunt demand for the surrender of the Army of the Tennessee based on the terms Grant had offered Lee at Appomattox. He showed both messages to Grant before sending them.

Sherman saw nothing alarming about the developments thus far. What he was unaware of was the fact that Grant was temporarily withholding the last paragraph of the Stanton letter, which could be the cause of radical action:

The President desires that you proceed immediately to the headquarters of Major-General Sherman, and direct operations against the enemy.[3]

Fortunately the term "direct operations" was open to interpretation. Quite possibly Stanton desired Grant to actually relieve Sherman of command. Grant, however, chose to read it in his own way. He did everything he could to minimize the effect of his presence at Raleigh. He made no move to supplant Sherman, and actually stayed out of sight of the troops. He studied the situation and waited until the twenty-seventh, when Sherman received Johnston's acceptance of the demand for surrender and then left, satisfied that Sherman was handling matters well. As a result,

Sherman still saw nothing in the situation to disturb him. He regretted the expression of dissatisfaction with his services, but was content that he had followed orders and terminated the truce.

Sherman was frank in admitting that he had exceeded his authority by dealing in political issues. Probably he realized that he had been over-zealous in his desire to see the Confederate soldiers back on their farms by fall. But despite his admission of violating protocol, Sherman still thought that he had done right in making the terms as attractive as possible to Johnston. He wrote a letter to Grant in which he sought to express his concern about the future:

> I now apprehend that the rebel armies will disperse; and, instead of dealing with six or seven States, we will have to deal with numberless bands of desperadoes, headed by such men as Mosby, Forrest, Red Jackson, and others, who know not and care not for danger and its consequences.

And in a letter to Secretary Stanton, he was blunt, even hostile. After admitting his "folly," he went on:

> I still believe the General Government of the United States has made a mistake; but that is none of my business—mine is a different task; and I had flattered myself that, by four years of patient, unremitting, and successful labor, I deserved no reminder such as is contained in the last paragraph of your letter to General Grant. You may assure the President that I heed his suggestion.

Notably, Sherman omitted the usual elaborate complimentary close of "obedient servant" or the like. He ended with a mere, "I am truly, etc."

In so writing Stanton, Sherman was inadvertently making a bad situation worse, exacerbating the personal venom that Stanton seemed to have developed toward him. The secretary had already set out to reduce Sherman's stature by ordering two other armies outside of Sherman's command to move against Johnston. He also removed a couple of other units that were at least nominally in Sherman's area of responsibility.

Sherman now began to realize how serious the situation was. As he was about to head for Charleston to supervise the surrender of that Confederate garrison, he was given a copy of *The New York Times* that carried a bulletin sent by the war department on April 22, the day Stanton had received Sherman's recommended "terms." The bulletin carried a touch of the frantic. It described in detail everything that had transpired, with two paragraphs added:

WAR DEPARTMENT WASHINGTON, April 22, 1885.

The orders of General Sherman to General Stoneman to withdraw from Salisbury and join him will probably open the way for [Jefferson] Davis to escape to Mexico or Europe with his plunder, which is reported to be very large, including not only the plunder of the Richmond banks, but previous accumulations.

A dispatch received by this department from Richmond says: "It is stated here, by respectable parties, that the amount of specie taken south by Jeff. Davis and his partisans is very large, including not only the plunder of the Richmond banks, but previous accumulations. They hope, it is said, to make terms with General Sherman, or some other commander, by which they will be permitted, with their effects, including this gold plunder, to go to Mexico or Europe. Johnston's negotiations look to this end."

This publication from the war department created a new dimension to the enmity between Sherman and Stanton. First of all, Sherman had expected that the exchanges between Stanton, Grant, and himself were the business only of the government; he had expected them to be kept secret. But even more outrageous was Stanton's baseless implication that Sherman had ordered his cavalry commander, General George Stoneman, to withdraw from Salisbury to allow Jefferson Davis to make an escape to

Mexico or Europe in exchange for great amounts of stolen specie.* It was a thinly disguised accusation of bribery. Sherman resolved at that point that he would always hold against Stanton what he termed a "resentment." Nevertheless, he had things to do in the South, and he set about to do them.

Besides inspecting the condition of his troops, Sherman had to provide for their sustenance. Even though nearly all the Confederate armies had surrendered, the population surrounding the Union garrisons was still hostile. Fort Fisher, Savannah, and Wilmington, all situated on the ocean, were no problem. Nor was the garrison at Charleston. But a sizable Union force was located near Augusta, Georgia, 135 miles up the Savannah River, and provision had to be made to supply that force—which Sherman did.

With the war essentially over, Sherman could now indulge himself with a sentimental visit to Charleston. Here he was in for a saddening experience. Nearly all the friends he had associated with so fondly twenty years earlier were dead or departed. Part of the family of one lady, Mrs. Pettigru, was still there, but almost nobody else. Furthermore, the buildings of the center city had been virtually destroyed. No other city, he observed, had been so damaged. It was necessary for him to rationalize that it had been South Carolina, especially Charleston, that had historically been the perpetrator of rebellions. It had been at Charleston Harbor, in fact, that the first guns of the late Civil War had been fired on Fort Sumter under the command of P. G. T. Beauregard. But that reasoning was intellectual, not emotional.

Insults from Washington had not ceased during Sherman's trip south. While Sherman was stopping at Hilton Head, a second article appeared in

---

* The term "specie," no longer in wide use, meant coinage, either gold or silver. It would have been ridiculous for Davis to make off with paper Confederate money. The whole accusation was later proved false.

The New York Times, this time citing a letter from Halleck, now commanding Union troops in Virginia, to Stanton. On his own authority he had ordered Union generals not to obey Sherman's orders while they were located in the territory of Virginia.[4]

Somewhat sadly, this sorry mess resulted in the end of the lifelong friendship between Sherman and Halleck. The rift was puzzling, because it transcended a mere disagreement over policy. There seems to have been no logical reason for the virulence of Halleck's insulting actions toward his erstwhile friend.

Few students of this period excuse the actions of Stanton, Halleck, or even President Andrew Johnson. Nevertheless, it is difficult to reconstruct, after all these years, the panic pervading Washington following the Lincoln assassination. The drama of John Wilkes Booth's actions is etched in everyone's memories; it is almost forgotten that Booth was actually only one part of a cabal that was intended to murder others as well. Another assassin, at least, made a serious and nearly successful attempt on the life of Secretary of State William Seward. While Seward survived the attack, he sustained a severe wound, as did his son.

It is understandable, therefore, that Stanton, one of the top officials of the government, should have every reason to fear for his own life. Sherman's brother John, who lived across the street from the secretary, reported that Stanton had stationed a heavy armed guard around his house for protection. In what appears to have been a somewhat deranged state of mind, Stanton was levying charges against the six persons allegedly responsible for Lincoln's assassination. Even President Andrew Johnson, a citizen of Tennessee and former Democrat, was caught up in the confusion and rage against the people of the South. Stanton and Halleck were in widespread company.

Fortunately Grant, almost alone, seems to have kept his head. While he conceded that Sherman's terms with Johnston were wrong by venturing into politics, he never lost faith in Sherman's good intentions. Having been with Sherman and Lincoln at City Point and witnessed the warm exchanges between the two men—and having heard the expressed desires of Lincoln for generous terms so long as the Union was preserved and slavery abolished, he was understanding. As he described the situation in his memoirs:

> Sherman thought, no doubt, in adding to the terms that I had made with General Lee, that he was but carrying out the wishes of the President of the United States. But seeing that he was going beyond his authority, he made it a point that the terms were only conditional. They signed them with this understanding, and agreed to a truce until the terms could be sent to Washington for approval. . . . As the world knows, Sherman, from being one of the most popular generals of the land . . . was denounced by the President and Secretary of War in very bitter terms. Some people went so far as to denounce him as a traitor—a most preposterous term to apply to a man who had rendered so much service as he had. . . . If Sherman had taken authority to send Johnston with his army home, with their arms to be put in the arsenals of their own States, without submitting the question to the authorities at Washington, the suspicions against him might have some foundation.

But Grant ended on a high note:

> But the feeling against Sherman died out very rapidly, and it was not many weeks before he was restored to the fullest confidence of the American people.[5]

With the various Confederate armies dispersed, President Johnson now decided that the main Union armies could be disbanded. He had no intention of ending the war with a whimper, however. He would do so with ceremony—a grand parade to be held in the nation's capital. He therefore ordered Meade's Army of the Potomac and Sherman's Army of the West to move to the vicinity of Washington.* While awaiting the event, Meade was to encamp on Arlington Heights and Sherman to the south of the Potomac, in and around Alexandria. Accordingly Sherman left Raleigh on April 29.

His route through Virginia took him to Richmond near City Point, where Halleck was still in command. For some reason, Halleck had decided to mend fences. He was, however, dealing with the wrong man. When Sherman reached Fort Monroe, he received a message from Halleck "professing great friendship" and inviting him to visit him when he reached Richmond. He answered by stating that he had seen Halleck's dispatch of April 26 to Stanton, which he regarded as insulting. He declined Halleck's hospitality, and added that he "preferred we should not meet as I passed through Richmond."[6]

He went on, declaring that:

> I will march my Army through Richmond quietly and in good order without attracting attention, and I beg you to keep slightly perdu [lost], for if noticed by some of my old command I cannot undertake to maintain a model behavior, for their feelings have become aroused by what the world adjudges an insult to an honest commander. If loss of life or violence result from this you must attribute it to the true cause, a public insult to a Brother officer when he was far away on public service, perfectly innocent of the malignant purpose and design.[7]

That was not quite all. At Manchester, Sherman found to his satisfaction that both the right and left wings of his army had arrived and were

---

* Somewhere along the line, having gone so far from Mississippi, the name of Military Division of the Mississippi in the field had been changed to the Army of the West, a much more sensible name.

in camp. At the same time he learned that Halleck, on his own, had ordered a review, to be conducted in his own honor, by one of Sherman's corps. Sherman forthwith forbade the review, finishing off his final insult. These gestures may have seemed petty, but in Sherman's mind they were important for the morale of his troops. They were keenly aware of the insults he had suffered from both Halleck and Stanton, and he was conscious, rightly or wrongly, that they were watching him to see whether he would take those insults lying down. He would not.

On May 10 orders came from Grant sending his army on to the vicinity of Washington. Sherman crossed the James River on May 11, 1865, and marched through the streets of Richmond. His armies traveled in two wings, Slocum, as always, on the left and Logan on the right.[8] It was a leisurely march, and Sherman's men were able to witness many of the battlefields on which the Army of the Potomac had fought. The left wing did best by way of sightseeing, visiting Hanover Courthouse, New Market, Culpeper, Manassas, Spotsylvania, and Chancellorsville. The right wing marched by a more direct route, by Dumfries and Alexandria. Sherman himself was not bound to stay with his troops, and he set his route so as to see every battlefield. On the nineteenth his force reached its designated camping ground, a space about halfway between Alexandria and Long Bridge.*

On arrival at Washington, Sherman accepted an invitation from Grant to visit the various governmental authorities. When he met them, he was perhaps surprised to receive such a friendly reception. Grant took him to visit many old friends and, most important, President Andrew Johnson himself. Johnson was particularly congenial, and when Sherman mentioned the two insulting bulletins that Stanton had sent to the *Times*, the president claimed that neither he nor any of his cabinet—with the exception of Stanton, of course—had ever seen them before they were sent.

---

* Long Bridge was the principal crossing of the Potomac between Washington and Virginia. It was located approximately where Memorial Bridge now stands.

But the reconciliation could go only so far. Neither Sherman nor Stanton made any move toward each other despite Grant's efforts to bring the two men together.

May 19 was a busy day. Not only did Sherman arrive in Washington, but on that day President Johnson specified the format for the grand review. It was to be held on Tuesday, May 23, and Wednesday, May 24. The troops were to march down Pennsylvania Avenue from the Capitol past a reviewing stand in front of the White House. As Meade's army was closer to the city than Sherman's, the Army of the Potomac would march on the twenty-third, Sherman on the twenty-fourth. It was a good arrangement, because the sizes of the forces were such that it took a whole day for each to march by.

Fortunately, the weather on both days was beautiful. Sherman had no role in the review on the twenty-third; while the president and his cabinet viewed the spectacle from their own stands, Sherman joined other distinguished guests in a separate stand. Notified sufficiently ahead of time, Sherman had sent for his wife, Ellen; her father, Thomas Ewing; and the Sherman son Tom.

The next day, however, at nine a.m., Sherman formed up in front of his troops and began the mile-long march to the White House. As they approached the stands along Lafayette Square on the north, he, who had been advised beforehand, rode over to the building on the southeast corner and raised his hat to Secretary of State William Seward, who had been placed at a window where he could witness the spectacle. A delighted Seward returned the salute and Sherman rode on.

Having passed the reviewing stand, Sherman and his staff peeled off and joined the presidential party to witness the rest of the parade. Sherman was introduced first to the president and then to each cabinet member in turn—with one exception. When Sherman reached Stanton, he ostentatiously refused to take the secretary's outstretched hand, a gesture of revenge noted by all, to Sherman's intense satisfaction.[9] The group then settled back for the six-hour parade to pass, the troops leaving the city at the west end of Pennsylvania Avenue.

Aside from the elation of celebrating the end of the war in triumph, the grand review of two days served as an eye-opener for the viewers, because it demonstrated the difference between Meade's and Sherman's armies. The Army of the Potomac was neat, well dressed, and well drilled— an impressive sight. But Sherman's men were different. As Sherman described it,

It was, in my judgment, the most magnificent army in existence— sixty-five thousand men, in splendid physique, who had just completed a march of nearly two thousand miles in a hostile country, in good drill, and who realized that they were being closely scrutinized by thousands of their fellow-countrymen and by foreigners. Division after division passed, each commander of an army corps or division coming on the stand during the passage of his command, to be presented to the President, cabinet, and spectators. The steadiness and firmness of the tread, the careful dress on the guides, the uniform intervals between the companies, all eyes directly to the front, and the tattered and bullet-riven flags, festooned with flowers, all attracted universal notice. Many good people, up to that time, had looked upon our Western army as a sort of mob; but the world then saw, and recognized the fact, that it was an army in the proper sense, well organized, well commanded and disciplined; and there was no wonder that it had swept through the South like a tornado. For six hours and a half that strong tread of the Army of the West resounded along Pennsylvania Avenue; not a soul of that vast crowd of spectators left his place; and, when the rear of the column had passed by, thousands of the spectators still lingered to express their sense of confidence in the strength of a Government which could claim such an army.[10]

A few days later Sherman took extended leave of the Military Division of the Mississippi. The war was over for him.

CHAPTER TWENTY

GENERAL OF THE ARMY

Almost immediately after the grand parade passed in review in Washington, Sherman said farewell to the Army of the West. At the end of May he joined Ellen and his family, and on an extended leave of absence from the army they became reacquainted. They visited the University of Notre Dame, where two of their sons were students, and went on to Chicago to attend an affair designed to raise money for wounded veterans. On the Fourth of July, 1865, Sherman attended the mustering out of a couple of his previous corps at St. Louis.

At the end of his period of leave, Sherman was given a temporary command in the West while the army was being reorganized. It took a while, and not until mid-1866 was he given a solid berth: as commander of the West. It was a position that made him nearly coequal in status with Grant, as no corresponding command was established in the East. Grant had undergone no such period of uncertainty that Sherman endured, because as commander in chief of the U.S. armies before the end of the war, he simply remained in place.

The vast volunteer army that had mobilized during the Civil War was inevitably disbanded at that time. According to Sherman's figures, its wartime strength had been about one million five hundred thousand names on the muster rolls, of whom about eight hundred thousand men were present for duty. The act of July 28, 1866, reduced it to a regular establishment of about fifty-four thousand, organized into ten regiments of cavalry, five of artillery, and forty-five of infantry. The command structure of the peace establishment was fixed at one general (Grant), one lieutenant general (Sherman), five major generals (Halleck, Meade, Sheridan, Thomas, and Hancock), and ten brigadiers (McDowell, Cooke, Pope, Hooker, Schofield, Howard, Terry, Ord, Edward Canby, and Lovell Harrison Rousseau).

A notable aspect of this command structure was the retention of several officers who had performed poorly during the war. Among the brigadiers being retained were three men who had once been in command of the Army of the Potomac (or its predecessor): McDowell, Pope, and Hooker. Other generals were reduced all the way back to their regular ranks. George A. Custer, for example, was reduced from the grade of major general (volunteers) to lieutenant colonel (regulars). To ease the pain of the demotion, such officers were addressed informally by their wartime rank.

The assignment as commander in the West was ideal for Sherman. He was by nature a Westerner, and he never lost his special distaste for Washington in general and politicians in particular. Unlike many residents of the Eastern states, he did not sentimentalize the great hordes of buffalo or the "noble redskins" who inhabited the plains. Always practical and forward-looking, he quickly became absorbed in the country's next great task, that of completing two lines of railroad tracks being laid across the continent. That effort had begun as far back as the 1850s, when Sherman was a banker in California.

One of Sherman's overriding characteristics was his loyalty, and at the top of the list of those who enjoyed that loyalty was Grant. Sometimes that commendable trait worked to Sherman's inconvenience. One such example occurred in the fall of 1866, while Sherman was on an inspection trip in New Mexico. There in the wilderness Sherman received a message from Grant in Washington ordering him to report to army headquarters without delay. Sherman did not welcome the order, especially because it involved a journey down the Arkansas River with only a small escort through country inhabited by tribes he described as "disaffected." Nevertheless, it never crossed Sherman's mind to protest. Fortunately, he made it back to Washington and reported to his chief.

When Grant greeted him, Sherman quickly sensed that his superior was in an angry state of mind. President Johnson, Grant confided, was in the process of drawing up orders for him to go on a mission to Mexico, a mission Grant regarded as an insult: The general in chief was to accompany an envoy that Johnson was planning to send to the entourage of Benito Juarez, the leader of a Mexican movement opposing the French-installed Emperor Maximilian. Grant agreed with Johnson's policy of supporting Juarez, but he had no intention of obeying the president's order, regardless of the consequences.

The crisis in Mexico had been long in coming. In early 1864, at about the time that Sherman was fighting the battle of Dalton, Emperor Napoleon III of France had set out to establish a European emperor in Mexico City, one over whom he himself would exercise hegemony. The puppet he chose was a thirty-five-year-old Hapsburg prince, Ferdinand Maximilian Joseph. To place Maximilian on the throne—and to keep him there—Napoleon had allocated a division of twenty-eight thousand French troops to occupy Mexico City. The United States protested, but was helpless at the time to interfere. Maximilian, accompanied by Empress Carlota, landed at Veracruz, and by late May 1864 he was established as emperor on the throne at Chapultepec Castle, Mexico City.

Napoleon, however, was in for a surprise. Maximilian, it turned out, did not act as the puppet he had expected. Within a short time he developed a sincere affection for his Mexican subjects and strove to do his best for them. But he never had a chance to succeed. The Mexican people resented being ruled by a foreigner, and the United States, once the Civil

War was over, was in a position to take action against him. The Mexican people themselves might not have possessed the power to remove Maximilian, but the United States did.

As of late 1866, President Johnson was not yet ready to undertake military action against Napoleon and Maximilian, but he felt free to take the diplomatic step of sending a minister to Juarez. The emissary he selected was to be Lewis D. Campbell, of Ohio, and Johnson assumed that sending a man with the stature of General Grant to accompany him would emphasize American support.

Grant sensed that the president had an ulterior motive. As with most vice presidents who have ascended to the presidency, Johnson had decided to run for a second term on his own. Grant suspected that Johnson viewed him as his greatest rival, because Grant was the most popular man in the country. Even though Grant had not as yet professed an interest in running, perhaps the presidential bug had already bitten him. He had developed a strong suspicion that Johnson, by sending him to Mexico, was seeking to remove him from the political scene. Sherman had his own suspicions: that he himself would become embroiled in the matter of Grant's mission.

Sherman's conjecture was borne out. When he reported to President Johnson, the president quickly told him of the plan for Grant to go to Mexico. He had sent for Sherman, he said, to function as acting general in chief of the army during Grant's absence. On receiving this word, Sherman did not hesitate. He advised the president that he already knew of the plan for Grant's mission but divulged, possibly to Johnson's surprise, that Grant would refuse to go. He sugarcoated Grant's defiance by saying that Grant was far too busy with more important matters and could not possibly comply. On the other hand he suggested that he, Sherman, could more easily be spared to go on the mission. A surprisingly cheerful President Johnson accepted the offer and sent instructions to the war department to substitute Sherman's name for Grant's.

That matter settled, Campbell and Sherman had a practical problem to face: Nobody knew where Juarez was located. For lack of a better prospect, the two decided to head for Veracruz by way of Havana, where the Spanish authorities might be able to help. They left New York by steamer on the evening of November 10, 1866. The mission seemed to entail no urgency, for the two emissaries lounged around Havana for several days while the Spanish governor lavishly entertained them. They enjoyed the warmth of the climate, which contrasted starkly with the cold of the North. Eventually they sailed for Veracruz, still hoping that Juarez would be there.

They could not have been more misguided. On arrival at Veracruz, Sherman and Campbell found no sign of Juarez. Instead they found the harbor full of French ships. The French emperor, they learned, had given in to American threats, and was withdrawing his force. The ships were busily preparing to evacuate Maximilian and his court. Maximilian was still in Mexico City, but everybody was expecting him to leave from Veracruz before all the troops were gone. Eleven hundred packages of furniture had already been shipped out.

The French showed them no hostility despite the reason they were there. When General François Bazaine learned of Sherman's presence in Veracruz, he quickly sent an invitation for Sherman to visit Mexico City. Sherman would have liked to accept, but since he was on a mission accredited to the "court" of the man rebelling against Maximilian, he decided that such a visit would be improper.

All this was a sideshow to Campbell and Sherman, who were seeking Juarez, not Maximilian, so they set out to find him. Northern Mexico seemed to be promising, so they visited, among other places, Lobos Island, Tampico, and Matamoros. Nowhere did they find a sign of him. Campbell even went into the interior of Mexico, to Monterrey. Finally they gave up and headed for New Orleans. There Sherman requested and received permission from Grant to give up the chase and return to St. Louis. He was home by Christmas.

He was not the least perturbed by the failure of the mission; in fact, he seemed to have enjoyed the jaunt. His mission, as he saw it, had been accomplished by the time his ship had slipped out of New York Harbor on November 10: He had prevented a break between Grant and President Johnson.

———

The next year, 1867, saw Sherman in Washington more often than he would have liked, playing the strange role of providing comfort to a beleaguered President Andrew Johnson, who was running out of people he could trust. What got Sherman in such an awkward position was not his interest in Washington affairs, but his lack of interest. The only inclination he felt regarding the nation's capital was to stay out of politics. For that reason Johnson trusted him.

The troubles in Washington stemmed from a clash that had developed between Congress and President Johnson over the fundamental question of how to handle a defeated and prostrate South. The followers of Abraham Lincoln advocated compassion and quick restoration of the Union. But the Republican Party—the Democrats had no say—was split by a second group called the "Radical Republicans," dedicated to punishment of the South for the crime, as they saw it, of bringing on the Civil War. President Johnson and most of his cabinet were Lincolnians; the Congress, on the other hand, was dominated by Radical Republicans. Johnson soon found the attitudes of the Radical Republicans too harsh for his tastes, and tempers rose. Even in his own cabinet, Johnson had to contend with one Radical Republican who sided with the Congress, none other than Secretary of War Edwin W. Stanton. With the passage of time, Stanton became more and more of a thorn in Johnson's side.

The congressional elections of 1866 had been a disaster for Andrew Johnson. A contributing factor was his mistake of campaigning personally for moderate candidates. With Johnson's abrasive personality, and the public's nostalgia for the martyred Lincoln (despite his own role as a Lincoln supporter), Johnson wound up facing a Congress two-thirds of the members of which were Radical Republicans. From then on the president was helpless in dealing with his enemies.

The Radical Republicans showed Johnson no mercy. In April of 1867 they passed the Tenure of Office Act, which forbade the president from firing any official in the executive branch who had been confirmed by the Senate. Though the act was manifestly unconstitutional, it was passed over Johnson's veto. To add to his woes, Johnson had already lost the confidence of Grant by attempting to micromanage the army. He also attempted to substitute Grant for Stanton as secretary of war on an interim status. Grant interpreted that ploy as trying to make use of his "celebrity." And Grant was now convinced of Johnson's intentions to run for a second term as president, a fact that further cooled their relationship.

Sherman was once again unwillingly drawn into this imbroglio in early January 1868 when he was summoned to Washington to head a board of officers charged with rewriting army regulations. The task was easy and readily fulfilled, but the working conditions were nearly intolerable. The officers were forced to do their work at army headquarters, across the street from the White House.[1] Grant and Secretary Stanton wandered in and out at will. Sherman was all too aware of the power struggle going on between President Johnson on the one hand and Congress on the other, with Grant and to a lesser extent himself as pawns in the chess game. For Sherman the situation was made all the worse because he was torn by divided loyalties. He was punctilious in his respect for the office of the presidency, but Grant was his close friend, whom he would never let down. The only answer, as he saw it, was to stay out of the melee—so far as possible. Though often summoned by the president, who remained confident of his loyalty and judgment, Sherman attempted always to keep the welfare of the United States, not of one partisan group, at the forefront.

The Sherman board finished its work and submitted the results to the adjutant general on about the first of February, 1868. Though Johnson was reluctant to let him go, Sherman was somehow able to depart Washington.

The reprieve was short. Before long President Johnson came up with another idea affecting Sherman. He proposed to establish a new headquarters on the East Coast with Sherman in command. It would be called the Eastern Command and would correspond in status to his present Western Command. In an effort to gain Sherman's agreement, Johnson promised to establish the rank of brevet general, four-star, to which Sherman would be elevated. Such a prospect would have been a strong temptation for any officer who would place personal ambition over the public good, but Sherman was not that man. Interpreting the plan as an effort to further decrease Grant's powers, he flatly turned it down. He felt so strongly that he was willing to resign from the army rather than accept the offer.

On February 14, 1868, Sherman wrote his concerns to Grant:

Your dispatch is received informing me that the order for the Atlantic Division has been issued, and that I am assigned to its command. I was in hopes I had escaped the danger, and now were I prepared I should resign on the spot, as it requires no foresight to predict such must be the inevitable result in the end. I will make one more desperate effort by mail, which please await.

Sherman accordingly wrote a strong letter to Johnson, and this time the president accepted his plea and retained him in St. Louis. Other issues were moving fast, out of Sherman's range.

On February 23, 1868, a bill for the impeachment of President Andrew Johnson was introduced on the floor of the House of Representatives. On March 23 it was passed by a near-unanimous vote, and three days later it was taken up for trial by the Senate. It took until May 20 before a verdict was reached: thirty-five in favor of impeachment as opposed to nineteen against.

President Andrew Johnson was acquitted in his impeachment trial by the margin of a single vote. A couple of days after the verdict, Edwin Stanton resigned as secretary of war, to be replaced by one of Sherman's previous subordinates, Major General John M. Schofield. And William T. Sherman was allowed to resume full command at St. Louis, at least for the short time left of the Andrew Johnson presidency.

Sherman did not have very long to enjoy his command in St. Louis after escaping Washington and the Johnson impeachment proceedings. Only a few months were left before the 1868 presidential election, in which Ulysses Grant was comfortably elected. Sherman, as the next-highest-ranking officer and Grant's closest associate, was his logical successor as general in chief, and Congress so appointed him, creating a new rank, that of general of the army. Lieutenant General Philip Sheridan took over Sherman's old post in St. Louis as commander in the West. In theory this was the obvious arrangement, but in practice it proved not as smooth as it had been during the war. Grant and Sherman were no longer in the field fighting an enemy; they were in Washington, where politics could mar any relationship.

One issue caused a brief rift between Grant and Sherman. It stemmed from a flaw in the American military system that had plagued the army since President James K. Polk and General Winfield Scott clashed during the Mexican War (1846–1848)[2]: the powers and prerogatives of the secretary of war as contrasted with those of the top general. The term "general in chief," as applied in 1869, was misleading, because it implied that the holder possessed power over the entire army—under the authority of the secretary, of course. But such was not the case. The so-called "technical services"—adjutant general, quartermaster general, chief of engineers, chief of ordnance, etc.—reported directly to the secretary, not to the general in chief. In point of time they antedated the existence of a general in chief, which office had been established only in 1821. The general in chief, in practice, was only the senior combat general of the army.

Sherman had hopes that this flaw in organization might be rectified, as General in Chief Grant had unsuccessfully importuned President Andrew Johnson to do. And on March 8, 1869, on assuming his duties in Washington, he received this welcome letter:

> By direction of the President, General William T. Sherman will assume command of the Army of the United States.
>
> The chiefs of staff corps, departments, and bureaus will report to and act under the immediate orders of the general commanding the army.
>
> Any official business which by law or regulation requires the action of the President or Secretary of War will be submitted by the General of the Army to the Secretary of War, and in general all orders from the President or Secretary of War to any portion of the army, line or staff, will be transmitted through the General of the Army.

Apparently, with a "military" president, a thorn in the army's side had been removed by a single stroke of the pen. Sherman had every reason to feel optimistic. It appeared that Grant would consult Sherman on all things pertaining to the army.

In a short while, however, Sherman detected disturbing signs. Grant replaced John Schofield, appointed by Johnson, as secretary of war with his own previous aide, John Rawlins, who was terminally ill. Further, Sherman picked up word that the technical services were "restive" under the arrangements whereby they reported to the general in chief rather than to the secretary. As Sherman explained it, they had never considered themselves to be part of the army. Rather they saw themselves as part of the war department. Apparently they had their way. On March 26 Sherman received the following order:

By direction of the President, the order of the Secretary of War, dated War Department, March 5, 1869, and published in General Orders No. 11, headquarters of the army, Adjutant-General's Office, dated March 8, 1869, except so much as directs General W. T. Sherman to assume command of the Army of the United States, is hereby rescinded.

All official business which by law or regulations requires the action of the President or Secretary of War will be submitted by the chiefs of staff corps, departments, and bureaus to the Secretary of War.

JOHN A. RAWLINS, Secretary of War.

By command of General SHERMAN:

E. D. TOWNSEND, Assistant Adjutant-General.

Sherman could not take this reversal without protest. He crossed the street from army headquarters to the White House to confront his commander in chief. Grant was noncommittal, even hostile. Rawlins was dying, he said, and it would be wrong to hurt him. But Sherman suspected that the technical services commanded enough influence in Congress that they had forced Grant to back down.

Sherman showed his displeasure in the only way proper: He stood stiffly, saluted, and said, "Mr. President, if that is your desire it will be carried out."

———

The constant demands for Sherman's presence in Washington did not require him to be at his desk all the time. The railroads had cut down travel time between Washington and St. Louis immensely. For two years he actually moved army headquarters to St. Louis. Thus he was able to stay in touch with his real interest, the building and the protection of the Union Pacific Railroad. His two obsessions—the railroad itself and settling the Plains Indians on the reservations—he regarded as parts of a single whole.

He was no passive or aloof supervisor. With every section of track laid, he rode out to inspect it. He was happiest, so it was reported, when he was in the field with troops, sleeping in a tent as in the old days. He mixed with the workers, many of whom were ex-soldiers, and some of whom still addressed him as "Uncle Billy." He was talkative and reportedly would talk "half the night" of old campaigns and old comrades.[3]

The timing was favorable for securing workers. With demobilization of the Union and Confederate armies, many former soldiers, ill at ease in their home surroundings and needing jobs, joined the road gangs. The man in charge of the construction was an ex–Union Army officer named Grenville M. Dodge, who enjoyed a mutual understanding with his workers and also a mutual admiration with Sherman.

Sherman was called to Washington to be the general of the army before the task was finally completed, with the driving of the Golden Spike between the Union Pacific and the Central Pacific at Promontory Summit, Utah Territory, on May 10, 1869. Despite Sherman's absence, Dodge had not forgotten his role. In reporting the event to Sherman he wrote,

> The tracks of the Union and Central Pacific Railroads were joined today . . . 2,000 miles west of the Atlantic and 790 miles east of the Pacific Oceans.
> Your continued active aid, with that of the Army, has made you a part of us and enabled us to complete our work in so short a time. I congratulate you for all you have done for us.[4]

The construction of the railroad was an unqualified success, but it was accomplished at the expense of the Indian tribes who inhabited the plains. Much as sensible people can sympathize with a proud nomadic race who can see the destruction of a cherished way of life, few would expect the white people of the coasts, especially uprooted by a great civil war, to allow the Great Plains to remain practically empty. Sherman had his own solution: that the Indian tribes should be absorbed by the Anglo culture, and quickly. In September of 1867 he met at Fort Laramie, Wyoming, with many Indian tribes—Cheyennes, Oglalas, and Brules. To them he issued a warning:

> *If you don't choose your homes now it will be too late next*
> *year. . . . You can see for yourselves that travel across the country*
> *has increased so much that the slow ox wagons will not answer the*
> *white man. We will build iron roads, and you cannot stop the*
> *locomotives any more than you can stop the sun or the moon. . . .*
> *Our people East hardly think of what you call war out here, but*
> *if they make up their minds to fight, they will come out as thick*
> *as the herd of buffaloes, and if you continue fighting you will all*
> *be killed.*
>
> *We now offer you this, choose your homes and live like white*
> *men and we will help you. . . . We are doing more for you than we*
> *do for white men from over the sea. . . .*
>
> *We will be kind to you if you keep the peace, but if you won't*
> *listen to reason we are ordered to make war on you in a different*
> *manner from what we have done before.*[5]

Sherman's message to the Indians was similar to his message to the Confederacy: We will be kind so long as you comply with our terms.

———————

Aside from his interest in Indian affairs, Sherman's tenure as general of the army was not a significant period. As in the wake of other major wars, the country found interest in other things. The army of which he was head for thirteen years bore no resemblance to the Army of the West that had followed him from Chattanooga to Goldsboro. The British military historian John Keegan has called George A. Custer's 7th Cavalry in 1876 a "poor thing." The soldiers, he claimed, were "under-trained and miserably paid . . . recruited from the country's unskilled poor." Many were immigrants, principally Irishmen and Germans, who had joined up in the absence of any available employment despite the booming economy. A third of them were recruits.

As to the officers, Keegan claims that many of them were "returned rank-holders from the Civil War who had avoided risk-taking in combat and shrunk from the risks of making a new career in the aftermath."

He concludes, referring to Custer's 7th Cavalry in 1876,

A British cavalry regiment in a similar state of training would have been on the home establishment, working up for active service, not posted to active duty in a theatre of war.[6]

Keegan does not hold Sherman responsible for this state of affairs, though he notes that Sherman "revealed in his formulation of a strategy for pacifying the plains something of that disgust with warfare as an instrument of policy which was to overwhelm him in his declining years."[7]

———————

Sherman stayed on as general of the army for more than thirteen years. He resigned his position in late 1883, and on February 10, 1884, his sixty-fourth birthday, he retired from the service of his country.

CHAPTER TWENTY-ONE

TAPS

At about the time of Sherman's retirement from the army, he was hit by devastating news: His friend Grant, who had left the presidency seven years earlier, had been diagnosed with terminal cancer. This was not the first misfortune that had beset Grant since the end of the Civil War. His presidency, while not so corrupt as his enemies like to picture, was no howling success. After leaving office, he had come on hard times in his personal civilian life, due to investing with crooks. By the summer of 1884 he was in dire financial straits.

Fortunately for Grant—and even more so for his family—a way to redeem his reputation and his fortune suddenly appeared. His friend Mark Twain offered him a highly lucrative contract to write two volumes of his memoirs. They would cover his life from birth through the Mexican War and then the Civil War, but omitting his presidency. At first things went well. The task seemed to restore the confidence that he appeared to have lost for twenty years, practically since the end of the Civil War. He had hardly begun his memoirs when the shocking diagnosis hit in late 1884. The thousands of cigars he had smoked over the years had taken their revenge. As the result of the throat cancer, the doctors prognosticated that his days were limited to only a few months. The little time left to him made the completion of his writing efforts all the more urgent. To stay out of public view and give himself a chance to concentrate, Grant retired to a cabin on Mount McGregor, in New York, and focused on his writing efforts.

Sherman, always his most loyal friend, went out of his way frequently to visit him. Grant appreciated this loyalty deeply. Sherman took a certain pride when he quoted Julia Grant's statement that Sherman's visits had done him more good than all the doctors.

Grant completed his work on the memoirs on July 19, 1885, and four days later he died. Newspapers offered Sherman large sums for articles on Grant, but he refused; he was not going to make money from the tragedy of his friend's death. And he may have indulged in some hyperbole when he declared that it would take a thousand years for historians to appreciate Grant's greatness.

Sherman's later years, even including those when he was still in the army, continued to be dominated by refighting the four years of war between 1861 and 1865. By and large his previous hostilities toward his former enemies, and even rivals both Union and Confederate, mellowed. When Henry Halleck died in 1872, for example, Sherman wrote kindly to his widow. On March 1, 1886, Sherman also wrote concerning Stanton, who had died in 1869:

> We were good friends for years before his death. . . . Stanton had some magnificent qualities which I have ever recognized and applauded, but he had others which brought him into conflict with his best friends.[1]

His friendship with Joseph E. Johnston, which began during the last days of the Civil War, continued to flourish. The two men met in Washington from time to time.

The one man with whom Sherman never made peace was Jefferson Davis, who remained unwilling to accept the outcome of the war and promote Reconstruction. Davis held a special animosity toward Sherman, based largely on the passage in his memoir in which Davis is described as being "out of his mind" during the time that Sherman was occupying Atlanta. As part of his personal vendetta, Davis contended that Sherman, not the Confederate Hood, had ordered the burning of Columbia, South Carolina, on his march northward from Savannah. (Sherman denied that allegation.)[2] He pictured the tragedy as an act of revenge on Sherman's part for the Palmetto State's role in launching the war.

The two men also fought over such trivialities as the unanswerable question of the relative greatness of Grant and Lee as generals. Sherman always remained steadfastly loyal to Grant as the greatest of all generals. When he was asked to give a rating, he placed Grant at the top, then George Thomas, and Lee third. When enraged Southerners howled about Thomas, Sherman answered that at Nashville in December 1864, Thomas had annihilated Hood's army. Lee had never, in the course of the war, won a victory of annihilation.

And of course there was the matter of Joe Johnston, whom Davis blamed for failure to attack when Sherman was driving from Chattanooga to Atlanta. The relations between Davis and Johnston had never healed, and Sherman's friendship with Johnston was well established. The two men—Sherman and Davis—never reconciled up to Davis's death in 1889.

Sherman spent most of his last seven years in New York City, experiencing by and large what appears to have been a happy old age. He patronized the theater, attended veterans' affairs, and luxuriated as the central figure at lavish parties. He carried on some flirtations with prominent actresses, but nothing to endanger his marriage to Ellen.

Ellen, afflicted by a weak heart, did not participate in Sherman's social activities, insisting on staying at home while he covered the town. Their relationship was strange, because although their deep affection remained, they had grown apart from many years of separation. It sometimes appeared that they were held together only by the memory of their son Willie, who had died at Vicksburg. Religious differences also damaged their relationship. Ellen, like her mother, was a devout Roman Catholic, whereas Sherman did not hold religion as a matter of any importance. He had been baptized as a Catholic at the insistence of Ellen's mother, and to humor Ellen he sometimes attended Roman Catholic Mass. But he was upset for a while when their son Tom became a priest, possibly because he had more earthly ambitions for the boy, although Sherman seems to have eventually reconciled himself.

Ellen preceded Sherman in death by two years. Her chronic heart condition worsened, but since she had always been something of a hypochondriac, Sherman attributed her bedridden condition to her imagination. On November 28, 1888, however, he was called upstairs to her bed in terms that alarmed him. Tom Ewing, Ellen's nephew, described the scene:

> The General was seated in his office when the nurse came to the head of the stairs and called to him that Mrs. Sherman was dying. Though he had known she was in danger, I think this was the first moment when he realized the imminence of her death. He ran upstairs calling out, "Wait for me, Ellen, no one ever loved you as I love you"; if she was alive when he reached her bedside it was only for a moment.[3]

As time went on, Sherman's distaste for war and politics grew. An extremely popular man, he was always being considered as a candidate for public office. Up until 1876, however, the possibility of a presidential candidacy had never become serious, because Grant, elected in 1868, was in office until then. When, during the last days of Grant's term, Sherman was approached by Republicans seeking to run him as Grant's successor, he uttered his most famous words: "If nominated I will not run; if elected, I will not serve." The declaration has come to be known as "Shermanesque." Many politicians have denied any interest in running for public office; Sherman meant it.

Sherman has often been characterized as the heartless brute who finally saw the light and became an avid pacifist. In fact he was neither. As a soldier, he showed no enjoyment in killing. His casualties in the Army of the West were minuscule compared with those of the Army of the Potomac. As to his allegedly harsh treatment of civilians, he gave orders for his soldiers when marching through Georgia to respect personal property that was of no potential use to the Confederacy or of value to his own army. His affection for his old friends in Charleston, whom he tried to visit at the end of the war, was genuine, so long as they were no longer capable of being of help to Jefferson Davis. But he was ahead of his time in recognizing that to bring down a proud and resourceful people such as the Southerners, one had to involve the civilian population as well as the armies. Hence the Hart description as "the first modern general."

Much has been made of Sherman's repeated statement that "war is hell," and rightly so. The occasion most noted occurred at a meeting of the Grand Army of the Republic, a Civil War veterans' organization, on August 11, 1880. It was a favorite theme, repeated more than once. And yet there is no sign that Sherman had his spirit broken more than that of the other generals, many of whom hated war as much as he did. It was principally his reputation for harsh measures, as contrasted with his peaceful professions, that caused the apparent dichotomy to be noticed. Sherman's postwar friendship with Joe Johnston was a personal matter, though a happy one. The real Sherman—courageous physically and morally, warm, practical, loyal, and singularly devoted to the Union—was not the man of the Sherman legend.

Sherman's death, or at least the circumstances surrounding it, was nearly as controversial as his life. He died from an illness that lasted ten days, though during that time nobody really knew how dangerous his condition was.

On the evening of February 4, 1891, Sherman left his New York home to host a party for some army friends at the Casino Theater. The weather was foul, and he woke up the next morning with a cold. He apparently gave his condition little thought, because he wrote letters in the morning and attended a wedding later in the day. Three days later, his skin broke out in a rash. Two doctors were called in, and they were sufficiently concerned that they summoned all of Sherman's children, including Father Tom, who was currently performing church duties in the Vatican.

By February 12, eight days after his first exposure, Sherman's illness was made known to the public. He was strong enough, however, to climb out of bed and sit in a chair. He professed a desire to see his children but he emphasized Tom. "Tom," he said. "I want to see Tom."[4]

It was now generally assumed that Sherman's death was imminent, although he rallied for a couple of days. As the end drew near, a controversy arose over his religious status. All of his children, in deference to Ellen Sherman's fervid desires, had been baptized as Catholics, and the consensus among them was that, since their father had also been so baptized, he should receive extreme unction, the last rites. Apparently Sherman himself was never consulted; nor did he much care. He had never been a believer in the doctrine of the Church; nor had his brother John. However, his children argued that the rite could be administered to anyone known as "friendly to the Church," and he had once been heard to say that he was now comfortable with Tom's becoming a priest, and that statement sufficed. His brother John was not charitable; he protested that the newspapers had taken advantage of his own absence to interpret the comings and goings of priests to mean that extreme unction was to be administered.[5]

In any event, the children had their way, and on February 14, at one fifty p.m., Sherman died of the disease that had plagued him all his life: asthma. According to his wishes, his body lay at rest for a full five days awaiting Tom's arrival from Rome, on the nineteenth. The funeral service was held that same afternoon, with Tom presiding.

The service was a spectacular event. Thirty thousand soldiers, including the entire corps of cadets from nearby West Point, marched proudly by. President Benjamin Harrison and his cabinet were among the attendees, along with former presidents Rutherford B. Hayes and Grover Cleveland. The casket, according to military custom, was drawn by a team of horses with boots turned backward in the stirrups. It was taken from New York City across the Hudson River and transported by train to St. Louis, where Sherman was placed beside Ellen.

By his own wishes, the train bearing Sherman's body avoided any large cities on the way to his final resting place. Of the cities to be avoided, at the top of the list was Washington.

ACKNOWLEDGMENTS

Mrs. Dorothy W. Yentz has now been my assistant and mainstay for nearly a quarter century. She remains in that capacity, and there is little to add except my thanks for her long service and help. My wife, Joanne, also provides suggestions and encouragement.

I also wish to thank E. J. McCarthy, my agent, and Brent Howard, my editor, for all they did on this book.

Friends have also helped. I would like to make special mention of the contributions of Dr. Mitchell Yockelson, of the National Archives, who is an authority on army history. I am also grateful (in alphabetical order) to John H. (Jack) Cushman, Kimberly Fernley, Robert H. Ferrell, Beverly Jarrett, June Koch, Alex Marshall, and his brother, Brian Marshall, both my stepsons.

Fortunately, Chris Robinson has once again been available to provide maps, also vital to a military book.

Susan Eisenhower's note: We are also indebted to Allison Jordon of the Civil War Institute of Gettysburg College, for stepping in at a moment's notice to help in the final stages of this book.

APPENDIX A

SHERMAN'S ORDERS FOR THE MARCH TO THE SEA

[SPECIAL FIELD ORDERS, NO. 119]

*HEADQUARTERS MILITARY DIVISION OF THE MISSISSIPPI
IN THE FIELD, KINGSTON, GEORGIA, November 8, 1864*

*The general commanding deems it proper at this time to inform
the officers and men of the Fourteenth, Fifteenth, Seventeenth, and
Twentieth Corps, that he has organized them into an army for a
special purpose, well known to the War Department and to
General Grant. It is sufficient for you to know that it involves a
departure from our present base, and a long and difficult march to
a new one. All the chances of war have been considered and
provided for, as far as human sagacity can. All he asks of you is to
maintain that discipline, patience, and courage, which have
characterized you in the past; and he hopes, through you, to strike
a blow at our enemy that will have a material effect in producing
what we all so much desire, his complete overthrow. Of all things,
the most important is, that the men, during marches and in
camp, keep their places and do not scatter about as stragglers or
foragers, to be picked up by a hostile people in detail. It is also of
the utmost importance that our wagons should not be loaded with*

any thing but provisions and ammunition. All surplus servants, noncombatants, and refugees, should now go to the rear, and none should be encouraged to encumber us on the march. At some future time we will be able to provide for the poor whites and blacks who seek to escape the bondage under which they are now suffering. With these few simple cautions, he hopes to lead you to achievements equal in importance to those of the past.

By order of Major-General W. T. Sherman,

L. M. DAYTON, Aide-de-Camp.

[SPECIAL FIELD ORDERS, NO. 120]

HEADQUARTERS MILITARY DIVISION OF THE MISSISSIPPI IN THE FIELD, KINGSTON, GEORGIA, November 9, 1864

1. For the purpose of military operations, this army is divided into two wings viz.:

The right wing, Major-General O. O. Howard commanding, composed of the Fifteenth and Seventeenth Corps; the left wing, Major-General H. W. Slocum commanding, composed of the Fourteenth and Twentieth Corps.

2. The habitual order of march will be, wherever practicable, by four roads, as nearly parallel as possible, and converging at points hereafter to be indicated in orders. The cavalry, Brigadier-General Kilpatrick commanding, will receive special orders from the commander-in-chief.

3. There will be no general train of supplies, but each corps will have its ammunition-train and provision-train, distributed habitually as follows: Behind each regiment should follow one wagon and one ambulance; behind each brigade should follow a due proportion of ammunition-wagons, provision-wagons, and ambulances. In case of danger, each corps commander should change this order of march, by having his advance and rear brigades unencumbered by wheels. The separate columns will start habitually at 7 a.m., and make about fifteen miles per day, unless otherwise fixed in orders.

4. The army will forage liberally on the country during the march. To this end, each brigade commander will organize a good and sufficient foraging party, under the command of one or more discreet officers, who will gather, near the route traveled, corn or forage of any kind, meat of any kind, vegetables, corn-meal, or whatever is needed by the command, aiming at all times to keep in the wagons at least ten days' provisions for his command, and three days' forage. Soldiers must not enter the dwellings of the inhabitants, or commit any trespass; but, during a halt or camp, they may be permitted to gather turnips, potatoes, and other vegetables, and to drive in stock in sight of their camp. To regular foraging-parties must be intrusted the gathering of provisions and forage, at any distance from the road traveled.

5. To corps commanders alone is intrusted the power to destroy mills, houses, cotton-gins, etc.; and for them this general principle is laid down: In districts and neighborhoods where the army is unmolested, no destruction of each property should be permitted; but should guerrillas or bushwhackers molest our march, or should the inhabitants burn bridges, obstruct roads, or otherwise manifest local hostility, then army commanders should order and enforce a devastation more or less relentless, according to the measure of such hostility.

6. As for horses, mules, wagons, etc., belonging to the inhabitants, the cavalry and artillery may appropriate freely and without limit; discriminating, however, between the rich, who are usually hostile, and the poor and industrious, usually neutral or friendly. Foraging-parties may also take mules or horses, to replace the jaded animals of their trains, or to serve as pack-mules for the regiments or brigades. In all foraging, of whatever kind, the parties engaged will refrain from abusive or threatening language, and

APPENDIX A

may, where the officer in command thinks proper, give written certificates of the facts, but no receipts; and they will endeavor to leave with each family a reasonable portion for their maintenance.

7. Negroes who are able-bodied and can be of service to the several columns may be taken along; but each army commander will bear in mind that the question of supplies is a very important one, and that his first duty is to see to those who bear arms.

8. The organization, at once, of a good pioneer battalion for each army corps, composed if possible of negroes, should be attended to. This battalion should follow the advance-guard, repair roads and double them if possible, so that the columns will not be delayed after reaching bad places. Also, army commanders should practise the habit of giving the artillery and wagons the road, marching their troops on one side, and instruct their troops to assist wagons at steep hills or bad crossings of streams.

9. Captain O. M. Poe, chief-engineer, will assign to each wing of the army a pontoon-train, fully equipped and organized; and the commanders thereof will see to their being properly protected at all times.

By order of Major-General W. T. Sherman,
L. M. DAYTON, Aide-de-Camp.

---

* Sherman, *Memoirs*, pp. 174–76.

"MARCHING THROUGH GEORGIA"

Bring the good ol' bugle, boys! We'll sing another song,
Sing it with the spirit that will start the world along,
Sing it as we used to sing it fifty thousand strong,
While we were marching through Georgia.

Chorus

Hurrah! Hurrah! We bring the jubilee.
Hurrah! Hurrah! The flag that makes you free!
So we sang the chorus from Atlanta to the sea,
While we were marching through Georgia.
How the darkies shouted when they heard the joyful sound!
How the turkeys gobbled which our commissary found!
How the sweet potatoes even started from the ground,
While we were marching through Georgia.

Repeat chorus

Yes, and there were Union men who wept with joyful tears,
When they saw the honored flag they had not seen for years.
Hardly could they be restrained from breaking forth in cheers,
While we were marching through Georgia.

APPENDIX B

Repeat chorus

"Sherman's dashing Yankee boys will never reach the coast!"
So the saucy rebels said, and 'twas a handsome boast
Had they not forgot, alas! to reckon with the host
While we were marching through Georgia.

Repeat chorus

So we made a thoroughfare for freedom and her train,
Sixty miles in latitude, three hundred to the main;
Treason fled before us, for resistance was in vain
While we were marching through Georgia.

Repeat chorus

APPENDIX C

OB—DEPARTMENT OF THE MISSISSIPPI, ATLANTA

The following order of battle for the Department of the Mississippi is shown as it existed for the Battles Around Atlanta, because that was the time when Sherman's force was at its peak. Sometime after the occupation of that city, Confederate general John B. Hood departed for Nashville, and Sherman sent the Army of the Cumberland after him, now under the command of George Thomas.

A word about the military formation called the corps. It was the building block of the army—about ten thousand men. (A Confederate corps was about twice that size.) As Sherman's force existed in the summer of 1864, these corps were assigned to three armies, under McPherson, Schofield, and Thomas. This apparent overorganization was necessitated by the legal powers granted to army but not corps commanders, such as the power to decree a death sentence.

At times in this text I have referred to a commander without tedious repetition of the corps he commanded. The reason is that the corps had no special character other than the commander himself. They had no traditions. Thus I often say "Sherman's corps" rather than "Sherman's XV

Corps." With that in mind, here is the order of battle for Sherman's Military Division of the Mississippi.

THE ARMY OF THE CUMBERLAND

MG George H. Thomas

MG Oliver O. Howard	IV Corps	Stanley, Newton, Wood*
MG John M. Palmer	XIV Corps	Johnson, Davis
MG Joseph Hooker	XX Corps	Williams, Geary, Butterfield

THE ARMY OF THE TENNESSEE

MG James B. McPherson

MG John A. Logan	XV Corps	Osterhaus, Smith
MG Grenville M. Dodge	XVI Corps	Sweeney, Veach
MG Frank P. Blair Jr.	XVII Corps	Leggett, Gosham

THE ARMY OF THE OHIO

MG John M. Schofield	XXIII Corps	Judah, Cox
MG George Stoneman	Cavalry Corps	McCook, Garrard, Kilpatrick

---

* Division commanders.

APPENDIX D

SHERMAN LETTER AFTER DEATH OF WILLIE

GAYOSO HOUSE, MEMPHIS, TENNESSEE

October 4, 1863, Midnight

CAPTAIN C. C. SMITH, COMMANDING BATTALION
THIRTEENTH UNITED STATES REGULARS.

MY DEAR FRIEND: I cannot sleep to-night till I record an expression of the deep feelings of my heart to you, and to the officers and soldiers of the battalion, for their kind behavior to my poor child. I realize that you all feel for my family the attachment of kindred, and I assure you of full reciprocity.

Consistent with a sense of duty to my profession and office, I could not leave my post, and sent for the family to come to me in that fatal climate, and in that sickly period of the year, and behold the result! The child that bore my name, and in whose future I reposed with more confidence than I did in my own plan of life, now floats a mere corpse, seeking a grave in a distant land, with a weeping mother, brother, and sisters, clustered about him. For myself, I ask no sympathy. On, on I must go, to meet a soldier's fate, or live to see our country rise superior to all factions, till its flag is adored and respected by ourselves and by all the powers of the earth.

But Willie was, or thought he was, a sergeant in the Thirteenth. I have seen his eye brighten, his heart beat, as he beheld the battalion under arms, and asked me if they were not real soldiers. Child as he was, he had the enthusiasm, the pure love of truth, honor, and love of country, which should animate all soldiers.

God only knows why he should die this young. He is dead, but will not be forgotten till those who knew him in life have followed him to that same mysterious end.

Please convey to the battalion my heart-felt thanks, and assure each and all that if in after-years they call on me or mine, and mention that they were of the Thirteenth Regulars when Willie was a sergeant, they will have a key to the affections of my family that will open all it has; that we will share with them our last blanket, our last crust! Your friend,

W. T. SHERMAN, Major-general

---

* Sherman, *Memoirs*, p. 349.

BIBLIOGRAPHY

BOOKS

Castel, Albert E. *Decision in the West: The Atlanta Campaign of 1864.* Lawrence: University Press of Kansas, 1992.

Fiske, John. *The Mississippi Valley in the Civil War.* Boston and New York: Houghton, Mifflin, and Company, 1900.

Flood, Charles Bracelen. *Grant and Sherman: The Friendship That Won the Civil War.* New York: Harper Perennial, 2005.

Glatthaar, Joseph T. *Partners in Command: The Relationships Between Leaders in the Civil War.* New York: The Free Press, 1994.

Goodheart, Adam. *1861, The Civil War Awakening.* New York: Knopf, 2011.

Hearn, Chester G. *Admiral David Dixon Porter: The Civil War Years.* Annapolis: Naval Institute Press, 1996.

Howe, M. A. De Wolfe (ed.). *Home Letters of General Sherman.* New York: Charles Scribner's Sons, 1909.

Kagan, Neil, and Stephen G. Hyslop (eds.). *Atlas of the Civil War: A Comprehensive Guide to the Tactics and Terrain of Battle.* Washington, D.C.: National Geographic, 2009.

Keegan, John. *Fields of Battle: The Wars for North America.* New York: Alfred A. Knopf, 1996.

Lewis, Lloyd. *Sherman: Fighting Prophet.* New York: Harcourt Brace, 1932.

Marszalek, John F. *Sherman: A Soldier's Passion for Order.* New York: The Free Press, 1993.

Meyers, Christopher C. *Union General John A. McClernand and the Politics of Command.* Jefferson, NC: MacFarland & Co., 2010.

Moody, Wesley. *Demon of the Lost Cause: Sherman and Civil War History.* Columbia, MO: University of Missouri Press, 2011.

Peters, Charles, *Autobiography of Charles Peters.* Sacramento: The LaGrave Co., 1915.

Reed, Germaine M. *David French Boyd, Founder of Louisiana State University.* Baton Rouge: Louisiana State University Press, 1977.

Sherman, William T. *The Memoirs of General William T. Sherman.* Bloomington: University of Indiana Press, 1957. Originally published in 1875, in St. Louis, Missouri.

Symonds, Craig L. *Joseph E. Johnston: A Civil War Biography.* New York: W. W. Norton & Co., 1992.

Tenney, William J. *The Military and Naval History of the Rebellion in the United States.* New York: D. Appleton & Company, 1866.

Thorndike, Rachel Sherman. *The Sherman Letters, Correspondence Between General Sherman and Senator Sherman from 1837 to 1891.* New York: DaCapo, 1969.

Tower, R. Lockwood (ed.). *A Carolinian Goes to War: The Civil War Narrative of Arthur Middleton Manigault.* Charleston Library Society, 1983.

Trudeau, Noah. *Southern Storm: Sherman's March to the Sea.* New York: HarperCollins, 2008.

Vetter, Charles Edmund. *Sherman: Merchant of Terror, Advocate of Peace.* Gretna: Pelican Publishing Company, 1992.

Von Hassell, Agostino, and Ed Breslin. *Sherman: The Ruthless Victor.* Nashville: Thomas Nelson, 2011.

Watson, Ronald G. (ed.). *Death Does Seem to Have All He Can Attend To: The Civil War Diary of an Andersonville Survivor.* Jefferson, NC: McFarland Press, 2014.

Weintraub, Stanley. *General Sherman's Christmas: Savannah, 1864.* New
    York: Smithsonian, 2009.

PERIODICALS

Boyd, David French. "General W. T. Sherman as a College President."
    Louisiana State University, *University Bulletin,* 1910.

ENDNOTES

PROLOGUE

1   Boyd, David French. "General W. T. Sherman as a College President." Louisiana State University, *University Bulletin*, 1910.

CHAPTER ONE | EARLY LIFE

1   Sherman, *Memoirs*, Vol. I, p. 2.

2   Howe, *Home Letters of General Sherman*, p. 7.

3   Sherman, *Memoirs*, p. 12.

4   "I remember seeing his name on the bulletin board when the names of all the newcomers were posted. I ran my eyes down the columns and saw there 'U.S. Grant.' A lot of us began to make up names to fit the initials. One said, 'United States Grant.' Another, 'Uncle Sam Grant'; another said 'Sam Grant.' That name stuck to him." Flood, *Grant and Sherman*, p. 23.

CHAPTER TWO | CALIFORNIA

1   Brigadier General Roger Jones.

2   Howe, p. 45.

3   In a letter to Ellen Ewing, Sherman mentioned Washington Irving, Shake-

speare, a history of the Reformation, and the Wandering Jew, among others. Howe, p. 68.

4   Howe, p. 63.

5   One report has it that the official name of San Francisco was still Yerba Buena, and that the name was changed to San Francisco within a couple of days of Sherman's arrival. However, he refers to the place as San Francisco in all his correspondence previously, and it is possible that he was referring to the mission rather than the small town of Yerba Buena.

6   Howe, p. 105.

7   Ibid., p. 88.

8   By convention, the spelling Monterrey is used for the capital of Nuevo León, in Mexico. The city in Northern California is spelled Monterey.

9   For details of this trip, see Sherman, *Memoirs*, pp. 47–51.

10   Thorndike, *The Sherman Letters*, p. 40.

11   Ibid., p. 42.

12   Sherman, pp. 66–67.

CHAPTER THREE | THE BLEAK YEARS—1850–1861

1   Vetter, p. 52.

2   Flood, p. 26.

3   Vetter, p. 55.

4   Ibid., p. 55.

5   Sherman, p. 125.

6   Ibid., p. 130.

7   Flood, p. 34.

CHAPTER FOUR | THE UNION ABOVE ALL

1   Later named Louisiana State University (LSU).

2   W. T. Sherman to Ellen Sherman, February 13, 1860, quoted in Howe, p. 177.

3   Vetter, p. 61.

4   Boyd, Sherman as college president, cited in Vetter, p. 71.

5   W. T. Sherman to Ellen Sherman, February 1, 1861. Cited in Vetter, p. 69.

6   Sherman, pp. 167–68.

7   Thorndike, pp. 112–13.

8   Ibid., pp. 117–18.

CHAPTER FIVE | BULL RUN

1   Sherman, pp. 181–82.

2   Lewis, *Sherman: Fighting Prophet*, p. 169, gives some startling statistics. He points out that of McDowell's other two division commanders, Heintzelman was the only one who had ever seen battle. Hunter had been only a paymaster during the Mexican War. Of the brigade commanders, R. C. Schenck, a political appointee, had never worn any kind of uniform. The secessionist army, on the other hand, was commanded by such luminaries as Beauregard, Joseph E. Johnston, Nathan "Shanks" Evans, Thomas J. "Stonewall" Jackson, J. E. B. Stuart, and E. Kirby Smith, among others.

3   Sherman, pp. 185–86.

4   Howe, p, 209.

5   Sherman, pp. 188–89.

6   Ibid., p. 189.

7   Ibid., p. 190.

8   Ibid., pp. 190–91.

9   Ibid., p. 193.

CHAPTER SIX | SHERMAN FINDS HIS NICHE—WITH GRANT

1   Sherman does not specify the date in his *Memoirs*.

2   Sherman, p. 197.

3   Vetter, p. 92.

4   Ibid., p. 93.

5   Ibid., p. 94.

6   Ibid.

7   Sherman, pp. 214–15.

8   Ibid., pp. 216–17.

9   Flood, p. 78.

10 Grant, *Memoirs, I*, pp. 74–75.

11 Ibid., p. 311.

12 Ibid., p. 312.

13 Sherman, pp. 219–20.

14 Grant, p. 315.

CHAPTER SEVEN | SHILOH RESTORES SHERMAN'S REPUTATION

1   Johnston held detachments on the Columbus, Tennessee, and Mississippi rivers, including Island Number Ten, a strong bastion located on a narrow, twisting part of the Mississippi, heavily garrisoned.

2   Grant, p. 126. Halleck started out with C. F. Smith, not Grant, in command. It was a foolish move on Halleck's part, and it is widely accepted as having been motivated partly by personal jealousy but also justified to some extent by Grant's independence of action. In any event, the arrangement was short-lived. Halleck soon reinstated Grant, it is also widely assumed, by pressure from President Lincoln himself.

3   C. F. Smith, a true hero of the Mexican War, had contracted a fatal illness.

4   Sherman, brigadier generals Benjamin M. Prentiss, W. H. L. Wallace, and Stephen A. Hurlbut. Another division, that of Major General Lew Wallace, was at Crump's Landing, five miles down the river.

5   In his *Memoirs*, pp. 138–39, Grant excuses the fact that his men had not dug defensive positions by insisting that they needed drill and training more than picks and shovels—a lame excuse.

6   In the Battle of Pea Ridge, Arkansas, fought in early March 1862, the Confederate force under Major General Earl Van Dorn was shattered. Many of the survivors were expected to make their way across the Mississippi and join Albert Johnston's force at Corinth.

7   Major generals Braxton Bragg, William Hardee, Leonidas Polk, and Brigadier General John Breckenridge.

8   W. T. Sherman to Ellen Sherman, April 11, 1862. Howe, pp. 230–31.

9   Flood, p. 114.

10   Ibid., pp. 222–23.

11   Howe, p. 222.

12   Prominent among the reporters was the twenty-three-year-old Whitelaw Reid, of the *Cincinnati Gazette*. Lewis, p. 233.

13   Ibid., p. 234.

CHAPTER EIGHT | **A HARD WINTER AT VICKSBURG**

1   Sherman, pp. 254–56.

2   Flood, pp. 127–28.

3   Flood, pp. 132–33.

4   Grant described McClernand as "unmanageable and incompetent," based on experiences at Fort Donelson and later at Shiloh.

5   Grant offered his appraisal of the fortified riverfront city that had a peacetime population of forty-five hundred, the second-largest city in Mississippi next to Natchez: "Admirable for defense. On the north it is about two hundred feet above the Mississippi River at the highest point

and very grown up with cane and underbrush by the washing rains; the ravines were much cut up with cane and underbrush while the sides and tops were covered with a dense forest." Flood, p. 149. Grant, p. 212.

Federal forces had tried to take Vicksburg before, in the summer of 1862. After Admiral David G. Farragut's seizure of New Orleans in April of that year, he had attempted to open the Mississippi by the use of some twenty-three mortar boats, finally reaching Vicksburg. There he found the bluffs too steep, and on July 18 he gave up the effort, returning to New Orleans.

6   Flood, p. 141.

7   Porter journal, p. 436. Cited in Glatthaar, *Partners in Command*, p. 168.

8   Howe, p. 235.

9   Ibid., p. 140.

10   XIII Corps, McClernand; XIV Corps, George H. Thomas; X Corps, Sherman; XVI Corps, Hurlbut; XVII Corps, McPherson.

11   W. T. Sherman to Ellen Sherman, January 28, 1863. Howe, p. 238.

12   Flood, pp. 151–52.

13   A similar effort against Fort Pemberton, at Yazoo Pass, had been launched earlier, but it had failed and the force had not yet been extricated; in fact it was still in peril.

14   Grant, pp. 177–78. Sherman, pp. 308–11.

CHAPTER NINE | THE GUNS OF VICKSBURG

1   In the East, Lee had defeated Ambrose Burnside at Fredericksburg the previous December. Chancellorsville was yet to be fought. Halleck's "siege" of Corinth could hardly be called a battle.

2   Flood, pp. 154–56.

3   Ibid., p. 156.

4   Glatthaar, p. 174.

5   Sherman, p. 316.

6   W. T. Sherman to Ellen Sherman, April 17, 1863, quoted in Howe, pp. 249–53.

7   Grant's force at Grand Gulf consisted of McClernand's XIII Corps.

8   Sherman, p. 319.

CHAPTER TEN | THE BASTION FALLS

1   Grant, p. 192.

2   Grierson's regiments were the 6th and 7th Volunteer Illinois cavalries and the 2d Iowa.

3   Sherman, p. 327.

4   Meyers, pp. 147–49. Fiske, pp. 240–42.

5   Grant, p. 216.

CHAPTER ELEVEN | CHATTANOOGA

1   Sherman, p. 346.

2   Ibid., p. 349. See Appendix D for the entire text.

3   Tower, p. 119.

4   Sherman, pp. 364–65.

CHAPTER TWELVE | COMMANDER IN THE WEST

1   Despite its modest-sounding name, the Military Division of the Mississippi was a tremendous command, both in terms of territory and the number of troops involved. It included the Departments of the Ohio, Cumberland, Tennessee, and Arkansas, commanded respectively by major generals Schofield, Thomas, McPherson, and Steele. Sherman, II, p. 5.

2   Sherman, pp. 399–400.

3   Sherman, II, p. 15.

4   Watson, p. 111.

5   Grant, p. 278.

6   Sherman, II, pp. 27–29.

7   Ibid., p. 29.

CHAPTER THIRTEEN | **THE BATTLE OF KENNESAW MOUNTAIN**

1   W. T. Sherman to Ellen Sherman, May 4, 1864. Howe, pp. 287–88.

2   Sherman, II, p. 34. The memoirs were written much after the fact, and by then McPherson had been killed and was considered a great national hero. Given the magnitude of the failure, it is safe to assume that Sherman, at the moment, was not so mild.

3   The name can be confusing. McPherson commanded the Union Army of the Tennessee. Johnston omitted the article, thus calling his force "The Army of Tennessee."

4   Cooper was the adjutant general, not a commander.

5   Eicher, John, and David Eicher, *Civil War High Commands*, p. 69.

6   Sherman, II, p. 59.

7   W. T. Sherman to Ellen Sherman, June 26, 1864. Howe, p. 298.

8   W. T. Sherman to Ellen Sherman, June 30, 1864. Howe, p. 299. The reference to Kilkenny cats comes from indefinite sources. Apparently British soldiers at Kilkenny, Ireland, in the last of the eighteenth century reported two cats who fought so fiercely that they ate each other up except for their respective tails, all that remained.

9   Johnston claimed the loss of only 808. Sherman, p. 61.

CHAPTER FOURTEEN | **THE FALL OF ATLANTA**

1   Castel, pp. 379–82.

2   Sherman, II, pp. 82–83.

3   Vetter, p. 213.

4   Sherman, II, p. 96.

5   Ibid., p. 105.

CHAPTER FIFTEEN | MARCHING THROUGH GEORGIA

1   Vetter, p. 217.

2   Sherman, II, pp. 141–42.

3   Ibid., p. 141.

4   Vetter, p. 233. At least some of this is in Sherman's *Memoirs*.

5   Grant, p. 378.

6   Sherman, II, p. 179.

7   Ibid., p. 182.

8   Ibid., p. 186.

9   Ibid., p. 189.

10 Hardee was the author of a drill manual used by both sides in the Civil War. He had been commandant of cadets at West Point.

11 It was incidentally the division that Sherman had commanded at Shiloh and Vicksburg, a matter of pride and confidence on his part.

12 Sherman, II, p. 231.

CHAPTER SIXTEEN | SAVANNAH

1   W. T. Sherman to Ellen, January 15, 1865. Quoted in Howe, p. 329.

2   Sherman, II, p. 236.

3   "... its streets perfectly regular, crossing each other at right angles; and at many of the intersections were small inclosures in the nature of parks. These streets and parks were lined with the handsomest shade-trees of which I have knowledge, viz., the willow-leaf live-oak, evergreens of exquisite beauty; and these certainly entitled Savannah to its reputation as a handsome town more than the houses, which, though comfortable, would hardly make a display on Fifth Avenue or the Boulevard Haussmann of Paris." Sherman, II, p. 230.

4   Sherman, II, pp. 233–34.

5   Yet Sherman was prescient in what he feared for the future of the freed slaves. On January 15 he wrote Ellen, "I have said that slavery was dead and the Negro free, and want him treated as free, and not hunted and badgered to make a soldier of, when his family is left back on the plantations. I am right and won't change." Howe, p. 328.

CHAPTER SEVENTEEN | MEETING AT CITY POINT

1   Grant claimed that he had always favored Sherman's plan to come overland but had doubted its feasibility. Sherman, II, 237–38.

2   Sherman, II, pp. 237–38.

3   Admiral Dahlgren and many of his army colleagues had blamed General Franklin Butler's lack of aggressiveness for the latest failure.

4   Throughout most of the war Lee had been in command of a single army, the Army of Northern Virginia. On January 31, 1865, however, President Jefferson Davis appointed him as commander of all the Confederate armies. By that time Lee was located under siege in Richmond.

5   Once Sherman's reinforcement arrived (Schofield's Army of the Ohio), he would have eighty thousand men.

6   Glatthaar, p. 131.

7   Sherman, II, pp. 326–27.

8   Sherman later made some changes to allow him to fight Lee and Johnston at the same time.

9   Sherman, II, p. 328.

10   Ibid., p. 326.

CHAPTER EIGHTEEN | SURRENDER

1   To the modern reader, the designation of "army" for a formation about the size of a corps can be explained by the type of function that headquarters was to perform. The army, an administrative unit, could convene courts-martial and perform many other administrative function denied the corps.

2   The Neuse was a significant waterway that flowed from the Piedmont of the Alleghenies past Raleigh, Durham, Smithfield, and Goldsboro, and emptied into the Pamlico Sound at New Bern.

3   Sherman, II, p. 343.

4   Ibid., pp. 356–57.

CHAPTER NINETEEN | TROUBLED PEACE

1   Tenney, pp. 700–1.

2   Ibid., 701.

3   Sherman, p. 359.

4   Flood, p. 351. Grant described the entire situation clearly and succinctly: "Halleck had been sent to Richmond to command Virginia, and had issued orders prohibiting even Sherman's own troops from obeying his, Sherman's, orders. Sherman met the papers on his return, containing this order of Halleck, and very justly felt indignant at the outrage. On his arrival at Fortress Monroe returning from Savannah, Sherman received an invitation from Halleck to come to Richmond and be his guest. This he indignantly refused, and informed Halleck, furthermore, that he had seen his order. He also stated that he was coming up to take command of his troops, and as he marched through it would probably be as well for Halleck not to show himself, because he (Sherman) would not be responsible for what some rash person might do through indignation for the treatment he had received. Very soon after that, Sherman received orders from me to proceed to Washington City, and to go into camp on the south side of the city pending the mustering-out of the troops." Grant, p. 453.

5   Grant, p. 447.

6   Sherman, p. 374.

7   Flood, p. 353.

8   Howard had been ordered to Washington to make preparations for the army's arrival.

9   So obvious was the gesture that Grant mentions it approvingly in his *Memoirs*.

10   Sherman II, pp. 377–78.

CHAPTER TWENTY | GENERAL OF THE ARMY

1   The other members were Major General Philip Sheridan and Brigadier General C. C. Augur.

2   The first war in which the United States had had a single army chief.

3   ". . . he acted like a boy turned loose—threw off reserve—asked 1,000 questions of everybody—never at a loss for a story or joke—a comic twinkle in his eye—a toss of his head—a serio-comic twitch to his wrinkled features—with a long stride he passed up and down constantly, never weary—a prodigious smoker and talker—stretched in blankets before the fire in the shadow of mountains, he talked the night half away." Lewis, p. 596.

4   Ibid., p. 599.

5   Ibid., pp. 597–98.

6   Keegan, pp. 284–85.

7   Ibid., p. 282.

CHAPTER TWENTY-ONE | TAPS

1   Lewis, pp. 637–38.

2   See Sherman and Howard, *Who Burnt Columbia*.

3   Lewis, p. 645.

4   Ibid., p. 650.

5   Ibid., p. 651.

INDEX

ABOUT THE AUTHOR

JOHN S. D. EISENHOWER was a brigadier general (Army Reserves), a U.S. ambassador to Belgium during the Nixon administration, and the author of numerous works of military history and biography. The son of Dwight D. Eisenhower, he lived in Maryland.